DEREK A. BARDOWELL is a wri[...] former director of programmes at [...] and Laureus Sport for Good. He [...] World Service, *The Source* and MTV, and currently hosts the podcast *Just Cause*, which explores the intersections of race, culture and social justice. *No Win Race*, his first book, was a *Sunday Times* Sports Book of the Year and was longlisted for the William Hill Sports Book of the Year Award in 2019. Derek is a Churchill Fellow.

Twitter: @DerekABard

'Personal, political, powerful and about so much more than race and sport.'

BERNARDINE EVARISTO, author of the Booker Prize-winning novel *Girl, Woman, Other*

'This searching exploration uses sport to examine questions of race and identity ... Bardowell does an excellent and passionate job of refracting the issues within sport – the dearth of black football managers, the lack of activism from black athletes who have made it into the spotlight – into wider society.'

Financial Times

'A painful reflection of racism in British sport ... Bardowell ably demonstrates the power of the media to determine the narratives around these sporting lives. He flags up the false binaries often promoted between good (patriotic) and bad (self-centred) black sportswomen and men ... it's a valuable act of remembrance of sporting stars who put their careers on the line in pursuit of a moral right.'

Observer

'*No Win Race* has the feel of James Baldwin's *The Fire Next Time* ... *No Win Race* will stimulate much discussion across generations of readers – both black and white. I would love to see it on secondary school and university curriculums, and with the breadth of what it covers, it should feature on the reading list of many creative disciplines.'
                                                                    Words of Colour

'And before you think it's some kind of sociological tome, that is best left for A-Level students studying Race and Sport – it's a really good read. There's lots of very personal recollections about sport, and the beauty of sport, and the power of sport to inspire and bring families together, and plenty of you will reminisce about watching sport growing up with your own parents and watching great sporting moments. You won't be reading this book and feel like you're being lectured at, trust me on that one, it's an enjoyable read.'

NIHAL ARTHANAYAKE, BBC Radio 5 Live

'A must-read for anyone interested in the cultural politics of sport, the question of English and British nationalism, and what sport can (and can't) do to produce a more convivial society.'

BEN CARRINGTON, Associate Professor of
Sociology and Journalism in the USC
Annenberg School for
Communication and Journalism

DEREK A. BARDOWELL

NO WIN RACE

A MEMOIR OF BELONGING, BRITISHNESS AND SPORT

MUDLARK

HarperCollins*Publishers*
1 London Bridge Street
London SE1 9GF

www.harpercollins.co.uk

First published by HarperCollins*Publishers* 2019

This edition published 2020

1 3 5 7 9 10 8 6 4 2

A catalogue record of this book is
available from the British Library

ISBN 978-0-00-830514-7

Printed and bound in Great Britain by
CPI Group (UK) Ltd, Croydon

MIX
Paper from
responsible sources
FSC™ C007454

This book is produced from independently certified FSC™ paper
to ensure responsible forest management.

For more information visit:
www.harpercollins.co.uk/green

To Elle & Keithus
For Meadow & Marlowe

CONTENTS

INTRODUCTION

My two kids ran up the stairs to wash their faces, clean their teeth and put on their pyjamas while I stayed downstairs to pour a shot of rum. I turned on the television. A documentary about Margaret Thatcher had just started. Couldn't think why she'd be on the telly. I had a feeling she'd died. So, I grabbed my iPhone to find out if that was indeed the case. She had died of a stroke, aged 87.

It had been our first night on holiday in an old cottage in Suffolk. The cottage, beautifully worn with creaky floors, low-hanging ceilings, stained rugs, and dusty, stale smells also featured all the modern trimmings required to make it a contemporary holiday retreat for kids, like a PlayStation and an iPad docking station.

I stood, ceiling hovering close over my head, watching the documentary, which covered Thatcher's unlikely rise to Conservative Party leadership in 1975, her battles with 'Heathite' Tories, her election victory in 1979, Bobby Sands, the IRA, the recession, the Brixton Riots, the Falklands War, the Miners' Strike, her battles with the trade unions, the breakthroughs she made for women in politics, the grinding shift from 'society to self', her loathing of the European Community, the end of the Cold War,

1

the introduction of the Poll Tax, the Poll Tax Riots and her eventual downfall at the hands of her Tory Party colleagues.

My son, two and a half years old at the time, cute and rashy, smiley and whiney, came down the stairs, walked up to me, rubbed his eyes and said in a dull voice, 'Take me [to] bed.'

He put his arms up, so I picked him up.

'You watching TV?' he asked.

'Yes,' I replied, 'it's about Margaret Thatcher.' Didn't elaborate, eyes barely shifted from the television screen.

Paused.

I realised I had started to squeeze him tightly. The back of my throat had started to tickle. My hands and my toes were cold and clammy. Not the rum. Should have been thinking about the immediate future, like playing games with the kids in the morning, country walks and beautiful landscapes. Instead, my mind was situated in the past. Always is. I took my son upstairs to bed, the documentary swirling through my head. I thought less about Thatcher's death and more about her legacy.

I remembered what it had been like as a child in the eighties. I grew up in Newham in the East End, which for many black and brown folks meant racially motivated attacks and police harassment, and a general denial that these problems existed from the services that were there to help you. It had been a time when fear, paranoia and insecurity consumed me. From a young age, I felt like an outsider. Felt as if my options, crafted by the grit and hard work of my Jamaican parents, were impossibly narrow. Felt like a problem to the state. Never knew comfort. Never really felt at ease. Bus stops, shops, school, trains, my everyday spaces, brought conflict, stares, stop and searches, anxiety, false accusations and a fear of other people's fear. I liked my home, my birthplace. England. But never quite felt at home in my birthplace. Never made to feel at home in my birthplace. It had been difficult to feel like a true citizen in a place where you were considered an outsider, in a place where many of the nation's heroes were often my forefathers' oppressors.

Too late for me, I thought. Always be this way for me. Caged, enraged. But what should I tell my son? Things have changed. Things have improved. He is unlikely to experience racism in the same way I had when I was growing up. So how do I prepare him without infecting him?

For me, sport had always been a great leveller. Something that brought me solace, an escape in times of trouble.

It was how my father, Keith, and I bonded. Before I could grip a mug, my father had already shoved a cricket bat and ball in my hands. We would go into our 30-foot back garden and play, my father bowling, me batting. He'd always bowl googlies at me, a deceptive delivery where the ball spins into the batsmen's legs instead of going straight. A magic trick. As my father watched me swing wildly, and miss, his shifty eyes would tighten, and his soft, narrow, light-brown face would break into a cheeky smile before he'd launch into a story about 'back home' – in Jamaica. My father's yearning for Jamaica and the role cricket played in transporting him 'back home', albeit for brief moments, made me recognise that sport was more than a game.

It had often been the case that white people assumed that the colour of my skin and my height ensured athletic excellence. Upon first meeting me, most would ask, 'Do you play basketball?'

'No,' I'd reply, never knowing what else to say. I would later come to realise that, for well-meaning white folks, in bowing to a more favourable stereotype (black people being good at sport) they were addressing their own discomfort. For them, a conversation starter and some solace. For me, a conversation closer and anxiety.

Sport offered positive images of black folks at a time when we were bombarded with negative images in the media. Back in the seventies and early eighties, the few shows that featured black actors like *Mixed Blessings*, *Rising Damp* and *Love Thy Neighbour* always emphasised the difference between Caribbean or African culture and the English. They forever depicted us as aliens – sources of fundamental difference, conflict and unrest. The gags were often cheap, cruel and exploitative. Sport, to some degree, balanced out these negative images.

It has always been difficult for me to separate 'race' and sport. Alongside music, sport has for many years been a platform where blacks have excelled. Where we've been allowed to excel. Whether you liked sport or not, black athletes were the most visible contributors to British society. Black people had of course built Britain, literally. We had constructed, supplemented and indeed strengthened the country. We had done so under forced labour, under poor conditions, with little or no rights, little or no credit. The black athlete's impact had been more difficult to conceal, their contributions measurable. Goals. Runs. Times. Wickets. Knockouts. Tries. This led to wins, which led to larger audiences, which led to more money, which led to more media coverage, which led to more sponsorship, which led to a higher profile for the black athlete. They were symbolic. Symbolic of everything we had achieved in this country, for this country. In addition, they seemed to be the only black people in the public eye who were embraced by whites, even if they had to win adoration through a torrent of boos and unconditional allegiance to Jack or George.

Yet at the same time, so much of what happened to black athletes on the field of play reflected the issues faced by black people in British society.

Growing up in the eighties, the popular racism being trumpeted by the mainstream media – moral panics about blacks being a threat to cohesion, to jobs, to safety – weaved its way into sport. The crowds were often hostile towards black athletes and commentary was often stereotypical, preoccupied with our physical attributes while constantly underestimating our sporting IQ. Institutional racism also restricted any hope of black people attaining positions of power or commanding the authority to complain about their treatment.

Thatcher told the nation how Britain had given so much to the world. She told the masses how much she loved Britain, wanted to protect Britain, valued Britain. Didn't doubt it for a second. But she also encouraged a climate where you were either with us (Britain) or against us. She made it a point that to question power and privilege as a root cause of social disparities would only make you an enemy of the state. Not the state's fault. Your fault. You are free to dream, free to succeed in a cage. Not our fault you can't break free.

You were in or out. Immigrants, well, those of colour and/or those who spoke a different language, were out. You want in? Shut up, be happy. Be grateful that Britain has given you a safe place, safe from the police, safe working conditions, safe housing.

Safe. You are here because we saved you, not because you are helping the British economy, not because of slavery, not because the Empire had left your country in ruins through colonialism. Don't worry about the fact that Britain compensated the slavers and not the enslaved, justified oppression in the name of God, in the name of science, in the name of the arts.

I had for many years understood that for any outsider Britain would always promise more than it could deliver. You achieved despite the system, not because of it. Yet the eighties appeared to make an already unequal society even more unfair, even more divided.

Later that evening, while reading *Handa's Surprise** to my son, Turner Prize-winning artist Jeremy Deller's *Joy in People* exhibition popped into my head. At London's Hayward Gallery I had seen, amid the colours and the quirks, amid the joy and the pain, the joy in pain, images of the Miners' Strike and police brutality. It brought the eighties back to me again and revealed just how many people across the UK Thatcher had displeased. Yet she remained in power for such a long time. Three election victories, remember? Impressive. Why did so many people vote for someone deemed so divisive? Must have found a way to appeal to the true blue within, right? Must have played patriotic games better than any other politician. Enough, therefore, for people to forget what the policies and the economy had really been doing to them all along.

---

* *Handa's Surprise* is an illustrated children's book, set in southwest Kenya. Handa is taking fruit to her friend Akeyo in a basket on her head. One by one, various animals take a piece of fruit from her basket without Handa realising. Will she have any fruit left by the time she finally sees Akeyo?

Suddenly I felt guilty and anxious. How could I let Thatcher interfere with this moment with my son? She had already interfered with my childhood. How could such feelings that I thought I had long since buried resurface so swiftly? The thoughts came, they went. They hurt. They died. Like my soul.

My soul finds solace in sport and indeed the success of black athletes. Rio Ferdinand on a football field, as smooth as Rakim on the mic. Lennox Lewis, an under-appreciated champion despite being Britain's greatest post-war boxer. Ian Wright, the working-class hero who taught everyone that you could succeed with hard work and without compromise. Anthony Joshua, Denise Lewis and Jessica Ennis-Hill, each winning with class. Lewis Hamilton, winning with style. Well, not just winning but transcending. He may be British sport's GOAT (greatest of all time). Don't care about their politics. Or how they self-identify. I need sport like I need friendships. I need to see those positive images, because it always feels as if they represent something more than athletic excellence. They represent you. The best of you; the *you* that the media and history tend to ignore, deny, conceal, suppress, revile.

The reality for people of colour in Britain is that our skin tone is a barrier. It limits opportunities. Things have improved. But for all the success displayed on the field of play, black people remain the poor relations in British society. We are still over-represented in the criminal justice system, in unemployment, in mental health institutions, in school exclusions. We remain absent in positions of power, around decision-making tables, in government. The black athlete may often be triumphant, they may create an illusion that we make up a more significant percentage of the population, but some gross disparities still exist in Britain for black people.

For all our success on the playing field, it is still hard for me to use the word 'we' and 'us' when referring to my place of birth. Why? Because in so many British people's eyes, we (black people) remain outsiders, visitors, not the ideal conception of Britishness or Englishness. As a friend once said to me, 'I only feel English when I'm abroad.' Another friend recently said to me, 'The only time I've ever seen true diversity on television was during the coverage of the Grenfell disaster.' So, while sport provides a remedy in the form of positive images of black people, does this also mask society's deep-rooted rejection and ignorance of Black-Britishness? Can blackness and Britishness ever be compatible?

This book aims to answer these questions. Primarily covering the period between the Brixton Riots (1981) and the Brexit referendum (2016), it looks at 'race' and racism in modern Britain through the prism of sport. It explores sport's role in reflecting, reinforcing or challenging common ideologies about 'race'.

I use the West Indies cricket team to explore the conflict of supporting colour (shared experiences) over your country (shared birthplace), I look at how London 2012 concealed the racial tensions of the time, I examine the Americanisation of Black-British culture through Michael Jordan and the re-emergence of athlete activism. I profile some of our major sporting heroes such as Lewis Hamilton, Eniola Aluko and Ian Wright. I also revisit major sporting events, such as Lennox Lewis *v.* Frank Bruno and some of our major sporting conflicts, like Linford Christie *v.* Lord Coe, and John Terry *v.* Anton and Rio Ferdinand. In each case, I uncover what these athletes and these events told me about 'race' relations in modern Britain.

This is not a *history of,* or a who's who, of black people in British sport. It does not attempt to cover every single event and every single athlete. Nor is this an academic study of 'race' relations through sport even if, at times, it draws on the excellent work of scholars such as Ben Carrington and Kevin Hylton. This is personal, telling true stories from a black perspective, my perspective, one informed by having worked as a journalist and in civil society for over 25 years. One informed by having loved sport practically all my life, because it is something that has bonded three generations of males in my family.

I cannot be saved. It will always be this way for me. Enraged, caged. Frustrated. Frustrated knowing that 'race' does not exist. Knowing it is a social construct. One of the biggest lies in history. That is why I refer to 'race' in this way. Cannot give it credence. Yet it is real: real in the minds of people, real in history, real in the way it equates Britishness to whiteness. The Empire state of mind.*

My partner once said to me, the only thing that exists is the way people see 'race'. See me. Limit me. I'm frustrated knowing that Britishness for many people isn't blackness. Well, Britishness nor Englishness isn't blackness. I veer between the two. My experience, the experiences in this book, are English. But the Empire state of mind is British.

Yet for him, my son, 'race' will affect his life chances. For him, my son, the playing field will also look extremely different to

---

* 'Empire State of Mind' was a song performed by Jay-Z featuring vocals by Alicia Keys. In the song, 'Empire State' means New York. Here, the West Indies exposed the fragility of the British Empire.

mine. He does not see colour. But people see his colour. As he gets older, those perceptions of his colour will become more vivid, more twisted, more restrictive.

So how do I prepare him for a society that, on the surface, is great, functions well, provides opportunities; a society I am glad to be in, yet I also understand will disadvantage him due to the colour of his skin? How should I impart knowledge without sinking his confidence? How do I achieve this without giving him my baggage, without afflicting? Without infecting?

How and when exactly do you tell a child that so much of what they will hear in school and read in newspapers is only half the truth; not our truth but a clouded, colour-blind version of the truth? How do I give him the confidence to fight when everyone around him will think that you can't win with 'race', that the only race you can win is on the playing field?

I often struggle to convey this to my white friends with children. We all have our problems. We all have our issues. I understand that. But I also know that they will never have to worry about whether their children will be welcome in some neighbourhoods or not. My white friends are unlikely to teach their kids about how to deal with the police, because their child will less likely be profiled and stopped without reason. They will not have to instruct their kids about the way they walk, through fear that this may reflect badly on how their behaviour is perceived. They will not have to worry about their child wearing a hoodie or having their child's athletic achievements being attributed to natural ability. They will not have to worry about their child being exposed to an overwhelming number of negative images in the media or having any academic failure implicitly attributed to 'race'. They will never have to edit their child's assertiveness in public through fear of their child being perceived as angry or aggressive. They will not have to prepare them for multiple taxis driving past them, low expectations and stereotypes from teachers, or multiple clubs, restaurants and bars refusing them entry. It is unlikely that their children will ever be mistaken for 'the help' at fancy gatherings. They will not have to worry about how 'race' is represented in school, or if their history is non-existent in textbooks. They will not have to worry about their child's skin being a determining factor around whether an employer thinks s/he can fit in or not, or whether they are deemed suitable for housing. They will not have to prepare their child for a society where white folks will continually explain how you (as a black person) should feel about racism.

My father grew up in the era of West Indian batsman Collie Smith, under colonial rule where the divides in society and on the playing field were written in the law. I grew up in the John Barnes era under Thatcherism, where the violence of racism enabled me to see how discrimination made the playing field uneven. My son is growing up in the Anthony Joshua era where the uneven playing field is not quite so clear, not quite so blatant, but the impact on black people remains overwhelmingly negative.

How, then, do you prepare your children for a society where they will be sent 'to the crease, only for them to find, as the first balls are being bowled, that their bats have been broken before the game ...'[1]

CHAPTER 1

HYMN OF HATE

THE FIRST TIME IS OFTEN THE WORST. You never forget that feeling. Never quite forget how you responded or how you wish you'd responded. You hate yourself. Hate yourself for the way you felt. And that hate, hatred of the incident, hatred of your response to the incident, it never leaves you. Always stays, always scars. It never leaves you because every time an incident like it happens again, whether explicit or implicit, your immediate emotion harks back to that first feeling, back to that first response. Fright. Fight. Distrust. Disgust. You may know how to respond differently now, how to be more assertive, maybe more passive. But fundamentally, at that moment when you are confronted by racism, you dive right back to that first feeling, to that first response. Fight. Fright. Disgust. Distrust.

My first time occurred at Wembley Arena on 27 September 1980. I was seven. Wasn't there in person. Observed it on TV. On screen, the Arena resembled a backstreet pub in the East End: smoky, uninviting, hostile and undeniably white and working class. You didn't need to see the faces of the patrons in attendance to grasp their attitudes. Their fanatical moans painted a picture of flushed-faced, testosterone-charged, agitated men. The Arena may have been playing host to the world middleweight championship fight between Alan Minter and Marvin Hagler, but on this night, the world-famous venue had been transformed into a scowling theatre of hate.

I watched the fight with my father in our comfy living room in Second Avenue in Manor Park. We were one of maybe seven black families on the street, which was in the north side of Newham, one of the most racially mixed parts of the East End. My father was a painter and decorator while my mother had just started working for Laker Airways. I lived in the three-bedroom terrace with my two older sisters and my grandmother, who had her own bedroom and kitchen in the extension. I planted myself chest down on our rug in my usual posture, elbows grinding into the rug to support my head, which was perched on my hands. My father took his place behind me on our sofa, with its black synthetic armrests and orange seat covers, which sat in front of our lantern-patterned wallpaper, coloured three shades of brown.

I didn't know Minter or Hagler at the time. However, I remember my father putting down his newspaper to concentrate on the fight, which signified its importance. It wasn't too often that our 19-inch colour television commanded my father's full attention. He had purchased it with my mother's premium bonds winnings in 1970, just in time for the World Cup in Mexico, the first finals to be televised in colour. Ever since, it had become the most vocal member of our family. It was always on, whether anyone was watching it or not. It drowned out the noise of cars speeding down our street, the screeches of kids playing knock down ginger and the metal on metal bangs from our neighbours working on their cars. My father controlled the TV, always claiming to be watching something even if he was asleep or reading the *Sun*. I was his personal remote control.

On screen, the fighters were standing in opposite corners in the ring. Minter, a white boxer from Crawley in West Sussex was the reigning world middleweight champion, having wrestled the title from Italian-American Vito Antuofermo in Caesars Palace, Las Vegas in March 1980. Minter's victory had been controversial. Most of the boxing writers sitting ringside thought Antuofermo won the fight. An informal poll of ringside writers had 10 siding with the Italian-American, five with Minter with two scoring it even. Two of the three judges on the night were split in their scoring between Minter and Antuofermo. However, the third judge, Roland Dakin from England, gave Minter 13 rounds to just one to Antuofermo with one round even, causing *Boston Globe* writer Bud Collins to remark: 'He [Dakin] wasn't the usual burglar, stealing in the comfort of the home precinct. He had gone into another man's country to perform the overwhelming act of larceny, and never tiptoed.'

So, Minter had to defend his title against Antuofermo in June. The return, at Wembley Arena, was not controversial. Minter dominated, slicing Antuofermo's face to pieces and causing the referee to stop the fight in the Brit's favour in round eight.

Minter had been the golden boy of British boxing. A 1972 Olympic bronze medalist, he looked like a young Clint Eastwood, with a hard face but pretty features and a constant expression as if the sun was shining directly in his eyes. Out of the ring he wore tight flashy suits with his shirts unbuttoned to reveal his chest and gold chains. Minter had a flat nose, a wide face with a natural tan and a bouncer's confident posture. His victory over

Antuofermo made him the most famous sports star in Britain, sought after for sponsorship deals and ads. American fight critics didn't think much of him though. Not surprising. American fight critics didn't think much of most British fighters. These writers tended to load their articles with lazy jibes about what British fighters did outside of the ring (primarily drinking tea) and insults about how they fought in the ring (stiff and upright). Minter certainly did not move with the fluidity of fighters like the American Sugar Ray Leonard or Mexico's Salvador Sanchez. And his biggest problem through the seventies had been his susceptibility to cuts, the core reason behind most of his defeats. But he was a gutsy performer, relatively light on his feet, with a piercing jab.

His opponent Marvin Hagler was bald, black and expressionless. Brought up in Brockton, Massachusetts, Hagler had earned his title shot the hard way, fighting for little or no money against a series of the division's toughest contenders, many of them from Philadelphia. He too had fought Antuofermo, in 1979, but failed to win the title after their contest had been declared a draw. Most boxing critics thought Hagler had won the fight. Hagler thought he'd won too. But Antuofermo's camp had refused to grant a rematch, instead preferring a contest against Minter. The result left Hagler bitter, moody and even more menacing. He even claimed credit for Minter's title victory stating, 'Minter is only champion because he gained the benefit of the beating I gave to Antuofermo in Las Vegas.'[1] Hagler had an immovable presence on screen. Though his features were soft, his bald head, sharp cheekbones and steely glare gave him an intimidating look.

At Wembley the fighters bobbed and weaved in their corners as they readied themselves for the national anthems. The crowd heartily booed the 'Star-Spangled Banner' while their slurred, groaning harmonies accompanied the British anthem. 'Minter led the singing of the British anthem, which was bellowed out with such intensity by the capacity crowd that it was more a hymn of hate than an expression of pure patriotism,' recalled Harry Mullan in *Boxing News*.

I didn't understand the crowd's hostility. Indeed, the anthems and the pageantry of boxing were all a blur to me, lost in the murky setting. Wembley Arena looked little more than a school gym. The spotlights were straining to shed light on the ring. Maybe it had been our television. Either way, I had no idea how big the arena was because it looked so dark, so congested. The entire crowd seemed as if it was within spitting distance of the ring.

As I watched Minter and Hagler in the ring that night, I knew who I wanted to win. So, when my father asked me to select my favourite, my response was instant and firm.

'Minter.'

My father was taken aback. 'Minter? Do you know what he said?'

'What?'

'He said a black man can't beat a white man. Can you really support someone who says that about us?'

I had no way of checking if it was true or false. I had no response. As far as I was concerned, Minter was English, and being English myself, I wanted him to win.

*   *   *

Nineteen eighty had, so far, been a fantastic year for sport. In my mind, Minter–Hagler was not at this point living up to the other sporting events I had watched. It was the first year that sports stars rivalled Batman and Superman as the heroes we all wanted to be on the school playground.

It started in May when West Ham United, my local football team, won the FA Cup. Football in the late seventies and early eighties was not glamorous. The balls rarely moved, rarely bounced because the pitches were always so muddy. The players didn't look like athletes: a combination of wild facial hair, unkempt Afros, mullets and perms, thick 'porn' 'taches, rolled-down socks and ill-fitting football kits made it unattractive.

Trevor Brooking, the Hammers' stylish midfielder with the leathery face of a miner, had been one of the few players during that period to shine on those boggy pitches. Brooking scored the winning goal against Cup favourites Arsenal. He was already a hero to football fans in the East End. But when he scored that goal, he became a sporting idol to every East Ender.

After the FA Cup, I spent most of the summer watching sport. Not really by choice. My parents rarely let me out to play in the street. Didn't know why, but I kind of knew. They never told me directly, but my sisters' stories revealed that the environment I had been growing up in was violent.

Manor Park was bleak. People were nice. But Manor Park seemed to lack ambition. Most of the older kids I knew would leave school at 16, find work, get married and, if they had airs about them, move 20 minutes up the road to Ilford. Nothing wrong with that, but it didn't feel as if much existed beyond Newham's borders.

Manor Park suffered from the usual inner-city problems: kids carrying knives, frequent robberies, high unemployment, little or no green space, little for kids to do. But racism had been among the borough's biggest problems. Felt it. Nothing direct. Heard the rumours. Saw the looks. Sensed the tension.

The National Front (NF), a violent, extremist, far-right movement, used to distribute racist leaflets outside my primary school (Avenue) and my two older sisters' secondary school (Little Ilford). I had heard rumours about black families, not far from where I lived, who had petrol poured through their letterboxes and had their houses set alight. I overheard the story of some white youths who had dressed in Ku Klux Klan outfits and set alight either a four-foot cross or a black kid. Didn't know which. The term 'P*ki bashing', which would involve skinheads beating up Asian people, had been a part of the daily vocabulary in primary school. Indian and Bengali kids were frequently beaten up by white youths on their way home from Little Ilford, our local secondary school. At my school, some white kids just wouldn't befriend you. I could take the constant questioning, about the colour of my skin ('were you burnt?'), about my heritage ('where are you really from?'), about my name. But some kids would just flat out refuse to play with me ('you must stick to your own').

My reality was not so bad in comparison to other black and brown people in Newham. Blacks and Asians had been regularly terrorised throughout the borough. There had been unsolved racially motivated murders, school children violently beaten up inside the school gates (not just outside), arson, and frequent unjustified assaults and arrests by the police. You never knew the names of the victims. No one, it appeared, was ever caught.

Didn't seem to make the news. Only made the news if blacks and Asians fought back, which would then be reported more as a reason for moral panic than a right to protest.

Black and Asian families had also been historically discriminated against by Newham Council and other local services. They were systematically put to the back of the housing priority line. They faced problems at work, often enduring the worst conditions. They had to cope with an education administration that followed the Minister of Education's policy that 'no one school should have more than 30 per cent of immigrants'.[2] I didn't know there had been a policy that problematised black and brown kids. I didn't know that black and brown kids were regarded as a threat to cohesion. I didn't know that schools were deliberately excluding black or brown pupils to keep numbers down or sending them to schools for the educationally subnormal. That's what alternative provision for 'troubled' pupils was called back then. Always wondered what happened to some of my school mates. They didn't do what was best for black pupils. We were treated as unwanted statistics.

I didn't know about the Virk brothers, the Ramsey family, Akhtar Ali Baig, Kennith Singh, the Toussaint brothers.* They

---

* The Virk brothers were racially abused and attacked by five white youths in East Ham. The brothers fought back and one of the white youths was stabbed. The Virks called the police and they were arrested. When they went to trial, the police's chief prosecution witnesses were the white youths. The Virks were found guilty and served time. The Ramsey family had been subjected to frequent harassment from the police including a raid on their home when 11 family members were arrested. Akhtar Ali Baig was killed in East Ham by two young men and two young women aged 15 to 17 years who spat in his face, racially abused him before stabbing him in the heart. One of the assailants allegedly said, 'I've just gutted a

were the victims or survivors with no names. The sources of rumours that were in fact a reality.

No freedom. That's what it meant for me. My parents had clearly been aware of the challenges in Newham, so they essentially locked me in the house during the evenings and in the holidays.

During the summer of 1980, I watched England fail miserably at the European football championships in Italy. My only memories were of Ray Wilkins lobbing two defenders and then casually lifting the ball over the goalkeeper in England's draw against Belgium and the tear gas used by police to restrain English football hooligans. Crowd violence would be the norm in English football through the eighties.

I saw my first live sports event that summer, when my father took me to Lord's to watch the second Test between West Indies and England. West Indies' opening batsman Desmond Haynes hit his highest Test score in that game with 184, while Viv Richards won man of the match for a typically destructive 145.

The Moscow Olympics followed, my abiding memories being Seb Coe's sulky face after surprisingly losing the 800 metres final to Steve Ovett, Scottish sprinter Allan Wells running as if breaking down a door in a police raid to win the 100 metres gold and Ethiopian Miruts Yifter 'The Shifter', who looked about 50, winning the 5,000 and 10,000 metres double with finishing bursts that Mo Farah would have been proud of.

P*ki.' Ten-year-old Kennith Singh never returned home after going to the shops in Plaistow. His dead body was found under some old carpets several days after he went missing. The Touissant brothers were racially abused and attacked by the police and eventually taken to a police station for no apparent reason.

By the time I returned to school that September, sport had taken on greater meaning. I would re-live sporting contests in my mind in the classroom, while walking down the street, while eating dinner, and pretty much at most points during the day. My love of sport required no dependency on other people, except of course my father, who controlled the television. There were no restrictions on my imagination. And television was never boring because there was always another major sporting event around the corner.

In the lead up to the Minter–Hagler fight, Minter had reportedly said: 'It has taken me 17 years to become champion of the world. I'm not going to let a black man take it away from me.' Minter later claimed that he 'didn't mean it the way it might sound'.[3] If it had been a ploy to sell more tickets or gain more support, it was ill advised.

The rivalry between the two fighters allegedly began in Las Vegas when Hagler refused to shake Minter's hand. Minter's stablemate Kevin Finnegan, a former Hagler victim, added fuel to the fire by claiming that Hagler once told him, 'I don't touch white flesh.'[4] These were unsubstantiated claims from a man who had admitted to hating Hagler. Hagler had previously said, 'I make a point of never shaking hands with future opponents.'[5] He preferred to shake hands with his rivals after they had fought.

Minter's reported racial comment set the tone for the contest. By also wearing Union Jack underpants at the weigh-in for the fight and then entering the ring with an oversized Union Jack and St George banner, Minter did little to subdue the jingoistic atmosphere that had built up at a time when England had been bursting with racial tension.

England's economic depression made race relations sink to one of its lowest points. By 1980, England had entered recession and unemployment topped two million. The blame for the country's lack of jobs quickly turned to immigrant populations, fuelled further by Thatcher's Tory government and the mainstream press. Demonising blacks and immigrants of colour sold papers, won votes. How perverse. The National Front and their supporters needed no excuse to instigate random acts of violence against blacks and Asians; the people they blamed for just about every problem in society.

Minter's words and actions came across as anti-black, not patriotic. By fight night, the contest was not just the United States versus the United Kingdom. It was black versus white.

With the anthems out of the way, the MC took centre stage. He announced that the fight would be for the 'undisputed middleweight title of the world' as if presenting the next act at a circus. The MC then introduced Minter, who wore dark red shorts with a thick white trim. Before the announcer could finish his name, the crowd let out a lusty cheer as Minter, hands held aloft, drifted to the centre of the ring to acknowledge them.

'And from Brockton in the United States, the challenger ...' The crowd dampened the atmosphere with boos before the MC could announce Hagler's name. Hagler, bobbing up and down and with his head bowed, half-heartedly pumped his left fist in the air, but it was unclear whom he was acknowledging.

Minter towered over Hagler as they met face to face in the middle of the ring for the referee's instructions. Some fighters look away, shaking their nerves loose by moving from side to side. Others will stare at their opponent and try to intimidate them. Minter and Hagler barely moved as they gazed at each other in the misty arena. They looked as if they were each about to avenge a friend's murder.

Once the bell rang, Minter came out aggressively, hoping to impose his will, but Hagler kept catching him with leaping right hooks. Every time Hagler caught him with a punch, Minter looked distressed. It was like he couldn't see the punches coming. Within a minute, Hagler opened a cut under the champion's left eye. This had been common for Minter. Most of his six previous losses had been due to severe facial cuts. Undeterred, the Brit pressed forward, although Hagler's jerky movements and compact stance appeared to confuse him. Minter offered little movement. His head stuck out like a pelican's. Every time they exchanged, Minter appeared to throw more punches but Hagler landed the more damaging blows. Minter was bigger and quicker, but his punches were more like slaps than real decisive hits.

The two traded blows as if in a street fight. There was no rhythm to it, just malice and anger. They'd throw scrappy punches in close, take a breather, and then go tearing into each other again. By round two, Hagler's slashing overhand lefts and uppercuts were hurting Minter. The American's shot selection was mesmerising. Hagler could slug or box. He could fight on the back foot or come forward, or from an orthodox (leading with his left hand) or southpaw (leading with his right hand) stance. Hagler's ability to adapt in a fight was also legendary, so it was unsurprising that he became the aggressor to neutralise

Minter's attacks. The challenger had been winning the brawl, making the champion look amateurish, when Minter caught Hagler with a clubbing right hook. The punch stopped the American from advancing forward and momentarily buckled his knees. Minter had finally derailed Hagler's charge and he moved in for the kill.

This appeared to be the turning point of the fight, the defining moment when the contest would be won or lost. Would Minter finish the job? How would Hagler react? I thought Minter was about to knock Hagler out. But Marvellous Marvin was a bitter and determined man. He'd waited years to get a world title. If the hostility of the crowd could not deter him, nothing Minter could throw at him would push him back. As that right hook landed, Hagler probably had flashbacks to his early days fighting in grimy Philadelphian gyms, picking up little or no money. I'm sure he didn't want to go back to those days. So Hagler came right back at Minter. The American stole the initiative away from the Brit, who was now bleeding from the nose and had a mark under his right eye.

According to Harry Carpenter, commentating for the BBC, Hagler had said before the contest that the title was rightfully his. In round three, he became the stalker, throwing double jabs with his snaking arms, moving around, always changing angles, never allowing Minter to relax or ease his way into the fight. Minter could not set his feet, which would allow him to generate enough power into his punches to push Hagler back. Every time Minter planted himself, Hagler would either hit him or move out of punching range. Minter's hands were quick, but his feet and reactions were slow.

The crowd, undeterred, chanted *'Miiiin-tuh, Miiiin-tuh, Miii-in-tuh!'* But Minter's face was a bloody mess. He now had a cut over his left eye. I wondered how he could see Hagler through all the blood. Midway through the round, Hagler bludgeoned Minter with a right hook; the Brit grabbed his face with his gloves as if his nose, lips, eyes and cheekbones were about to collapse. I didn't know whether he was trying to stop his gum shield from flying out or his face from crumbling onto the canvas.

When you see fighters in pain or hurt while watching a contest on television, you're detached. You cannot smell the metallic fragrance of blood. You cannot hear the abused squeals of grown men in pain. You cannot see the saliva flying from the mouths of the fighters after absorbing a punch. You cannot hear the trainers shouting instructions or the audience urging their man to win. You cannot see the fighters' distorted expressions or the way their eyes roll aimlessly like a metal ball in a pinball machine. But after that shot, I could feel Minter's pain.

Soon after, the referee called timeout. He tugged a reluctant Minter to his corner for the ringside doctor to inspect the facial damage. Minter's face looked like someone had slashed him above and below each eye with a knife. The crowd's mood changed. Chants turned to grunts. Minter's father-in-law and trainer Doug Bidwell had seen enough. Bidwell stopped the fight. Minter lodged his arms on the ropes in frustration. Hagler sank to his knees in the middle of the ring as if in prayer. The title was finally his.

Then a beer can whistled towards Hagler's head. Before Hagler could get to his feet, another object flew over his bald dome, then another missile and another. Soon bottles and cans rained. The new champ curled into the canvas like a scared child at a fireworks display. The police jumped into the ring to apprehend a man who tried to attack Hagler.

I couldn't believe how quickly the crowd had soured. Nor could I tear my eyes away from the screen. Hagler's corner men Goody and Pat Petronelli came into the ring to protect him. They formed a human pyramid over the fighter as the crowd gathered ringside to shout racist abuse. Most of the press sitting ringside sheltered under tables or held chairs above their heads to avoid being hit by the alcoholic missiles. Objects struck Carpenter and ITV's Reg Gutteridge, British boxing's foremost commentators. These fans, it appeared, had not thrown empty cans and bottles. They had thrown half-full weapons in disgust and hatred.

I did not see Hagler again that night, maybe a knee on canvas or the shining glint of his beer-stained bald head. But his corner men, some officials in suits and the police scraped him through the bottom rope. 'He had to be smuggled away like a criminal from the scene of his triumph,' said the *Daily Mirror*'s Frank McGhee. They dragged him through the hostile crowd to his changing room as remnants of blood and beer sizzled in the ring.

'Disgusting!' was the headline on the front cover of the 3 October issue of *Boxing News*. Mullan opened his report by stating: 'The long-dead myth of British sportsmanship was finally buried at Wembley as a cascade of beer bottles and cans showered the ring and a racist mob howled obscenities at the black fighter who had taken Alan Minter's world middleweight title and at the black referee who had stopped the fight after one minute 45 seconds of the third round.'

In the same edition of *Boxing News*, American promoter Bob Arum, who staged the Minter–Hagler fight, had stronger words.

'This was a disgrace ... It was ridiculous the way this nationalism was built up before the fight.'

Once Minter had drawn the colour line, the fight had taken on a sinister tone. Black had beaten white. Black had beaten up white. Embarrassed white. England's ego had been bruised. And they couldn't accept it. My father was happy for Hagler, but the racial conflict had disturbed him into silence. England had lost more than just a boxing contest.

Until the first beer can flashed past Hagler's head, I had not completely inherited my father's support for the American. I couldn't grasp how Hagler's skin colour could be the cause of such fury. And sport seemed like such an inappropriate platform for such clashes. Didn't seem real. But then this was the first time I'd ever witnessed racially motivated violence.

Fright.

The fight sullied my impression of sport. Couldn't quite re-live sport in my mind anymore. Couldn't quite use sport to alleviate the boredom of school anymore. Couldn't quite hide as freely behind my daydreams anymore.

Distrust. Fright.

A year after the fight, my sisters were talking about a fight at Little Ilford where a white girl had called a black girl a 'black bitch'. When I heard this, I laughed. Paula, my eldest sister, turned to me and snapped, 'Why are you laughing?' I didn't know. I probably thought the word 'bitch' was naughty. 'Don't you understand?' Paula said, before explaining that the term was a racist insult. I didn't understand and walked off in a sulk.

*   *   *

The Minter–Hagler fight flashed back into my head a few months later, when my television screen was on fire. That was all I could see, flames bursting through our 19-inch canvas. I had been lying passively on the floor, waiting for the blaze to engulf me. However, my television was not about to burn down. My house was in no immediate danger. I just couldn't digest the images on the news. I felt troubled and anxious as I watched scenes from the 1981 Brixton uprising.

The 'riots' had been sparked by 'Swamp 81', a police operation launched in Brixton that allowed officers to stop and question anyone they thought looked suspicious of committing a street crime. The police stopped 943 people (over half were black) of which 118 were arrested in four days.[6] 'Swamp 81' had followed years of over-policing in black communities and over-policing at any events or venues frequented primarily by black people. This had followed years of mainstream press linking crime to black people as if an inherent character trait. This had followed Thatcher's warning that British people feared being 'swamped' by people from different cultures. This had followed the New Cross Fire in January 1981, when 13 black partygoers aged between 14 and 22 lost their lives. There was little or no mainstream press. No outcry, no mourning outside of the black and local communities. Despite New Cross being a hub for the National Front, police investigations had been swift, too swift, to rule the incident as an accident. To the wider public, the victims had no names, the incident went unnoticed. This led to the 'Black People's Day of Action', a 'general strike of blacks' where 20,000 people marched from Fordham Park in New Cross to Hyde Park on 2 March. The march had been largely peaceful. Despite this, the *Sun*'s headline read: 'Day the blacks ran riot in London.'

The New Cross Fire had been vague but haunting to me. I knew of it, but without detail. 'Thirteen Dead and Nothing Said.' The Brixton 'riots' had been more vivid. But my mind could not absorb the extreme violence and rioting taking place in my city. I was only eight and didn't know much about anything. All I knew was that I had never seen the night distorted so alarmingly as I watched the images on the news of overturned vehicles set alight, and blackened and shelled buildings. There were hundreds of police cowering under riot shields, pelted with Molotov cocktails and bricks, distressed black people dragged by coppers in riot gear, a pub with an erupting roof, incessant sirens, rushing crowds and confusion.

The morning after the uprising, the streets were dusty and empty, as though desperate for sleep. The skeletons of cars threw mournful shadows. Shops and houses were doorless, windowless and war torn. Brixton looked haunted and exhausted.

On the final day of the 'riots', I was having a late afternoon bath when my mother entered the bathroom. I stepped out of the bath while the washing machine, which was in our bathroom, was convulsing. My mother helped me dry myself. As I stood there, damp and naked, I said, 'Mum, I want to bleach my skin white.'

'Why?' my mother replied calmly, although startled by my confession. 'People don't like us,' I replied. I was too scared to say white people through fear they might be listening. She replied, 'Listen, your skin is beautiful, dark and smooth. You must always be proud of your skin and who you are.'

I listened. I took note. But I was entering a phase when racism would become part of my daily reality.

For some time after the Brixton 'riots', I could not sleep. Paranoid, I would listen for sirens. Couldn't hear much. But the slightest sound would make me shiver as if someone had been breaking into our house. Walking to school, I inspected nearby shops, trying to detect any visible signs of damage. My eyes flickered constantly as if someone had been waving a sword an inch from my face. My skin terrified me. Everyday experiences of racism, the period when rumour turned to reality, made me even more cagey, even more withdrawn, never quite knowing where I stood, never quite knowing how people perceived me. What did white folks really think of me? Didn't know. But my skin tone made me feel apologetic, guilty, watched, scrutinised, as if a constant Spotlight had been covering my every move.

I didn't know at the time, but this had been the double-consciousness American sociologist W E B Du Bois referred to, the conflict between trying to develop your own character while being cognisant of how you are perceived by white society.

Fright.

During my final years at primary school, as Hagler bullied his way through the middleweight division and Minter faded into retirement, racism had become an everyday struggle. Shopkeepers frequently told me to leave their shops for no reason or they would call the police, bus drivers refused to let me on their buses, old ladies clutched their bags in my presence and police stopped and searched me for no reason (ignoring my best friend, who happened to be white). I had an older white youth threaten to slash my throat with a bulb if I didn't shout a racist obscenity, and another older kid, a neighbour who I had invited round to my house to play, pin me down in my own living room and call me a black bastard.

It wasn't just the frequency of these incidents that troubled me. The settings, the timings, added to my distress. These incidents happened in the daytime, in sweet shops, at bus stops, on the way to school, on the high street, outside the school gates, in my home.

I tried to minimise my presence when out in public. Walked soft. As I was attempting to do so, Newham's black and Asian youths had started to fight back. This time I knew their names and I could see their faces.

Fight.

A group of elder Asian youths had taken to protecting younger children from racist attacks by accompanying them home from Little Ilford school. On 24 September 1982, three 'scruffily dressed' white men in bomber jackets and jeans jumped out of their car and started abusing this group of young and elder Asian youths, which led to a fight. Uniformed police were on the scene swiftly, resulting in eight Asian youths being badly beaten and taken to Forest Gate police station. It turned out that the 'scruffily dressed'[7] white men were plain-clothes policemen. The community mobilised swiftly around what became known as the Newham 8. This led to demonstrations largely frequented by Asian children and young people. The resulting national media coverage exposed Newham policing for what it had been at the time: meek in the face of racism and aggressive in its policing against black and Asian communities. The police had been placing the blame on the victims.

By the summer of 1984, racist violence had not subsided. I had been transitioning from primary to secondary school. At this point, Little Ilford had a mobile police unit situated within its school grounds. It had also erected spiked metal frames on the periphery of the school. My parents decided that it would be safer sending me to Langdon Secondary School in East Ham, some 30 minutes away from our house, instead of Little Ilford.

Disgust.

On 7 August 1984, a group of white youths randomly started carrying out acts of violence against black and Asian people. In one incident, a disabled Asian youth was hit on the head with a hammer. A group of Asian youths decided to confront the alleged white culprits outside the Duke of Edinburgh pub. A fight ensued but whereas five of the Asian youths spent seven weeks on remand for offences that did not warrant such length, their white counterparts were immediately let out on bail.

On 29 November 1984, 16-year-old black youth Eustace Pryce was stabbed in the head outside the Greengate pub in Plaistow. Pryce, his brother Gerald and some friends had confronted racists, which led to a fight in which Eustace was fatally stabbed. The police, on arrival, arrested Gerald and not Eustace's killer despite plain-clothes officers allegedly witnessing the tail end of the fight. Eustace's killer Martin Newhouse was eventually arrested. Yet while Newhouse had been let out on bail because 'it would be wrong to keep him in jail over Christmas', Gerald had been denied bail. He spent Christmas in prison and on release Gerald was prevented from going back into Newham, despite his girlfriend being pregnant at the time.

Fight.

The black and Asian communities rallied behind both cases under the guises of the Newham 7 Defence Campaign and the Justice for the Pryce Family Support Committee. This led to the National Demonstration Against Racism on 27 April 1985 with 3,000 demonstrators. A further 2,000 demonstrators marched on 11 May. The pressure from both campaigns led to national coverage about poor policing in Newham. This exerted pressure, symbolised by the demonstrations uniting blacks and Asians while also highlighting institutionally racist policing, contributed to justice being done. Newhouse was sentenced to four and a half years' youth custody for manslaughter and two years for affray, running concurrently. Gerald had not been criminalised. While some of the Newham 7 did time, the case highlighted that reasonable physical resistance against attacks would not automatically result in prison. The coverage of the Newham 7 and Eustace Pryce campaigns also demonstrated that cases like these could no longer be swept under the carpet and that blacks and Asians had the right to defend themselves.[8]

Black was not just a term that unified the African diaspora, it also became a term that united all black and brown people in the fight against racism. This had been my London. The London I grew up in. A London that had been hostile towards me from the beginning, a London where black and brown resistance had been unified and emphatic.

Minter–Hagler symbolised more than the racial divides of the time. It symbolised the choice you had to make growing up back then. Blackness or Britishness? Colour or country? Do you side with those with shared experiences or those with a shared birthplace? I had to choose. Rebel or comply. Be bold or be shy. Risk exclusion or be subservient.

I knew it would be impossible for me to remain anonymous being black. No middle ground. There were no hiding places for black athletes. No hiding place for blacks. And no hiding place for me.

CHAPTER 2

BLACKWASHED

IN MY HOUSE, THE ATHLETES my father and mother admired did not try to hide. The foremost sporting names had been the boxer Muhammad Ali and the West Indies cricket team. I kind of missed the Ali era, only catching the tragic tail end of the most magnificent career in sport's history. I grew up at a time when Larry Holmes ruled boxing's heavyweight division, from 1978 to 1985. In truth, there was little to choose between Ali and Holmes. Both were wonderful boxers, great thinkers, with piercing jabs and an ability to control the narrative in the ring, to improvise, to ensure they had the final say in the storyline. Both were technically gifted and incredibly tough with a frightening ability to absorb huge punishment without being knocked out. Both looked good too, like lighter-weight fighters. Most heavyweights are lumbering, crude, one-dimensional, mechanical. Imposing. But difficult to watch. Ali and Holmes had speed, mobility, fluidity.

Holmes couldn't scale to Ali's heights though. Couldn't come close. He didn't have the charisma. He didn't fight with the same balletic grace. Didn't have Ali's back story, the way he stood up for black people, his eloquence, his beauty, his ability to be vocal in situations when he had been expected to be compliant. Holmes, it seemed to many, stood more for money than politics.

And rarely would his fights have as much drama as Ali's. Holmes' fights were well scripted, technically sound, not expansive, unrepeatable, intimidating in their excellence. Ali won against the odds. Performed miracles. Against Sonny Liston in 1964. Against George Foreman in 1974. On both occasions people feared for Ali's health because, like Mike Tyson in the eighties, Liston and Foreman were frightening, more than human. Ali mocked fear and his opponents before the fight. He cracked jokes, made up poems, all while talking black politics, black liberation. All while spending as much time with ordinary people – signing autographs, delivering magic tricks, listening to their stories – as he was in training. Then he'd control the narrative in the ring. Perform a miracle. Then he'd crack more jokes afterwards. Talk more black politics, spend more time with people. Ali was the most grassroots megastar ever. Likely the first and only sports star crowned the most famous person on the planet.

Budd Schulberg, the Academy Award winning screenwriter of *On the Waterfront*, once wrote: 'Nothing reflects character more nakedly than boxing.' Schulberg once regarded the heavyweight champion of the world 'with a reverence just this side of religious fervour'. According to Schulberg: 'The heavyweight champion was no mortal man but stood with Lancelot and Galahad.' Ali stood with Lancelot and Galahad, perhaps more so than any of the great heavyweights, from Jack Johnson and Jack Dempsey to Joe Louis and Rocky Marciano.

Ali and Holmes faced each other on 2 October 1980, a few days after the Minter–Hagler fight. Ali was 38, Holmes 30. Ali had been retired for about two years. Holmes had graduated from being Ali's former sparring partner to world champion. Ali by this point had already started slurring his words, walking slower, talking slower.

Ali's biographer, Thomas Hauser, recalled on ESPN's *30 for 30* documentary episode *Muhammad and Larry*: 'Before the Nevada State Athletic Commission licensed Ali to fight, they asked him to go to the Mayo Clinic for a full report. That report said that when Ali tried to touch his finger to his nose, there was a slight degree of missing the target. He couldn't hop with the agility that doctors expected he would. He had trouble coordinating the muscles he used in speech. This is before he fought Larry Holmes.'

By fight night, Ali looked sedated. He was Chief Bromden from *One Flew Over the Cuckoo's Nest*. For ten rounds, Holmes hit him. Over and over. In round nine, Ali screamed. Ali didn't fight back, couldn't fight back. But he wouldn't give up, wouldn't go down. Holmes kept looking at the referee, he wanted him to stop the fight. He wouldn't. Eventually Angelo Dundee, Ali's long-time trainer, threw in the towel. Holmes cried.

I remember when highlights of the fight were shown on television. Not so much the details of what happened, more my father's response to the fight. I had little to no conception of Ali's full history, the 1960 Olympics, the poetry, Henry Cooper, Liston, the Nation of Islam, the Vietnam War, 'The Rumble in the Jungle', 'The Thrilla in Manilla'. My father cherished Ali's defiance and willingness to confront mainstream America, to defeat white America. If the Black-British footballers in the seventies, often victims of abuse from crowds, had symbolised what black people were going through in their everyday lives, Ali had been emblematic of what we could be. He did not bow when criticised for changing his name from Cassius Clay to Muhammad Ali and converting to Islam. He did not bow when he had been threatened with jail and lost his world titles because he refused to fight in the Vietnam War. He had been the highest profile athlete across the globe, yet he did not minimise his politics to attain or retain fame. He used his platform to highlight the plight of black people across the globe. With black history having been bleached, silenced and obscured, in education, on television, Ali was our great hero, our great king, a symbol of a heritage that had been denied, the black messiah.

I knew Ali had been an important figure to my father. My father would often pull an Ali pose in photographs with me. He'd pretend to be Ali when play-boxing against me. When Leon Spinks, a man who had no front teeth and the scowl of a demoted worker, defeated Ali in '78, our house mourned as if a major political figure had been assassinated or something.

At the point when the Ali–Holmes fight was about to start, my father put on his coat to leave the house. I thought my father's memory must have been fading. This was Ali. This was boxing. This was how we bonded. Yet what I had been seeing on the screen was not always what my father had been feeling. What I witnessed on the surface rarely reflected the reality of the situation. We were, in many ways, bonded by sport, but at times miles apart.

Maybe my dad knew the result. Maybe he knew the inevitability of the result. I didn't. I asked where he was going. Informed him that the Ali fight was about to start. He turned, and I'll never forget the look on his face. Anger mixed with hurt. A kind of disempowering look. Must have been the first time I'd seen my father display any level of vulnerability. When he said something like I don't want to see that fight, and then left, something sank inside of me.

Ali retired in 1981. At the time, I was still at an age where my parents' Jamaican culture conflicted with my external environment. I preferred chips to my mother's rice and peas. At home, the sounds of Max Romeo and Bob Marley were a constant. But I preferred Adam and the Ants. In my house, my father had two large speakers (roughly the height of an average year four pupil) in our living room. Never saw speakers that size in my white friends' houses. My father liked cricket. I preferred football. I was more cockney than Jamaican. Like two different worlds.

My attitude changed between 1981 and 1984. I had started to become more comfortable with my home world and friends with shared experiences. This gave me a sense of belonging, it welcomed me, strengthened me, put me at ease. Unlike the external environment – school, shops, transport – it had not been hostile or limiting. My emerging love of the West Indies cricket team played a fundamental role in that shift. The West Indies represented strength, they represented my parents' history, my heritage. No single team captivated me more than the West Indies side that toured England in 1984.

Cricket had always been a feature in the stories that my parents told me about Jamaica. They grew up in Galina, a small district in the hilly parish of St Mary in the northeast. St Mary had been the former residence of playwright Noël Coward who lived in a place called Firefly. Apparently, Coward did not like to entertain guests there, so he kept a guesthouse by the sea called Blue Harbour where he hosted major public figures such as Errol Flynn and Sir Winston Churchill. Author Ian Fleming's 15-acre Goldeneye estate was also in St Mary. As a teenager in the fifties, my mother, Magnore, would ride her bike from Galina to Goldeneye to deliver Fleming's groceries. It was not until my mother moved to England in 1961, a year after my father, that she found out that Fleming had been famous.

At an age when I was studying for my GCSE exams, my father had already left school, lived alone, and had been earning money by selling stones and limes by the side of Galina's dusty main road. His one-room shack had no running water, no toilet. My mother during her school years had been doing the books and shopkeeping for her uncle Frank or 'thumbing' a lift to go to the places where she could sell fabrics.

For my father, his childhood had been full of little ventures to earn money. He would go 'crabbing' at night, hoping that a little rain would entice the crabs to emerge from their burrows. Without a torch, my father made a light by filling a bottle three-quarters full of kerosene oil. He then wrapped a sardine tin lid round an eight-inch string of crocus, leaving about an inch exposed. My father dipped the tin covered crocus into the bottle leaving the inch-exposed crocus hanging outside of the bottle. To prevent kerosene leakage, he covered the bottle lid in soap and lit the exposed crocus to provide enough light to view and catch the crabs.

By morning, he would sell the crabs to people in the district or to local hotels. Once he'd made enough money, he bought a small rowing boat with his friend Jack Johnson to catch more fish to sell. They made wire fish pots (holes on either side) and used stale mackerel as bait. The method worked, but the only problem had been my father's limited tolerance for inhaling stale fish while moving back and forth on a boat. He aborted the scheme and turned to selling bananas. He would go to the port in Oracabessa to scrounge for bruised or small bananas. Then he'd load them into a wheelbarrow, wheel it four miles back to Galina and sell the fruit by the roadside.

None of these ventures were particularly lucrative, but my father never went without food. He'd also pick mangoes, sweetsop, soursop, paw or custard apples; he'd drink coconut water and eat the white jelly of the coconut with some sugar if he had no money to buy food. If he wanted a hot meal, he'd pick ackees and breadfruit or he'd dig up yams or plantain from the fields to cook in the bushes. He'd also play competitive games of dominoes for a loaf of bread or something to eat. My parents worked hard, living off their wits and imagination.

Cricket had given my father some conception of a world beyond Galina. He had been one of the best cricketers in the district, nicknamed 'HH' after bowler HH Hines Johnson and then 'Collie' after batsman O'Neil 'Collie' Smith. HH only played three times for the West Indies, all coming against England, when he was 37 years of age. Despite his advanced years, he had taken 13 wickets in those Tests. Collie was nearly as good a batsman as Sir Garfield Sobers. Sobers is universally regarded as the greatest all-round cricketer in the history of the sport. Smith and Sobers were good friends. Sadly, Smith died aged 26 in 1959 when a car driven by Sobers on the A34 near Staffordshire crashed into a 10-ton cattle truck. Jamaica was in shock. They took Smith's body back to Jamaica where an estimated 30,000 people mourned his death.[1]

Galina had no cricket coaches or scouts fawning over young talent because it was such a small district. Fantasies remained fantasies when you had to worry about what you were going to eat the following day. Cricket represented something much purer. The British elite had the money, the resources and the facilities. My father and his friends could not even afford cricket bats. They would cut a coconut branch and, when it dried, shape it into a bat. They did not have professional cricket balls (made of cork, wound by string and coated with leather) so they used tennis balls. There were no cricket grounds or even-surfaced pitches, so they played in the street, on the sidewalk or on any patch of open land, private or not. It would be those same qualities – enterprise, hard work, toughness, pride, resilience – that would underpin the West Indian cricket team's success and their determination not to hide. 'Cricket was a part of you,' my father would say. 'We played it every day, rain or shine.'

When the West Indies' matches were broadcast on the wireless, all the kids in Galina would gather round at Mr Reuben's grocery store to listen to the likes of HH, Collie and Sobers play. Those early West Indian teams were pioneers but also children of the colonial era. They played with pride and with passion, but there was little they could do to combat the history, the stereotypes and the infrastructure that governed their every move. The West Indies players were treated more like subjects than peers. They had some respect because of their sporting prowess. Not quite like other blacks. Beyond black. But not equal.

Cricket had been brought over to the Caribbean in part to demonstrate English dominance. The early West Indian players were pioneers, the first black players to break through internationally. The cricketing authorities admired them. Not only their brilliance and their resilience, but the way in which they conducted themselves. Compliant. Integrative. Rarely did they overtly challenge. This served to appease cricket's overwhelmingly white-led authorities, as they didn't perceive the growing presence of blacks in international cricket as a threat to the existing power structures of the game. In Simon Lister's book *Fire in Babylon*, he quotes what former England cricket captain Sir Pelham Warner said in 1950: 'The West Indies are among the oldest of our possessions, and the Caribbean Sea resounds to the exploits of the British Navy. Nowhere in the world is there a greater loyalty to, love of, and admiration for England.'

As such, those early West Indian teams endured stereotypes with little recourse to counter such views. They were regarded as subservient, ill-disciplined, likeable but a little lazy, jovial, enthusiastic. 'The erratic quality of West Indian cricket is surely true to racial type. At one moment these players are eager, confident and quite masterful; then as circumstances go against them you can see them losing heart.'[2] They were known throughout the world as 'Calypso Cricketers', a team that played for fun, a team that played to entertain.

West Indian cricket had also been governed as if a colony. There would not be a black president of the West Indies cricket board until the eighties. Black players were not allowed or indeed trusted to captain the team until 1959, when Sir Frank Worrell, after years of lobbying by writer, activist and historian

C L R James, became the first black captain of the West Indies. James had been supported in his efforts by Sir Learie Constantine, a cricketer, lawyer and politician who fought against racial discrimination during his years living in England and a man who would become the UK's first black peer.

There had also likely been a quota system in the West Indian team too, which meant that a certain percentage of the side had to be white. It's unlikely that the white West Indians earned their place on merit. From 1928, when the West Indies played their first Test match to 1960, when Worrell became captain, against the England team, white players only had a minor impact on the team in comparison to their black counterparts. A look at the batting and bowling averages during this period illustrates the point that black Test cricketers outperformed their white peers.[3]

These early black and brown West Indian players put the Caribbean on the map long before Bob Marley. And nothing was as sweet as a victory over England. Jamaica did not become 'independent' of British rule until 1962. So, every victory had been significant. Defeating the rulers went beyond national pride. It caused mayhem, hysteria. Galina would have a street party. The cricket team were the soldiers; cricket had been the tool to undermine the rulers.

By the time my father arrived in England in 1960, the West Indian team served another purpose; they incubated him and his peers from the hostile reception of English folks. Caribbean immigrants huddled together, sharing houses, jobs, money and resources to survive. For sure, my father attempted to fit in. Like the many workers from the Caribbean who arrived between 1948, when the *SS Empire Windrush* docked, through to the sixties, my father had arrived from a country in Jamaica that had been like a little Britain, with brown faces. He learnt more about the Empire than anything else. Black history obsolete. He had no major anxieties about being black in England. This was the mother country. Another country. He would be as much a citizen in England as he had been in Jamaica. He felt a great sense of loyalty before he had arrived on these shores. It was only in cricket where he felt any resentment towards his new homeland. Cricket had been the platform where England flexed its authority, epitomising its supremacy. A platform where, more than any sport, colonial attitudes had been reinforced.

Against this backdrop, it had been no surprise that my father started a cricket team in Balham on his arrival. It had been no surprise that he put a cricket bat and ball in my hands at such an early age. Couldn't say I liked cricket that much. But cricket soon became a part of me. The West Indies became a part of me. When I played cricket, I was not pretending to be Ian Botham. I was Michael Holding, Joel Garner or Malcolm Marshall.

If the West Indian teams that my father grew up listening to in the fifties were more compliant, the seventies' teams set the tone for the squad that toured England in 1984.

When Clive Lloyd captained the West Indies on its tour of Australia in 1975, they were humiliated by the pace and aggression of Aussie fast bowlers Dennis Lillee and Jeff Thomson. The West Indies lost the series 5–1. Soon after that tour, Lloyd realised he needed to change tactics. He started employing four quick bowlers to keep batsmen under constant pressure.

India toured the West Indies in 1975–76 and Lloyd unleashed four fast bowlers in the final Test, much to the dismay of the visitors. On an uneven Sabina Park surface in Jamaica, Michael Holding, Wayne Daniel, Bernard Julien and Vanburn Holder terrorised India, injuring three batsmen. By the time the Indian team came out to bat for a second time, they were battered and bruised. With five wickets down and only 97 runs on the board, Indian captain Bishan Bedi surrendered and ended the innings, losing the match. Three of his players were still injured from the first innings, two more were suffering from injuries too, so Bedi could not put any more players out. The West Indies won the series in brutal fashion and a new era was about to begin.

Had there been any doubt that Lloyd would use the same tactics against England later that summer, it was all but erased when England's South African born captain Tony Greig said: 'I think people tend to forget it wasn't that long ago they [the West Indies] were beaten 5–1 by the Australians and only just managed to keep their heads above water against the Indians just a short time ago as well ... You must remember that the West Indians, these guys, if they get on top are magnificent cricketers. But if they're down, they grovel, and I intend, with the help of Closey and a few others, to make them grovel.'

Coming from a South African commenting on a team comprising black and Asian players, Greig's statement carried racist connotations. The West Indies would make Greig grovel with one of the most brutal displays of fast bowling witnessed in England and one of the greatest batting performances by Viv Richards. During the Test matches in 1976, Richards scored 829 runs at an average of 118. The West Indian team won the five-match Test series 3–0 (two games were drawn) and all three one-day matches. The seventies version of the West Indies had been brought up in an independent Caribbean. They were more politicised, less willing to comply and keen, once and for all, to erase the image of Calypso Cricketers.

The West Indies' ascendancy coincided with a period of increased activism by Britain's black communities. The Windrush generation, the first set of Caribbean migrants to enter these shores en masse, were amenable. They had been 'hunted' down by the British. Post-war prosperity meant that Britain did not have enough workers, or at least enough willing workers to fulfil labour-market shortages in the new NHS, in transport. So, they sold the 'British Dream' to Caribbean citizens. The prospect of a new life, a better life. Britain did not have to pay for their schooling, their health or their housing up to that point. They were 'ready-made workers'. But Britain was not prepared for its new arrivals. Didn't think they needed to adjust. Wanted them to integrate. No questions asked. Shut up, be happy. All the run-down places and spaces that the now affluent white working-class people had vacated were now populated by the emergent Caribbean community.

For many of the Windrush generation, England had not been a dream. By the early seventies, opportunities and living conditions for their children had not vastly improved either. Jamaican-born poet Linton Kwesi Johnson encapsulated how many black people felt throughout the seventies when he sang 'Inglan is a bitch'. Two generations were fed up. Fed up of being forced to integrate without a say, to de-colourise; fed up of poor working conditions, fed up of poor schooling, poor housing; fed up of having to mini-mise to progress.

By the seventies, it had become difficult for Britain to ignore the rising cultural and political presence of black Britain. This included cultural theorist and sociologist Stuart Hall, the rise of the Notting Hill Carnival, the continued wisdom, writing and leadership of C L R James, the activism of Darcus Howe and Althea Jones-Lecointe, the victory of the Mangrove Nine which led to the first acknowledgement of racial hatred within the Metropolitan Police, the music of Aswad, Janet Kay and Steel Pulse.

Whether it was the poetry of Linton Kwesi Johnson, the rise of the Organisation for Women of Asian and African Descent and the Black Parents Movement, the proliferation of supplementary schools, the black publications that saw the light of day through Margaret Busby's Allison & Busby and John La Rose's New Beacon Books, or the Race Today Collective and the Institute of Race Relations holding power to account, black Britain had been gaining its identity, growing confident in its identity, creating platforms for self-knowledge and self-determination. So much of what these academics, artists, original intersectional feminists and activists fashioned had originally been ignored by main-stream institutions. We didn't exist. Black didn't exist. But these pioneers shoved their way through, often with minimal resource and against extreme opposition.

Fuelled by the activism and music of the Caribbean, Africa and the United States, the children of the Windrush generation took up the fight. They were actively fighting back with greater force, no longer fearful of the consequence and attracting white comrades to the struggle.

During this period, the West Indies continued to dominate cricket. They had won two World Cups (1975 and 1979) and been finalists in 1983, they had exacted revenge on Australia after the 1975 series and emerged from Kerry Packer's World Series 'Supertests' and one-day series against Australia and a World XI as arguably the world's most dominant side.

The 1984 West Indies team had a distinct set of characters, particularly its fast bowlers. Each had unique bowling actions that appeared to speak volumes about their approach to the game. They were led by Malcolm Marshall, Michael Holding and Joel Garner. Marshall would charge in and bowl at such pace that he appeared to be moving faster than the ball once it was released from his hands. But he had craft and guile. Holding was graceful, haunting, elegant. He would glide in to bowl effortlessly, quietly, only to unleash deceptively vicious balls, which is why he had the nickname 'Whispering Death'. And Joel Garner, all six feet eight inches of him, bundled in like an old man with a stitch running for the bus, only to uncoil at the last minute, lengthy like the Statue of Liberty, before delivering the ball so quick, so accurate, so full in length, he would make the batsmen jerk violently as if a rug had been pulled from beneath them. Missing from the 1984 tour was Andy Roberts: no-nonsense, stoic and the 'father' to all these bowlers, the man through which the West Indies' fearsome reputation had been established.

The West Indies remained the favourites in 1984, although there had been some belief that England could push them. In the 1983 World Cup Final, India surprisingly defeated the West Indies. India had made a modest 183 runs and it appeared as if the West Indies would run away with a third World Cup in a row. Inspired by captain Kapil Dev, India rattled the West Indies out for a paltry 140 in one of the greatest upsets in cricket history.

In 1982, the West Indies had also lost some of their best players to a rebel tour in South Africa, at that point banned from international cricket due to apartheid. South Africa had been desperate to get back on the world sporting stage, so they started offering large sums of money to teams, mainly in cricket and rugby, to tour illegally. Nelson Mandela would later say that the sporting ban contributed to his freedom and indeed the end of the apartheid regime.

The first target had been Viv Richards. By 1983, he was acknowledged by many of his contemporaries as the greatest player in the world, and the greatest batsman since Australia's legendary Don Bradman. Imran Khan, currently the Prime Minister of Pakistan and one of the great all-round cricketers in history, called Richards 'a complete genius ... no other batsman could attack me when I was at my peak'.[4] Dennis Lillee, arguably the greatest fast bowler in history, said, in his autobiography *Menace*, that 'for sheer ability to rip an attack apart, animal brutality and no fear in taking you on, I have to put Viv Richards on top of the list'. In 2000, *Wisden* would vote him as one of the five greatest players of the century, alongside Bradman, Sobers, Aussie spinner Shane Warne and English batsman Jack Hobbs.

His refusal to go to South Africa in 1983 had been symbolic. He was the best player in the world. The prize catch. If ever there had been a symbol of West Indies' shift from Calypso Cricketers, Englishmen with brown skin, and colonial subjects to antiracists, to independence, to rebels, it had been Richards. Wearing a red, gold and green wristband, the sight of Richards strutting from the pavilion to the batting crease was as dramatic and intimidating as watching Mike Tyson walk to a boxing ring. Richards would scan the audience and the opposing team as if they were his subjects. He would walk to the crease as if failure was not an option. In an era of hostile fast bowling, where Richards faced the likes of Lillee and Thomson from Australia, Imran Khan from Pakistan and his West Indian teammates, who he regularly faced in the English County Championship, Richards never wore a helmet. He had been a king without security, a superstar without a bodyguard, a target without protection.

Had Richards gone to South Africa, his departure would have signalled the premature death of West Indian cricket dominance and indeed all that the team had stood for since 1976. It would have opened the floodgates and made it acceptable for other Caribbean players to go.

'The whole issue [of race and apartheid] is quite central to me,' said Richards. 'I believe very strongly in the black man asserting himself in this world and over the years I have leaned towards many movements that followed this basic cause.'[5]

In the end, a West Indian team comprising world-class batsmen like Lawrence Rowe and Alvin Kallicharran, all-rounder Franklyn Stephenson and fast bowlers like Colin Croft and Sylvester Clarke went on tour, much to the wrath of the Caribbean. Each had been paid allegedly around US$100,000, huge sums at the time, for two tours against the banned South African team. Upon arrival in 1982, they had been honoured/insulted by being classified as 'honorary whites'. The tour had been a low point in the history of West Indies cricket. An unforgiveable stain. The 'rebel' players were less than 'house negros' and more like slave traders in the eyes of the Caribbean.

Former Jamaican Prime Minister Michael Manley summed up the feelings of Caribbean people in *A History of West Indian Cricket* when he wrote: 'To the members of the black diaspora the oppression which continues unabated in South Africa has become the symbol of more than a tyranny to be overthrown. Apartheid points like a dagger at the throat of black self-worth in every corner occupied by the descendants of Africa.'

In South Africa, these players became heroes. In the Caribbean, they became outcasts, banned for life from playing for the West Indies. Some of the players moved to the United States, hiding until the controversy died down. Others resumed their careers in England, away from the gaze of the Caribbean authorities, media and fans. For the lesser players on that tour, those who could not command interest in teams outside of the Caribbean, they were not so fortunate. Richard Austin, who would later be known as 'Danny Germs', ended up a cocaine addict, begging on the streets of Kingston. Herbert Chang would end up losing all his money. According to Robert Craddock of *The Courier-Mail*, Chang was last seen 'standing listlessly in the middle of the road … clearly out of it.'[6] Chang had allegedly been heard saying, 'Man, man, man, I just, I just wanna know which end I bowl from tomorrow.'[7]

The West Indies team that toured England in 1984 remained strong. In captain Clive Lloyd, opening batsmen Gordon Greenidge and Desmond Haynes, Viv Richards and fast bowlers Marshall, Holding and Garner, the team were fielding seven legends in every match they played. Think Brazil's 1970 World Cup football team, the All Blacks rugby union team from 2010 onwards, the Soviet Union's great ice hockey teams in the seventies or USA basketball's Dream Team at the 1992 Olympics. That West Indies team may have been the greatest Test side ever assembled.

In the first meeting between England and the West Indies that summer, a one-day international match at Old Trafford, Richards set the tone. He hit a then record 189 not out off 170 balls in what had been considered the greatest one-day batting performance in the history of the sport. But the one-day games had only been warm-up matches, starters. The main course would be the Test series.

Test cricket. Two teams. Five days. Two chances for each team to score the most runs. Team game. But a sequence of one-on-one challenges, bowler versus batsman. Difficult to follow all the way through. Long. Too long for even the most rational sports fan to follow. But surely one of the greatest of tests for any sportsman. Batting. Bowling. Fielding. Tactics. Weather. Violent weather. Control. Uncontrol. Beyond control. Pitches can dictate, be it hard, cracked, flat, great for batting, bad for bowling, bad for batting, great for bowling. It can all change from day to day. Momentum swings. Swinging all the time. Need for concentration, patience. Need your team, need all eleven men. Tuned in. Tuned on. Ready to battle, ready to roll, to play their role.

Couldn't imagine. I played cricket to a high level at school. At one point, I represented four teams. These were one-day games. A few overs. A few hours to compete. Half a Saturday or weekday evening lost to the game. Exhausting. Couldn't get over the powerlessness of cricket. During the many hours you play, you have a limited amount of time to have a direct impact. You may bowl five or ten overs. Can't bowl all of them. If you're batting and you're bowled out, you're out. No second chance. Better make the most of your time. The rest of the time you're either fielding while teammates are bowling or sitting in the pavilion watching the game while your teammates are batting. If you don't seize your moment with bat or with ball, you spend a lot of time limply thinking about what could have been, while trying to motivate your teammates to seize their moments. Too much damn time to think. Couldn't imagine having to do it for five days.

For the viewer, bliss. A friend for five days. You end your week on a high. In those days, a Test match in England started on a Thursday (the build-up), reached its peak over the weekend (when you could go to see it live if you had been working during the week) and, if you were lucky, it would reach a conclusion on the Monday (a great way to start the new week). A novel. A box set. For the live audience, unpredictable. They don't know what they'll get. Five days can at times blend into one. But the 1984 series was different. The games didn't blend. The results were predictable, but the drama within the games was unpredictable.

First Test: A Malcolm Marshall bouncer strikes English Test debutant Andy Lloyd in the head. Dramatic. As the ball rises towards Lloyd's head, he twists to avoid it. Too late. Hits. Hurts. In a split second, it looks as if the ball has spun Lloyd round 180 degrees. Pause. He's down, toppled, facing the stumps that had once been behind him. Lloyd is hospitalised. He never played Test cricket again. West Indies win.

Second Test: England are close to victory but West Indies' opening batsman Gordon Greenidge starts limping. Hobbling as if struck with cramp. Greenidge's limp is like Michael Jordan's tongue sticking out or Zinedine Zidane puking up on a football pitch. Something beautiful is about to happen. Greenidge scores 214 not out. West Indies win.

Third Test: Malcolm Marshall, the best bowler in the world, arguably the greatest fast bowler ever, a man at/near the peak of his powers, breaks his thumb. Larry Gomes is close to getting a century, but nine West Indian wickets are down. Either Marshall comes out to bat with a broken thumb (in two places) or Gomes will be disappointed. Marshall comes out. Cast on one forearm, holding the bat in his other arm. Batting with one arm, he fends off England's meagre attack. Gomes gets his century. Marshall returns, cast on forearm, cricket ball in the other. He is now bowling. Decimates England. Gets seven out of 10 English batsmen out. Michael Holding, a great bowler but a poor batsman at best, also demolishes the bowling of Bob Willis, hitting five sixes on his way to 59 runs. Willis retires from Test cricket. The West Indies win.

Fourth Test: Winston Davis is a fast bowler who cannot get a game for the West Indies because of Holding, Marshall and Garner. He gets his chance here and fractures English batsman Paul Terry's arm. Terry returns, arm in sling to help teammate Allan Lamb get a century. But he never plays for England again. Davis, like Holding, is a mediocre batsman. But he scores 77 runs. West Indies win.

Fifth Test: England blackwashed. West Indies win the series 5–0.

Gordon Greenidge was voted Player of the Series, with an average of over 81. Marshall, Garner and Holding scooped almost

70 wickets between them. For Viv Richards, it had been a relatively quiet series. He averaged just under 42 with the bat. But for the best part of the summer, Richards had been subdued, which was unusual for a player who saved his best for England.

During the 'grovel' series of 1976, Richards hit 291 in the fifth Test at The Oval. In the 1979 World Cup final at Lord's, it had been Richards' 138 not out against England that had been the game-winning performance to secure victory. Later, in 1986, in front of his home fans in Antigua, Richards would hit the then fastest Test century ever, in just 56 balls. The combination of Richards' cruel excellence and posturing on the pitch, his aloofness and politics off the field made England's cricketing establishment uncomfortable. He did not fit their notion of what a black man should be. Didn't come across as grateful enough.

Former *Wisden* editor Dave Frith once wrote, 'For me that should be the limit of aggression in Test cricket, but now we are in very serious times and all sorts of things are motivating people – religious belief and racial conviction – and most of all these resentments. And I think it's rather sad if you need a resentment like that to fire you up. You should glory in the gift that you've been given. I mean, he was a born athlete, Viv Richards. He surely could have gone out there and done just as well and retained his cool. I wish he didn't get angry so often, because I believed in him. But after that evening I was left quite worried, I thought, Well, he's talking to young kids, and if he preaches that sort of stuff, the world's not going to be a very peaceful place.'[8]

In Richards, cricket had found a player that had been fundamentally rupturing the status quo. Rupturing the norm.

Rupturing every conceivable notion of what a West Indian cricketer could and should be. He had been creating a new blueprint. Changing the narrative away from the compliance demanded by the civilising abolitionists. Richards' assertiveness was a threat. His politics became a proxy for radicalism. England had for many years treated the West Indies, both politically and in cricket, with contempt. It had not been right, in their eyes, for Richards to be fuelled by oppressions of the past; a past not relevant to the present or to the future.

My mum couldn't watch. The 'othering' of blackness, the casual racism, the biased commentary – my mum felt every remark, every dig, every complaint. She knew that most commentators had little or no conception of where these players had come from. Or where she'd come from. If in Ali–Holmes I saw for the first time vulnerability in my father, in my mother's response to the critics of the West Indies, I had seen where some of my politics had come from. A staunch and boundless love of black people. For the first time, I recognised that the fear I felt because of others' fear was in fact real. Not an abstract conception I had been internalising, running away from, trying to explain, failing to explain. The switch. A switch. I thought less about what we as black people were doing wrong and more about what the mainstream media had been claiming we were doing wrong. Not us. But them.

As the West Indies' dominance continued, the criticisms heightened. Not just Richards. Clive Lloyd – bespectacled, respected, more diplomat than cricketer – had been severely criticised for his tactics. The coverage of his captaincy often felt like he had betrayed his colonial masters; he had failed to follow in the footsteps of Sir Frank Worrell and others who never used such tactics. Lloyd had little or no respect for the former rulers. Didn't care what they said, or how they portrayed him.

In the eyes of the media and English public, it always appeared as if the West Indies were never worthy winners. They won because so many of their players developed their talent in the English county cricket system. They succeeded because of natural athleticism. They were successful because they cheated. Implied. Never really said. The bouncers unfair, the slow over rates an unsportsmanlike tactic. They made the game boring, they were boorish. The criticisms became a perverse obsession, lacking critical thought. The criticisms had frequently been vile. Often laced with what many would see as racist or stereotypical undertones. Usually delivered by the white establishment's recognised names.

'Until we can breed seven-foot monsters willing to break bones and shatter faces, we cannot compete against these threatening West Indians. Even the umpires seem to be scared that the devilish-looking Richards might put a voodoo sign on them!' from a letter published in *Wisden Cricket Monthly*.[9]

'The summer game, it had become something else. It had lost its romance, it had lost its sportsmanship, it had lost its lovely edge; it was now a place where people got frightened,' said David Frith, editor of *Wisden Cricket Monthly*.[10]

'Their game is founded on vengeance and violence and fringed by arrogance,' said Frith.[11]

'Most people on whose support English cricket depends, believe monotonous fast bowling to be both brutalising the game and boring to watch,' said the *Sunday Times*' Robin Marlar.[12]

English journalist Geoffrey Moorhouse was 'sickened' by 'the downright thuggery of fast bowlers working in relays to remove batsmen by hurting and intimidating them'.[13]

John Woodcock, editor of *Wisden Cricketers' Almanack*, wrote an article with a picture captioned 'the unacceptable face of Test cricket'.[14] He had also classified the West Indies' fast bowling as 'chilling' and warned that its 'viciousness was changing the very nature of the game'.[15]

'It seemed that cricket had been transformed into something really ugly,' said Frith.[16]

West Indian supporters felt every comment. And we probably only heard or read about a quarter of them. I did not realise until much later, when books such as Mike Marqusee's *Anyone But England* and Simon Lister's *Fire in Babylon* were released, just how bad the commentary and views published had really been. Seven-foot monsters, devilish-looking, vengeance, violence, brutalising, thuggery, viciousness, ugly. Shut your eyes. Hear those words and those phrases. Not describing slavery, colonialism or apartheid, but cricket. Twitter language. YouTube comments. Comments that can easily be traced to age-old stereotypes of black folks.

If you can't beat them on the field of play, change the rules of the game. How else do you undermine a movement? The media mediates, sways public opinion. There were calls for changes. Increase the over rate. Sanctions. Reduce the number of non-English players in the County Championship. Reduce bouncers. The media and authorities conspired to undermine the impact and indeed the legacy of the West Indies.

The West Indies never stood a chance. No infrastructure. No sway. Still dependent, colonialised. Beginning of the end. The

West Indies never controlled the narrative, never had control of the game in the areas where it really mattered. They always had a cricket board with no money, a board that bowed to bigger boards, aboard someone else's ship.

The colonial attitude of the establishment had not just been confined to the West Indies team. As a West Indies fan, I never followed the black players who represented the English national team. They felt like traitors, sell-outs. But those black players had been subjected to just as much hostility from the press as the West Indies team. And they were meant to be allies.

In 1980, Barbadian Roland Butcher became the first black cricketer to represent England. Through the eighties, a steady trickle of black players like Gladstone Small, Wilf Slack, Monte Lynch, Norman Cowans, Phil DeFreitas and Devon Malcolm played for England, alongside several white foreign-born cricketers. The eighties had been a bad decade for English cricket. An emerging narrative through this period had been the English team's identity crisis, born from the 'foreign' make-up of the team.

You could hear it in the commentary. You could see it in the press coverage. Nothing quite as blatant or emotive as the boos on a football pitch. But similar criticisms you'd hear about black footballers and whether they were loyal to England, bled for England.

In 1990, Tory MP Norman Tebbit would crystalise the sentiment when he questioned which side Britain's Asian population would cheer for in a game of cricket. The Tebbit test brought to the surface the issues of belonging and national identity when he said, 'Are they still harking back to where you came from or where you are?'[17] For Tebbit, living in England meant supporting

England over one's place of birth. By giving up your culture, this would signify true loyalty to England. As the story evolved, Tebbit would apply the theory to second-generation blacks too.

To me and my friends, Tebbit's question sounded archaic and of little relevance to us. Like many of the kids at my school, I supported the West Indies in cricket, Brazil in football and Great Britain in basketball. Sugar Ray Leonard was my favourite boxer. For me, shared experiences remained stronger than a shared birthplace. I felt safer around my black and Asian peers than white. Practically all the conflict I had faced during school had been the result of anti-black racism. I couldn't support England, because England rarely supported me. Not every black person felt the same, however. Tebbit's theory seemed to target people of colour. Not a nationality test. A colour test.

Tebbit's test mirrored much of casual racist commentary of the eighties. I couldn't think of a time, a moment, when I was watching cricket through the eighties and regularly buying cricket publications, that white foreigners had faced as much scrutiny. For much of the eighties, black English players, like the footballers, stayed mute.

Years later, when former civil servant Robert Henderson penned an essay in *Wisden Cricket Monthly* in July 1995 entitled 'Is it in the blood?', the casual racism and elitism of English cricket surfaced once more. Henderson, who referred to black people in the article as 'negroes', claimed that 'a coloured England-qualified player feels satisfaction (perhaps subconsciously) at seeing England humiliated, because of post imperial myths of oppression and exploitation'. *Myths*. He would go on to say that 'mixed groups' would never 'develop the same camaraderie as eleven unequivocal

Englishmen', describing foreign-born English players as 'interlopers' and describing West Indians based in England as 'generally resentful and separatist'.

The article was widely condemned by cricket legends such as Ian Botham, David Gower and Michael Atherton, who would resign from *Wisden*'s editorial board as a result. Black cricketers like fast bowler Devon Malcolm and all-rounder Phil DeFreitas, implicated in Henderson's piece, would later successfully sue the publication (despite being advised otherwise by cricket's players' union). But the cricket authorities had been at pains to cover up the fact that the legendary publication had just published an ill-informed, ill-researched piece of racist propaganda. That Frith, *Wisden*'s editor, couldn't see it, was hardly surprising. Frith once said that Jamaican-born Devon Malcolm 'acts, thinks, sounds and looks like a Jamaican. This hits the English cricket lover where it hurts.'[18] What qualified Frith to know what a Jamaican acts like, how they think, what they looked like, I don't know. I've never read all of Frith's articles. But I cannot remember him condemning South African-English players like Allan Lamb or Robin Smith for sounding South African. Did they look like typical South Africans? Translated: Malcolm is black and that hits the English cricket lover where it hurts. Even allowing for the time, the politics of the English press seemed embarrassingly dated, perversely discriminatory, lacking in self-reflection, humility or understanding. They may have known black players, been friends with them, gone to the West Indies, eaten jerk chicken and rice and peas, but they had little conception of what it meant to be black. They made little attempt to find out. The message seemed to be that blackness could not equal Englishness. Worse still, in

my mind it felt as if these writers and commentators were implying that English identity was some sort of proxy for racial purity.

Malcolm would later say in his autobiography *You Guys Are
History!*, 'My kids had all been born in England, for heaven's
sake. They went to integrated schools and had white godparents.
We all considered England our home, and colour wasn't an issue
in our choice of friends at school.'

Phil DeFrietas, who also had his Englishness questioned by
journalists throughout his career, continued to play for the
national team despite threats from the National Front to kill him
and his family if he played for England. DeFreitas turned down
the opportunity of going on a 'rebel' tour of South Africa during
apartheid when white national team members sacrificed their
England careers temporarily to cash in on the riches offered by
the racially corrupt regime. DeFreitas, in his autobiography
Daffy, said that he never had the 'desire to play for West Indies'
and given that he had learnt the game here, he felt he had a debt
to pay to England. Not all black folks the same. Just like white
English folks, there will be some who will die for England, and
others who will not. The problem had less to do with black
players and their motivations and much more to do with England
and its own fragile state. That appeared to be the barrier, or at
least a rarely questioned barrier, to true cohesion.

England attributed their failure to a crisis of identity because
they were trying so hard to hold on to the idea of Empire as the
bonding force for the team. But this conception was now dated.
Imaginary. The past. The English team no longer reflected
England's imagined self. And that's what really hurt.

*   *   *

My PE teacher and cricket coach in secondary school clearly did not, in my view, see blackness and Britishness as compatible. A stout, flushed-face man, more darts player than athlete, he often verbally abused pupils with his breathy, sour tones. I found him intimidating. I did not join the school football team in my first year because of his constant shouting and bullying. When, for the first time, he umpired one of our cricket matches, I had been captain. I dropped an easy catch. 'Why the hell were you made captain, Beardwell?' he shouted. Always called me that, Beardwell, with a dismissive tone.

He assumed I supported the West Indies. So, he would mock me and every other black kid during PE lessons when they lost. Can't remember ever saying I had been a West Indies fan. Thank God for Viv. It seemed like every time this teacher found fault, Viv, even in his later years, would do something to shut him up. In the 1987 World Cup, the West Indies lost their first match against England. This teacher prowled around making scornful comments. He'd probably call it banter. But it was offensive. Often discriminatory. But I had little option but to take it. I mean, who could I complain to? And what would they really do about it?

This had been a weakened West Indian team; no Marshall, Holding or Garner, no Greenidge or Lloyd. But to lose to England, still embarrassing. West Indies' following match came against Sri Lanka, then still a minor side. But given that the Sri Lankans were playing at home, I feared the worst. Richards once more rose to the occasion. He hit 181 runs off 125 balls, momentarily silencing my teacher.

Temporary reprieve. The teacher took the captaincy of the school cricket team away from me. No reason. Gave it to a white kid, one of his favourite players from the football team. The only white kid on the team. Under my captaincy, the team had been poor. Under the white kid's leadership, we were just as bad if not worse. I wanted the captaincy back. I'd been playing well. Felt as if I was still the best player in the team.

I approached the teacher and told him that I wanted to captain the team again, or to at least co-captain. He said no, insulted that I would ask such a thing. I asked him why. He refused to respond. So, I refused to play. He made me run laps around the sports field in every PE lesson. At the start of every session, he'd growl, 'Are you going to play?' I'd say no. And then he would make me do laps while the other kids played football or cricket.

I didn't know whether the teacher's decision to take the captaincy away from me had been racially motivated, even if I suspected it was. Wasn't the sole point. I didn't like the way he dismissed me, the way he treated me, the way he bullied me. Without prompting, the rest of the team agreed with my assertion. They didn't like my treatment either. So, they refused to play too. The cricket team went on strike.

A black teacher summoned me and the other black and brown players to his classroom to try and end the strike. I sat staring out the window as he tried to reason with us, make us aware that it was our duty to represent the school. The meeting ended in a stalemate.

The situation had become embarrassing to the school as it could no longer field a cricket team. The PE teacher relented. He made me co-captain. We ended up with three captains: one black, one white and one Indian.

The PE teacher continued to shout at me. He continued to try to intimidate me. I don't believe our results were significantly better, but it had been a slight victory. It was probably the first time that I didn't minimise myself. The first time I had not been hiding.

Cricket represented the first time that I can remember feeling a true sense of pride in my Caribbean heritage. At home, my cultural reference points were more Jamaican than they were English. Outside of home, black and Caribbean culture and its history had been non-existent. Indeed, the only black person I would learn about through my whole school life would be athlete Jesse Owens, and that had only been in the context of Hitler and World War II. Until I discovered West Indies cricket, there had been a whole side of me that did not exist to my white peers and teachers. When the West Indies forced its way into public consciousness, I didn't have to minimise as much. Didn't have to apologise or hide as much. In these cricketers was hope; hope that I wouldn't always be anxious about being trapped between blackness and Britishness.

Couldn't win though. Couldn't change this narrow perception of blackness. A perception that we were subjects. If we were not subjects then we were somehow extremists, enemies of the state. Couldn't change the perception that we were all the same. I was no different to my father. No different to a Nigerian. We were possessions. Guests. Barbaric, devilish-looking, ugly. Couldn't win by rebelling. Couldn't win by being compliant. Couldn't win for trying. Blackness had been a white problem, not my problem. I'd started to recognise this through cricket and the establishment's illogical response to black players. The establishment's inability to see blacks as equals, its inability to see blacks as truly English, its inability to acknowledge us on our own terms.

Blackness could only be seen through their eyes, their history, their struggles. Our version, our history, our lens did not exist. It didn't seem to exist to my PE coach and it didn't exist to the establishment.

'It was only long years after,' said C L R James, 'that I understood the limitation on spirit, vision and self-respect which were imposed on us by the fact that our masters, our curriculum, our code of morals, everything began from the basis that Britain was the source of all light and leading, and our business was to admire, wonder, imitate, learn; our criterion of success was to have succeeded in approaching that distant ideal —to attain it of course was impossible.'[19]

The West Indies cricket team had been the purest sporting experience I had witnessed. It was John Edgar Wideman on 'race',* Serena Williams' return to Indian Wells after being racially abused by its crowd early in her career, Public Enemy's 'Rebel Without a Pause', the Newham 7. This uprising had been televised. It was legal. Attractive. Brutal. In living black and white. It fractured whiteness (opening the doors for India and Pakistan to follow) and made the rulers the subjects, providing an image of what it would be like if you were us and we were you. England had been colonised. We had been decolonised.

I'm not sure I could ever support a team as much as that West Indies side. They meant more to me than Ali. They were activism, style, excellence *and* heritage. They amplified my parents' childhood stories. They never minimised, despite criticism. They

* John Edgar Wideman is an American writer and professor, and the author of ten novels and five non-fiction books. Wideman was the recipient of the Pen/Faulkner Award in 1990 and an American Book Award in 1991.

exposed the fragility of the Empire state of mind. They validated me, my past, my present. They represented a part of me, the heart of me, but not all of me. I was stillborn in England. Still more English than Jamaican. I needed to find the English me, the non-white-defined English me, the something that represented a side of me that my father could never be.

CHAPTER 3

THE SHOT

WHEN I STARTED WATCHING BASKETBALL, I discovered for the first time a side of Englishness that spoke to me, spoke about me and spoke for me. Through the mid-to-late eighties, I followed a group of basketball players, primarily children of the Windrush generation, who played the game with a distinct Black-English style. A 'hyphenated' style. A style that reflected the dual identity of being black and being English. A style that came to personify my experience.

Historian and academic Paul Gilroy once said that the song 'Keep on Movin' by British music group Soul II Soul 'is notable for having been produced in England by the children of Caribbean settlers and then re-mixed in a (Jamaican) dub format in the United States by Teddy Riley, an African-American'. Soul II Soul, he said, 'projected the distinct culture and rhythm of life of black Britain'.[1] These basketball players were the first athletes I witnessed who projected a similar culture and rhythm, a combination of the flash and brashness of urban America, the toughness of their inner-city upbringing, and the discipline and work ethic implanted by their Caribbean parents.

These players had the potential to dispel the myth that a mixed heritage team couldn't form a successful British national team.

They could have provided British basketball with an opportunity to take the sport mainstream. They could have provided a vision of what a cohesive multi-cultural Britain would look like. They could have been the first truly mixed team that Brits would root for.

I was compelled to watch basketball from a young age. As mentioned, everyone I met would ask, 'Do you play basketball?' I had no reply. I needed to find out more. So, when Channel 4 started to show live games in 1982, it became must-see television for me.

The opening titles featured two women, one with dour brown hair and the other with a sandy crop, dancing to a spineless soul-funk tune. They were dressed in gaudy orange leotards with matching rah rah skirts and sparkly blue bow ties. With dance moves as elaborate as ones you'd expect to see in a primary school play, the titles looked more like a cheap promotional video for a local leisure centre than the opening credits of a prime-time television show. Cheerleading had never looked so unflattering.

Once the cheerleaders departed, presenter Simon Reed came on screen. Reed, the younger brother of the late actor Oliver Reed, was likeable, unruffled and cool with hypnotic eyes and hidden upper teeth. Reed conveyed passion for a sport unfamiliar to the British public without being over-animated. Next to him sat the six foot seven American Miles Aiken, a former basketball player for Real Madrid. Aiken had the looks of a Motown singer, the deep, succulent voice of a soul DJ and an annoying habit of mispronouncing players' names. Together they looked as if they were commentating in different time zones. For me, and for most people in England, Channel 4's foray into the razzmatazz of

American sport in 1982 would have been their first experience of basketball.

The players from the competing teams, Crystal Palace Supersonics and Birmingham Bullets, ran onto a court at the Aston Villa Leisure Centre that had been painted green, like a football pitch. Palace, clad in tight white vests and equally snug shorts, looked like a bunch of swans flapping around in a pond full of algae. There was nothing remotely fashionable or cool about the sport. This was the time before baggy shorts, cornrow hairstyles, tattoos, customised trainers, earrings, headbands, armbands, leg bands and all the other cool accessories players wear nowadays. These were the days before rap music became basketball's soundtrack, before kids were sporting Air Jordans, before basketball had international sports stars like David Beckham and Thierry Henry sitting courtside. There wasn't even an enviable Afro to dote on.

I am not sure what the crowd expected. I am not sure what I expected. Like most watching on TV, who knew anyone played basketball in England? The 3,500 people in attendance, comprising primarily white male council-worker types, looked baffled too. They spent the best part of the game giggling hysterically at dunks and other spectacular plays as if they were observing a circus act. And why not? Here they were watching a game with an unusually high scoring rate played in what appeared like a breezy community hall with freakishly tall men in long socks.

Channel 4 joined the game in the second half. The Bullets led 42–38. Reed and Aiken spent much of their commentary building up the rivalry between two American players, the Supersonics'

Dave Shutts and the Bullets' Russ Saunders. The American players would often receive top billing over here. They came over to England with huge reputations. These sportsmen usually had the talent to play in the NBA (National Basketball Association), the best league in the world. But they came to these shores with some sort of baggage. They were either too small, too one-dimensional, too lazy, or too dependent on drugs or alcohol. But they were the stars of our league, the guys who scored all the points. Behind these Americans sat this group of homegrown players who created a Black-English style that I could identify with. These players could graft, play defence, do the dirty work, and make the Americans look good, like most British players of the time. But this generation were also less willing to play second fiddle to the Americans.

Perhaps no player symbolised English basketball's inability to harness black talent and the hyphenated style more than Joel Moore – someone who, I would later find out, had the talent to give the NBA a good shot.

Moore was just 18 in 1982, when I first saw him play in that first televised match. He had been considered British basketball's hottest prospect at the time. In a country where it was more common for a youngster to kick a ball than to bounce one, Moore had been the nearest Britain had to a natural talent. He had long arms, the shoulders of a rugby player, and although only eleven stone condensed in a six foot one frame, he had a chest with the hammering quality of a Graeco-Roman wrestler. Moore had been more athletic than most Brits in the sport and could do more with the ball too; he was also flashy and ambitious.

He discovered basketball after seeing the Harlem Globetrotters as a nine-year-old. Mesmerised by their flair, the sport soon became an obsession. Moore would dribble the ball to and from school. He would use estate signs as imaginary hoops. At times, he would sleep with the ball in his bed or sneak out on Christmas Day to practise his dribbling. Basketball gave him confidence, a platform to express himself more than he could in the school playground at Deptford Green or in class. Moore also felt that basketball was the most individual of team sports, where one man could truly make a difference to a team, and shine.

Besides basketball, Moore kept himself busy working part-time. He started by selling items in a friend's leather shop. He also worked in a factory washing dishes and stacking shelves. Moore could afford the latest sounds from Phyllis Hyman, Evelyn 'Champagne' King and Yellowman, and the latest fashions, the Farah slacks, Slazenger trainers and gold rope chains. Sport and work enabled him to avoid getting caught up in inner-city problems, the menace of the National Front, police harassment, petty crime. But basketball had been his real passion and Crystal Palace basketball club offered a potential pathway to riches.

Palace was British basketball's version of Liverpool in football, the Dallas Cowboys in American football or the New York Yankees in baseball. They were the most dominant team in the sport. An institution. A club that had outgrown the domestic league in which it had been competing. Palace had been successful in European competition; they hosted an annual tournament over the New Year period, which enticed Europe's best teams, and they attracted the best talent from the United States. This included Alton Byrd and Jim Guymon, arguably the greatest players in

British basketball league history, and six foot five Larry Dassie, a man who could score 40 points against the best teams in Europe and, legend has it, would drink Guinness for breakfast, outplay teammates wearing flip-flops and regularly turn up to morning practices straight from a punk gig. Palace also had the most dominant junior club in the country, led by coach Roy Packham.

By the early eighties, there had been an influx of black players into the junior programme. What had once been the domain of white players, largely from Crystal Palace's surrounding counties, now featured a crop of young black players from all over London. This may have been the result of so many schools diverting black youths towards sport. This had been a tactic of many schools to integrate or engage black male pupils, often at the expense of academic encouragement. Being pushed towards sport was actually one of the better options for black pupils in the seventies and eighties.

Guyanese academic Bernard Coard's book *How the West Indian Child is Made Educationally Subnormal in the British School System*, published in 1971, highlighted the problems black pupils faced in the education system. He wrote: 'There are three main ways in which a teacher can seriously affect the performance of a Black child: by being openly prejudiced; by being patronising; and by having low expectations of a child's abilities.' Power. Teachers had the power to dictate black pupils' prospects, whether entering them for lower exams, excluding them or directing them towards sport. I had experienced this myself.

I was pretty good at cricket. I would spend hours playing cricket (for the school, the borough or local clubs) or looking after junior players, but I received little encouragement academically.

Beyond cricket, and with the exception of four teachers through my five years, the school didn't really know me. The only time I had ever spoken to the head teacher occurred when I had been wrongly accused of stealing a pool table from the common room. When I left, my final report advised that I should take a vocational career path. I had no idea how they had come to that conclusion. All of my decent grades had come in humanities. It felt as if they had a template for black kids – nursing, trade, trains, sport, or exclusion. It felt as if they had already written my report before I had started secondary school.

We suffered in silence. Being pushed into sport was better than going to an alternative provision or being excluded, a fate that in these more lawless school days had been a distinct possibility.

Palace's junior team included Steve Bucknall, Michael Hayles and Trevor Anderson from schools in southeast London and Junior Taylor from northwest London. Each player came to the team with towering reputations. Each had been the best player in their schools and, like Moore, supremely confident in their own ability. The competition was fierce.

When Moore had an opportunity to play with the seniors in the first televised game, he hardly made a splash. He entered with less than 17 minutes to play. Other than a spin-move, which left Saunders flailing aimlessly as if trying to catch a £10 note in a violent wind, that had been the extent of Moore's contribution.

Soon after, Supersonics' coach Danny Palmer demoted Moore back to the bench. As he trudged slowly off the court, he snatched a towel out of oncoming teammate Dave Shutts' hand. His disappointment so evident, Aiken commented: 'Joel Moore wasn't too happy with that. He was just getting warmed up.'

The hero of the game ended up being Trevor Anderson, one of Moore's ex-teammates on the junior team. Within the space of about two and a half minutes, he scored eight points. With only a few seconds remaining on the clock, and the Bullets leading 77–75, Anderson bolted into the air as if being airlifted by a helicopter and shot from around 20 feet out. The ball clanged off the backboard smack into the net to level the score.[2]

Anderson looked like a child who had taken his first steps in front of giddy parents. The whole team high fived him. Moore awoke from his slump to hug Anderson. For Moore, it felt like a victory for the new generation. Anderson couldn't have picked a better time to become a hero. One dramatic moment – watched by over a million viewers – illustrated how basketball could be as theatrical as a boxing contest or as tense as a penalty shootout in football. Palace eventually won the game. Basketball had found its place. I was hooked.

As I continued to follow British basketball through infrequent coverage on Channel 4, occasional highlights on the BBC and primarily by reading Richard Taylor's *Basketball Monthly*, a pattern seemed to emerge. I knew the names of the American players Art Wearren, Russ Saunders, Steve Bontrager, Dan Davis more than the British players. I'd see players like Moore one year, then they tended to disappear the next. I never quite knew why or where they had gone.

The pathways for British players had never been clear in this country. British basketball did not have the infrastructure to support talent management and progression and even when money came in, little of it leaked into grassroots development. The most lucrative path was to go abroad via the American high school and college system. America offered superior coaching, higher level competition and training but, more importantly, it provided exposure to the NBA or a clearer route towards a paid career in the sport. But this had not been systemised in Britain. If a young player was lucky enough to have a coach with connections, then they could get a scholarship. But you would have to be lucky. Steve Bucknall had taken this route and Moore followed, when he received a scholarship to US International University in 1984. Moore didn't stay long, however, as he was homesick.

He returned to England to play for Portsmouth in 1985. John Deacon, Chairman of Portsmouth football club, invested in the belief that basketball would be the next big thing. Prime-time television, advertising and major sponsorship had enabled the league to entice high-calibre players, pay competitive wages and attract mainstream coverage.

Moore was reunited with coach Palmer and Palace teammates Joe White and Trevor Anderson. He also played with Dassie and fellow legends Alan Cunningham and Colin Irish. At 21, Moore had never had so much fun and he was earning a good wage (likely the equivalent today of £55k–£60k).

By the late eighties, British basketball looked completely different from a decade earlier. In the seventies, Crystal Palace's Paul Philp had been the only major black player in the English national team. Now, white players were in the minority. Palace had produced Moore and Steve Bucknall among others. Across the country, the rising stars included Kenny Scott (Birmingham), Karl Brown (Leicester), the Scantlebury brothers (Peter and Richard) from south London, Roger Huggins who played for East London, Manchester's Carl Miller and Sandwell's

Martin Henlan. These players were not marginal talents, extras, role players for flashy Americans. They had star potential. A full-scale takeover was about to occur, and it took an American to realise it.

The 32-year-old Connecticut-born Joe Whelton coached Great Britain's basketball team during the 1987–88 Olympic qualifying tournament. Moore and Bucknall joined seven other black or mixed-heritage players on the 12-man squad. They played the game in a hurried, dogged, defensively assertive style, intimidating their European counterparts.

Great Britain advanced to the finals of the Olympic basketball qualifying tournament by crushing Holland 85–65 in Holland. I remember purchasing a copy of *Basketball Monthly* (September 1988) and reading the headlines from the Dutch press, which labelled Great Britain as 'street fighters'. It had not been a compliment. The Dutch press at one point asked Whelton: 'How can you expect to play smart basketball with so many urban players?' While it had been common in English football for the media to riddle commentary with lazy stereotypes about black players, you didn't hear or read such views in the English basketball press. The reaction of the Dutch press came as a surprise to Whelton, who lashed out: 'We've taken a lot of criticism this week. I've been told I've got too many old players, too many black players and that we can't play smart basketball. Well it's my team, I'm sitting on top right now and it feels good.'

In the final group matches of the Olympic qualifying tournament, Great Britain played the giants of European basketball, with the top four teams out of the eight qualifying for the Olympic finals in Seoul, South Korea. Great Britain had to face seven foot three Lithuanian Arvydas Sabonis from the former Soviet Union, Croat Drazen Petrovic playing for the former Yugoslavia and Nikos Galis from Greece. They were all national treasures, as famous as any footballer, tennis player or track and field athlete in their home territories.

But Great Britain were not intimidated. Their hyphenated style, applying tireless pressure all game long and the way they could ignite a crowd with a flamboyant play, was like watching a lower league club continually embarrass Division One sides in the FA Cup. They defeated West Germany and France. They led Yugoslavia, possibly the greatest European basketball team of all time, at half-time before losing 102–85. In short, Great Britain showed the world they belonged and that they had a style that could compete with the greatest European nations. Bucknall had been the star. Moore, who had survived a car crash in 1985, a broken arm and the death of his close pal Larry Dassie in 1986, also played a significant role.

I finally felt that Black-Britain could compete with Black-America. And not only on the basketball courts of Britain. Through the eighties, the influence of Black-America had been getting bigger and bolder. Black culture in Britain, like basketball, remained on the margins. Crumbs. Something you had to actively find. Black-America was something I had been observing on prime-time television. Michael Jackson, blacker then than in later years, glittering glove and all, had the biggest-selling album in music history in *Thriller*. Whitney Houston, a voice that boomed from impossibly delicate features, rivalled Madonna as pop music's leading female artist. The seemingly perfect black family hit our screens in *The Cosby Show*. It was never as funny as the Black-English sitcom on Channel 4, *No Problem*. But while *No Problem* emphasised the idiosyncrasies of Black-English life, the people, the situations, and the humour that I could relate to, *The Cosby Show* enabled us to dare to dream, to live like the other half do.

If it wasn't Carl Lewis picking up four gold medals at the 1984 Olympics, Florence Griffith Joyner (Flo-Jo) with false but elaborately decorated fingernails, obliterating world records, Eddie Murphy smirking his way to becoming the biggest Hollywood star, Oprah Winfrey taking over the talk-show circuit or Mike Tyson, neck twitching in sweat-soaked black shorts, emerging as the biggest name in boxing since Ali, then it was the emergence of rap music replacing reggae as the soundtracks to our childhoods.

Black-America's history in sport had also been more familiar to me than Black-Britain's sporting history. African-American athletes had redefined every sport they had entered (or the ones they were allowed to enter). Perhaps no sport had been more important than boxing. Difficult to think of another sport in the early part of the twentieth century where the colour line had been broken and the black athlete had been so prominent.

Jack Johnson became the first black heavyweight champion in 1908. Previously, black fighters were not allowed to contest for the world heavyweight title. Johnson had been so good, there were calls for then world champion Tommy Burns to prove white superiority once and for all by defeating Johnson. Jack won. Worse still, he mocked his white foe, laughing in his face as he defeated him in front of thousands of white fans. He also married a white woman and remained champion until 1915. *Unforgivable*

Blackness, the title of Geoffrey Ward's biography of Jack Johnson, had been apt.

Joe Louis would become the most dominant heavyweight champion in history, defending his title 25 times in the thirties and forties. The 'Brown Bomber' became a national hero by defeating German Max Schmeling in a heavyweight title bout in 1938. He had dispelled Hitler's claims of Aryan supremacy by destroying Schmeling in front of 70,000 fans in New York, within a round. Louis would also take up military service in World War II.

It was not only in boxing that African-American athletes had been prominent. Sprinter and long jumper Jesse Owens went to the 1936 Berlin Olympics and won four gold medals in front of Hitler. Like Louis, he too became a national hero. There had also been Paul Robeson, among the first black professional American footballers. Robeson was also a lawyer, a stage and film actor, a global civil rights activist, a bass baritone singer, and a baseball, basketball and track athlete. This had been a man who fought for equal rights for blacks in the USA, supported the loyalist movement in the Spanish Civil War, studied Chinese, campaigned for better pay for Welsh miners, was almost killed by teammates while playing American football, performed at Buckingham Palace and met Albert Einstein. He is perhaps best known for singing 'Ol' Man River' in the movie *Show Boat* (he changed the words from the passive 'I'm tired of livin' and feared of dyin'' to the more defiant 'I must keep fightin' until I'm dyin'').[3] He counted among his friends writer Ernest Hemingway, scholar W E B Du Bois, Kenyan leader Jomo Kenyatta and Indian leader Nehru. He was a giant of the Harlem Renaissance, supported trade unions, donated money to Jewish refugees fleeing Germany, performed in *Othello*, *Ballad for Americans* and *Emperor Jones*, and refused to declare he was not a communist in front of the McCarthy committee. Robeson had been a giant. Every bit as important a figure as Muhammad Ali.

In 1947, Jackie Robinson broke the colour line in baseball, America's national game, becoming the first black player in a major American league. He would go on to become the Most Valuable Player in the National League in 1949 and he was one of only three professional athletes (alongside Ali and Pelé) to make *Time* magazine's 100 Persons of the Century. Althea Gibson would break the colour line in tennis and in professional golf. She had been the first black person to win a Grand Slam (French Open in 1956) in tennis, eventually winning five titles. Sprinter Wilma Rudolph overcame polio, numerous childhood illnesses and having to wear a leg brace until she was 12 to win three gold medals at the 1960 Rome Olympics. Rudolph was only 20 and became the first American woman to achieve such a feat in a single Olympic Games.

By the sixties, African-American athletes were even more outspoken and defiant than previous generations. During the height of the civil rights and Black Panther movements, Muhammad Ali may have been the most famous American athlete-activist of the time. But there were many others. Basketball player Bill Russell and American footballer Jim Brown candidly fought racism through much of their careers. Like Ali, they too were the best in their sports. Sprinters Tommie Smith and John Carlos's Black Power salute at the 1968 Mexico Olympics highlighted the plight of black people in America and became one of the most famous and iconic political statements in sport's history. Tennis player Arthur Ashe became the first black man to win the US Open title. In the seventies, he would become the first African-American to win the singles title at Wimbledon and the Australian Open. Ashe had also been a civil rights campaigner and a major figure in the anti-apartheid movement.

The black athlete in Britain did not have such a storied history. Sure, there had been many breakthroughs, from Viv Anderson becoming the first black player to represent England in football in 1978 to Roland Butcher's debut for the English cricket team in 1980. But very few of these advances carried the global or political significance of their African-American counterparts.

By the late eighties, no black sportsperson symbolised the advances of African-Americans or sold the American Dream quite like Michael Jordan. Jordan was dark-skinned. Bald. Six feet six. Playing a blacker-than-black sport. On the surface, he had been everything white folks feared and desired about blackness. Yet he became the biggest marketing phenomenon in sports history.

By the time Jordan arrived in the NBA in 1984, the interest created by Magic Johnson and Larry Bird's Los Angeles *v.* Boston, black *v.* white, flash *v.* blue-collar rivalry provided the ideal platform for Jordan to take the sport global. Upon turning pro with the NBA's Chicago Bulls, Jordan signed a $2.5 million five-year contract with Nike who created a signature shoe for him, the 'Air Jordan'.

Nike's Jordan 'Jumpman' swiftly became one of the most iconic logos across the globe once the Air Jordan I trainers had been launched in 1985. The Air Jordan I generated around $130 million in its first year. By 1986, Nike topped $1 billion profit for the first time. Over a 15-year period, Jordan products alone would surpass $3 billion. When Gatorade started the 'Be Like Mike' campaign in the early nineties, within a year their annual revenues increased from $681 million to over $1 billion. By 2015, it had been estimated by *Forbes* that Jordan products accounted for 8 per cent of Nike's $30.6 billion profits. 'The marriage of Michael and Nike is the biggest story in the history of sports marketing,' said Sonny Vaccaro, the man who brought Jordan to Nike.[4] The big, bald, black man ended up endorsing the most all-American of commercial products, from McDonald's and Coca-Cola to Chevrolet and Disney.

I first saw Jordan play in 1986 on Channel 4's basketball magazine show *Go 4 It!* It had been a three-minute highlights reel showing his most spectacular moments: an assortment of his slam dunks; 360-degree dunks, take-off-from-the-foul-line dunks, back-to-basket dunks, alley-oop dunks and one-handed dunks. Jordan's game was much more than that. But those highlights created an impression of athletic dominance unsurpassed by any other athlete in any sport. Those highlights transcended the uneducated basketball eye. Flair, imagination, grace. Jordan seemed to do everything better than anyone else; he seemed to leap higher, hang in the air longer, play at a swifter tempo. It had been like the most dynamic gymnastic floor-routine conceivable, full of dramatic leaps, stabbing karate movements, convulsive breakdancing. I was hooked. Jordan's style had been perfect for the MTV video generation. Style. Instant pleasure.

Pizzazz. But Jordan had substance on a basketball court too. Not just marketing.

Anything Magic and Bird could do, Jordan would do better. Magic won five NBA titles, Jordan won six. Magic and Bird were voted the league's best player three times apiece, Jordan won it five times. Magic won back-to-back titles (1987 and 1988), Jordan 'three-peated' on two occasions (1991 to 1993, then 1996 to 1998). Jordan was also the star of the first NBA team to win 70 games in a regular season. More than anything, it had been Jordan's ability to convert excellence on the court to brilliant marketing off it that helped globalise basketball to a point where it became the second most popular sport behind football. In a survey of Chinese schoolchildren in the early nineties, they placed Jordan next to Zhou Enlai, China's premier between 1949 and 1976, as the 'two greatest figures in twentieth-century history.'[5]

Jordan's style had been rooted in black culture. In Britain, Jordan remained more myth than reality. These were the days before YouTube, 24-hour sports talk or social media. You saw him in snippets. Too short to get bored. Too short to fully understand basketball. Too short to know how good he really was. Yet his fame went viral before there had been a platform to go viral.

Earlier in his career, in 1985, Jordan opened the Nike-sponsored basketball court at the Brixton Recreation Centre (better known as the Brixton Rec). The court was home to the Brixton Basketball Club, run by Jimmy Rogers, who had been a coach at Crystal Palace when Joel Moore played there. Jordan's presence was already being felt in England.

After the Brixton uprising in 1981, 70 volunteers started the New Education and Recreation Association (New ERA). New

ERA aimed 'to advance the education of young persons in Brixton (and the surrounding) area through the provision of facilities for physical recreation'. They used sport as a positive intervention, running 50 hours a week of physical activities in schools, youth clubs and sports centres in Lambeth. Rogers, a part of New ERA, left Palace to start the Brixton club in 1984.

Brixton would play in the red and black colours of Jordan's first Air Jordan trainers. When Rogers asked his players to come up with a nickname for the club, they chose the Topcats, in honour of the cartoon character Top Cat. The rationale being that these young players could relate to Top Cat's fractious relationship with the police. This wasn't just a basketball team. It was a movement.

Everybody knew the Topcats. The black and red vests. Practically an all-black team. Based in Brixton. A second-division club with greater fame than its first-division contemporaries. And led by a bull of a man in Rogers.

For all of Jordan's flashy play, he had been a fierce competitor. He was also technically sound at every element of the game, incredibly disciplined and he enjoyed playing defence. These qualities – being competitive, good technique, discipline, strong defence – underpinned the success of the Topcats. Rogers also thought that basketball could provide a basis for engaging disaffected youth. He believed that basketball inspired independence and bravery, perfect attributes for raising self-esteem. Rogers used sport for development, 'the intentional use of sport and physical activity as a tool to bring about positive change in the lives of people and communities',[6] long before the term had been defined.

He developed a philosophy for the club, 'winning is an attitude'. And Brixton soon became the place where young aspiring black players congregated. If Joel Moore personified the hyphenated style, then Rogers had a whole club playing this style of basketball.

Brixton may have been fractured by poverty, poor relations between the police and its local community and little or no provision for its youth. But it remained the black capital of Britain, home to the Race Today Collective, Black Cultural Archives, Nyam food, Blacker Dread Muzik, Red Records and C L R James. On any given week, one of the major reggae stars could be seen walking down Coldharbour Lane or Electric Avenue. And just as Michael Jordan had opened the Brixton Rec, every major black name – from Ali to Mandela – paid homage to a place that became a reaffirmation of the black diaspora's existence in the UK.

When the Topcats played their league matches, spectators would congregate underneath the Rec, a huge red-brick building that looked like it was being held up on high heels. Rogers had created a vision of how English basketball could grow. He prioritised local talent, he let them express themselves, be themselves, but without compromising discipline; he built up a following in the community which had been based on pride and spirit. His teams were fiercely competitive and he used sport as a tool to develop young people's character, not just their talent. For local fans, they could see their heritage reflected in the Topcats, which enhanced the sense of identity and belonging.

As Black-America continued to sweep through the UK, by the late eighties the Topcats had become the sporting the equivalent of the *The Voice* newspaper, Saxon Studio International sound system, the Black Arts Movement, the Jazz Warriors and Soul II Soul. Each were created out of a dire need for blacks to have their voices heard, powered by their communities, reflecting the needs of their communities, creating opportunities for their communities.

The Voice had been started by Val McCalla in 1982 to serve a black community that had been grossly misrepresented in the mainstream press, particularly after the '81 uprising. Not only did it receive significant readership and advertising from employers aiming to diversify their workforce, but *The Voice* supported the careers of many people, including former Commission for Racial Equality head Trevor Phillips, journalists Martin Bashir, Afua Hirsch, Dotun Adebayo, Joseph Harker and Henry Bonsu, and authors Leone Ross, Diran Adebayo and Vanessa Walters, among many others. Its legacy for representing the voice of the black community while nurturing or providing a platform for previously marginalised talent had been formidable.

Further east, towards New Cross, Saxon Studio had been started by Musclehead and D Rowe when they were teenagers in the mid-seventies. By the eighties they would become chief rivals to the Brixton-based Coxsone sound, where celebrity chef Levi Roots made his name. Saxon would become a world-leading sound system, regularly defeating feted Jamaican rivals in sound clashes and accompanied by a selection of artists that would take dance-hall music into the pop charts. Saxon helped Maxi Priest become the biggest global reggae star of the late eighties, Papa Levi to start the fast style of chatting prominent in contemporary urban music today and the late Smiley Culture and Tippa Irie to chart success.

These were just two of the many movements that emerged or thrived after the '81 riots. Many funding opportunities also opened the door for black people to initiate programmes that celebrated blackness, black Britishness and the African diaspora. These movements built on the foundations set in the seventies, enabling future generations of black folks to infiltrate the media, sport, politics, academia and other spheres. More importantly, they did so unapologetically.

This had been a period of celebrating black culture, but with a political undertone. It had been near impossible to ignore. You wanted to be a part of it, because they were you, all of you, the multiple layers of you, your identity, your rightful place in Britain. But it did not emerge without a struggle. For some, these movements had been a threat.

The basketball authorities used to treat the Topcats like some sort of feral mob. They were frequently denied entry to higher leagues, they marginalised Rogers and only reluctantly sent officials to the Rec to officiate games. Despite Rogers' success in developing England international players and in engaging supposedly hard-to-reach young people, I don't think he had been subject to a visit from any of the sport's major governing or funding bodies. Never elevated. Huge discomfort. They couldn't silence the Topcats, because Rogers had still been producing as many good players as any club in the country. The Topcats were treated less like an asset and more like a burden, a nuisance. To me, they were cool and successful, succeeding against the odds. But inaccessible if you were not a Brixton local. Like Moore, I couldn't understand why the powers that be had not been celebrating the Topcats more. I couldn't understand why they were not trying to replicate this formula.

In contrast, Jordan's fame continued to elevate. He had the street game, the middle-class talk. This had been crucial in enabling him to transcend basketball. Broad enough to appeal to kids in Hampstead or Harlesden, Jordan's language could neutralise his black game, and he had a smile that put white folks at ease. Jordan's agent David Falk once said, 'People don't look at Michael as being black,'[7] and that Jordan was 'apolitical by nature', and that 'when players of color become stars they are no longer perceived as being of color. The color sort of vanishes'.[8]

Vanishes. But people's attitude towards black folks didn't vanish. White folks may have been buying into black culture, but this did not translate into a greater understanding of black people in society. All surface. Aesthetics. Jordan's style of play had grown from the ghettos. An expression of black life. But that didn't appear to be part of the narrative around this style of basketball. The inner-city blues had been left behind. The wider socio-economic and indeed racial dynamics that fuelled basketball's global rise had been left behind. Not a part of the global narrative. The global narrative seemed to be more about super-human athletes, successful at this particular sport because 'white men can't jump'.

Like the Topcats, the message had been clear: you could attain the dream but make sure you leave your blackness at the door.

It had been difficult to argue against that approach given the African-American athlete's legacy in sport. Paul Robeson, after all, had been banished from the United States through much of the fifties, was hounded by the FBI, struggled to find work after returning from exile and suffered from depression in later life.

Even the more accommodating black athletes had suffered at the hands of white-led authorities. After the 1936 Olympics, Jesse Owens was stripped of his amateur status by the US Olympic

Committee for opting to earn some money after the Olympics rather than participate in a track meet. Owens had not been outspoken like Robeson. In fact, he had very much been compliant. But he wasn't invited to the White House after his return from Berlin, even though this was customary for victorious Olympic athletes. He struggled to gain endorsement deals, therefore prematurely ending his career at 24. He survived by racing animals and being a gas station attendant, among other jobs. He never competed in Olympic competition again. He would later say in a 1971 interview: 'When I came back to my native country … I couldn't ride in the front of the bus. I had to go to the back door. I couldn't live where I wanted. I wasn't invited to shake hands with Hitler, but I wasn't invited to the White House to shake hands with the president, either.'

Tax problems sent Joe Louis into debt, resulting in the 'Brown Bomber' fighting many years after his peak. While much of his problems stemmed from poor investments and advice, Louis had also been taxed for the charitable fights he contested in during the war, fights for which he did not see a penny. Post-career, his heroism long since forgotten, Louis took to wrestling and being a 'greeter' at Las Vegas casinos to earn money. He was broke when he died of cardiac arrest. Schmeling, along with other celebrities, paid for his funeral.

If Jack Johnson had been 'unforgivable blackness', Jordan seemed to be 'neutralised blackness'. In 1990 and 1996, black Democrat Harvey Gantt ran for a US Senate seat in Jordan's home state of North Carolina against former segregationist Republican candidate Jesse Helms. The same Jesse Helms that considered the Civil Rights Act in 1964 as 'the single most dangerous piece of legislation ever introduced in the Congress'.

But Jordan refused to endorse or even support Gantt, allegedly commenting, 'Republicans buy sneakers too.'[9] Helms won both races.

If Tommie Smith and John Carlos's Black Power rostrum salute at the 1968 Olympics had been a symbolic political act, Jordan covering the Reebok logo on his tracksuit with an American flag on the rostrum at the 1992 Olympics symbolised just how commercial sport had become.

Jordan's image adorned the food we ate, the drinks we consumed and the trainers we wore. Basketball apparel became the leisure clothing of choice for everyone from rappers to business women. But the price, as William C Rhoden once wrote, was a generation of contemporary black athletes who had been 'unwilling to collectively rock the money boat'. A new blueprint had been set.

This version of Black-America may have been different to the sixties, more commercial, but it was still attractive, still expansive. Britain remained narrow. Jordan ascended in public. Joel Moore, the Topcats, hyphen-nation ascended in the margins, restricted in a way that Mike didn't appear to be.

There was something empowering about looking like America's nightmare and still winning. You couldn't blame me for being seduced, particularly if the difference between the plights of Black-Britons and African-Americans during this period had been any gauge. Moore left Portsmouth in 1987 to play for Kingston. They were arguably the two most successful teams in Britain. By the end of 1988, both teams would fold. The remnants of Kingston and Portsmouth merged and relocated to Glasgow. The club had been owned by David Murray, a multi-millionaire who owned structural steel distributors Murray International Metals. Murray also owned Scotland's other dominant team, Livingston. After one season in which Glasgow, featuring Moore, won three out of the four domestic trophies, Glasgow was sold, relocating back to Kingston, and Livingston folded. These had been the four most successful clubs in Britain. Imagine if the same fate had befallen Liverpool, Manchester United, Arsenal and Chelsea?

By the early nineties, millionaires divested, England's top players spent less time in the BBL (British Basketball League) than a drug courier would in jail, a salary cap (basically where every team in the league has the same limit on what it can pay players and coaches) had been introduced that was so low that the league could no longer attract major players or indeed full-time players, and mainstream television lost interest in the sport. Even less money seemed to be going into grassroots basketball, while members of the English Basketball Association, the governing body for the sport, would later stand accused of misappropriating money and investing it into their own commercial enterprises.

Years later, I'd hear from several players that English basketball teams had limits on the number of black players. Successful black coaches were never brought into mainstream structures to develop the game on a national level. Closed shop. English basketball never received significant investment, despite high participation levels among young people and the demonstrable ability to reach kids that other activities couldn't. An inner-city game. Blacks, ethnics, working-class kids. An American sport. Privately educated administrators. Preservers of tradition. They didn't get it. Didn't value it. Didn't invest in it.

Future English national team coaches would end up paying for travel or training facilities out of their own pockets. Players went to qualifying tournaments across Europe with no means of transport to take them to their hotels, if, indeed, a hotel had been booked. Some players were left stranded at airports. Players had to purchase pot noodles in bulk to ensure they received a hot meal on trips. For those players who worked part-time, there was a £15 daily allowance. Domestic basketball had about as much stability as a two-litre bottle perched on the seat handle of a moving train.

For the first time, I needed something more than sport. I disliked the way the system minimised black basketball players. I disliked the way blackness in American sport increasingly became more cultural and fashionable. For all the greatness of Michael Jordan, Magic Johnson and boxer Sugar Ray Leonard, there was not one athlete I admired for being overtly political. And for me, the term black was political. As I transitioned from college to university in 1991, from east London to north London, from working-class friends to more middle-class friends, from lots of black and brown people to more white people, I needed something more than what sport could offer.

Rap music was that something more. The truth is, rap originally appealed to me because its main protagonists looked harder than your average skinhead. That simple. I feared skinheads more than anyone or anything in my childhood. In my mind, LL Cool J could beat those skinheads in a fight. He offered hope. Watching those rappers in their untied Adidas trainers, Kangol hats, leather jackets with thick gold rope chains dangling from their necks like anacondas – scowling, posturing, strutting, bragging about how great they were, how much money they made, how hard they were – had been a revelation, a revolution, an uncompromising black experience. A vision of empowerment. Not as pure as the West Indies team, but a vision at least of what it might look like to be in control.

By 1987, I knew something special was happening. Our Harlem Renaissance. Our generation's explosion of ideas, art, politics, beats, rhymes and noise. Every week, something new was emerging: gangsta rap, the intersection of rap and reggae, rap and faith, rap and politics, Afrocentrism, the rise of West Coast rap, authentic British rap (not poor American imitations), female rappers not trying to emulate the fellas, the birth of the dirty south (precursor to trap music).

The press demonised it. My parents thought it wouldn't last. White kids were fascinated by it. Everyone could find their place in it. If you couldn't rap, you could write (do graffiti). If you couldn't write, you could (break)dance. If you couldn't dance, you could DJ or sell mix tapes. Almost overnight, all the faceless artists I had been listening to on pirate radio were now appearing on *Top of the Pops*. The transformation had been swift. And no one in the mainstream saw it coming.

Rap music for me changed when Public Enemy released the single 'Rebel Without a Pause'. It was fury on vinyl, with furious, kettle-boiling horns from the JB's 'The Grunt' and front man Chuck D's sermonising. Public Enemy had come over to England as part of the Def Jam Tour in 1987, supporting LL Cool J and Eric B & Rakim. The combination of that tour, where they projected an image as distinctive and powerful as the Black

Panthers with frequent references to the politics of Malcolm X and Louis Farrakhan, shifted rap from the boasting and bragging of Run DMC and LL Cool J to a more political agenda. They made politics relevant and cool. Chuck D once famously said that rap was the 'Black CNN', a tool to inform black people about issues relevant to its community.

What made Public Enemy special had been the fact that they initially gained more popularity in the UK than they had in the USA. They used the 1987 Hammersmith concert as a backdrop to their classic album *It Takes a Nation of Millions to Hold Us Back* (1988), while Chuck D often proclaimed that Black-Britain would be at the forefront of a black diasporic civil rights movement.

Rap music swept everything aside. Football, cricket, *The Cosby Show*, Jordan, the Topcats. It became our news channel. Our voice. It redefined cool. The black youths owned it, while my white peers did everything they could to be a part of it. I no longer had to be coy about whether I supported England in sport or not. Now it was the white kids who were being coy about whether they liked rap music or not. At no point in my childhood had anything so distinctly black dominated youth culture, and crystalised what it meant to belong.

Rap and basketball would eventually marry. A perfect union. Perhaps in time, politics would re-enter basketball. Perhaps the might of Black-American influence, power and culture would open doors for the Topcats and Black-British 'ballers. It needed to.

When Joel Moore started playing for a London Towers team coached by Joe White, it had been an all-English cast. This included Moore's former Palace teammate Junior Taylor, ex-Topcats Ronnie Baker and Andrew Bailey, and the Scantlebury brothers.

The Towers finished third in the BBL in 1992–93, a significant achievement for an all-English squad in a league littered with American players. They finished fifth the following season. At last, the BBL had a team like the 1988 Great Britain side, with a distinct hyphenated identity and the potential to build a following. Yet the following season, the Towers released White, and brought in two American players.

Sky television swooped in, with a production style that British basketball had never seen before. NBA teams and players had started to regularly visit these shores too. There had been talk of an NBA franchise being based in the UK. The sport temporarily boomed with more investment. Money talked.

Then in 1996, the BBL introduced a rule that would allow teams to field up to five non-British players. This had increased from the limit of two foreign players. Each team could essentially field an all-American starting line-up. In Britain. What had been a healthy, balanced influence from America had become a takeover.

Joel Moore never got his shot at the NBA. Never reached the heights his talent deserved. His career faded soon after the Towers' all-hyphenated team disbanded. When I last caught up with him, he had been managing a major furniture store while continuing to coach on the side. But he had not been a part of any England or Great Britain management set-up.

Jimmy Rogers continued to produce the top talent in Britain. This would include England's greatest ever player, NBA star Luol

Deng, and English basketball's most capped international, Ronnie Baker. Other players who would pass through the Topcats' doors would include London's former Deputy Mayor and barrister Matthew Ryder and Grammy-nominated singer-songwriter Marsha Ambrosius. But the club continued to struggle for funding and Rogers, like Moore, was never a major part of any England or Great Britain setup.

But NBA basketball continued to grow and with it rap music. The gangsta rappers and the new generation of 'ballers did not shy away from the spotlight, they hogged it. Didn't care how history defined them. Didn't care whether they reinforced stereotypes. They embraced the stereotypes because it had become a key factor in making them wealthy. The narrative had changed. But we didn't own the narrative, the corporates did. And they commoditised it. Athlete activism died. Rap was no longer the 'black CNN'.

Apparently, among the first people Chuck D gave copies of *Nation of Millions* to were Dr Dre and Eazy-E from N.W.A. (N****s With Attitude). N.W.A. took things a step further than Public Enemy. The sound was not as hard, or incessant, but the lyrics were. 'F**k tha police'. 'Gangsta Gangsta'. Took the rage from the streets and put it on record, unfiltered. A documentary of urban street life in America. More profanity. More sales. Banned albums. More sales. Cancelled concerts. More sales. N.W.A. on the FBI watchlist. More sales. Their music had been insular, nihilistic and focused on the negative realism of black culture. But it was also dynamic and fearless, backed by expansive funk sounds and atomic basslines. No one quite knew how popular they were. But then in 1991, Nielsen SoundScan started assessing sales data and tracking units sold. Once the major record label execs recognised how many records N.W.A. had been shifting, gangsta rap became a focus for them.

After the success of Jordan, major sports companies scoured the inner cities of America looking for the next Jordan. Pre-teen prospects were buttered up, given free trainers, given promises, given hope that if they made it, they too could be rich like Jordan. Inner-city kids, parents of inner-city kids suddenly had a clear financial route out of the ghetto. Spoilt ghetto kids. By the time the very few in this pipeline made it to the NBA, they were no longer trying to 'out-Jordan' Jordan in the way Michael had been trying to surpass Magic and Bird. They were trying to attain more wealth than Jordan. For inner-city kids, their parents and peers, the agents, the corporates and the NBA, this would be the road to the riches.

This was America. 'Cash Rules Everything Around Me'.* It would cast an indelible Shadow over Britain, over Black-Britain. The Spotlight of British society, as identified by the systemic failure within British basketball, versus being in the Shadow of Black-America? The Shadow had to be the choice, even if it had been difficult to trust, even if it had been, ultimately, white-owned. Everything appeared green (American) before it appeared black. And the big sporting names, they didn't say much. Didn't try to change the status quo. Didn't try to change the narrative. They got paid well, but I also had a feeling that they got played well.

---

* 'Cash Rules Everything Around Me', a song by New York hip-hop group Wu-Tang Clan, from their 1993 studio album, *Enter the Wu-Tang (36 Chambers)*, on Loud Records.

CHAPTER 4

SO MANY TIERS

AFTER THREE ROUNDS OF HIS 1990 world welterweight title fight against Marlon Starling at the Indoor Sports Pavilion in Las Vegas, it was clear that Lloyd Honeyghan's anger had doomed him to failure. The Jamaican-born Brit had staggered Starling with a ferocious right hook in the third round. Starling shook off the punch as if it were a half-hearted slap from a jilted mistress. At the end of the round, Starling casually strolled back to his corner. In contrast, Honeyghan's legs did not look stable enough to support his upper body. He looked defeated. When a fighter cannot muster any confidence after scoring a solid blow, then you know something must be wrong.

Starling was a quick-tongued, cocky fighter from Hartford, Connecticut. He could have replaced Eddie Murphy as Axel Foley in *Beverly Hills Cop*, although you got the impression that Starling was more comfortable being the bad guy than a cop. Honeyghan too was brash. He nicknamed himself the 'Ragamuffin Man', a Jamaican term for a street-smart youth from the ghetto. Although based in Bermondsey, southeast London, Honeyghan had strong Jamaican roots. His language, while seasoned with a cockney twang, had a stabbing, broken Jamaican quality. Honeyghan was flashy. He could fill a room with his flamboyant personality and dress sense. Yet underneath that cypress pine complexion, squinty eyes and pout was a boyishly charming man who struggled to hide his emotions. He was unpredictable. You never quite knew what he'd say or how he'd say it.

Honeyghan and Starling disliked each other. They had cleared the welterweight division of all competition. In 1986, Honeyghan travelled to Atlantic City, New Jersey to face Donald 'The Lone Star Cobra' Curry, regarded as the best pound-for-pound boxer in the world. No one gave Honeyghan a chance. Curry, in the minds of the American writers, was the rightful heir to Sugar Ray Leonard. He had talent; a smooth predator with knockout power in both fists, innate defensive skills, and was ring savvy. But he did not have Leonard's charisma and he struggled to make the welterweight limit for his fights, which often left him weakened. Against the fearless Honeyghan, Curry had been overwhelmed. In a dimly lit banqueting suite, Honeyghan jumped on Curry from the opening bell, never allowing the 'The Lone Star Cobra' to settle into the fight. Curry retired in the seventh round and Honeyghan became an instant star.

In 1989, Starling had knocked out another American golden boy, the 1984 Olympic champion Mark Breland (heralded by many as the new Sugar Ray Robinson). Honeyghan's victory over Curry did not impress Starling. 'Anybody coulda beat Don Curry. You know who beat Don Curry that day? A rag'muffin man.' When Starling referred to Honeyghan as the 'rag'muffin man', he was probably not being flattering but literal to the term for someone scruffy or dirty. Regardless of Starling's opinion, the bookies made Honeyghan the 5–2 on favourite.

Starling thought the fight would be easy. After three rounds his declaration appeared to be correct. Every time Honeyghan threw punches, he did so with such venom his posture resembled a tennis player after a serve. Head leaning forward, arms flailing, body doubled. Whereas a tennis player has a few seconds to regroup before his or her opponent returns the ball, a boxer does not have that luxury. A skilled fighter, once he sees an opponent assume a vulnerable position, will strike before they can react. This is how Starling fought. He covered up and waited for his opponent to over-commit. When Honeyghan's head dipped or hands dropped, Starling would unravel and strike with swiping left hooks or over-hand rights. In truth, Starling did little more than that all night. He patiently fed off Honeyghan's wrath.

Starling rarely made mistakes, rarely took any risks. Perhaps when bored, he might edge forward. Get a little closer. Clown a little. Feel a breeze of danger. However, for Starling boxing was a waiting game. He had the gift of equanimity in the ring. Take away your opponent's strengths and quietly and efficiently grind him down once his confidence and ideas had diminished.

Honeyghan, while not nearly as assured in his use of the ring, not nearly at ease, had a greater repertoire. Honeyghan could have hit Starling to the body to bring his arms down, which protected the American's upper body like prison bars. Honeyghan could have out-punched Starling by throwing more shots, remaining aggressive but doing so in an educated way, forcing Starling to come out of his shell and come up with a plan B. Honeyghan could have danced a little, moved round the ring to create interesting angles and snap swift blows on Starling. Honeyghan could have combined the styles, slowing and quickening the pace like a Kenyan middle-distance runner, always keeping Starling off-balance. Honeyghan didn't, much to the frustration of his promoter Mickey Duff who urged him to change his attitude and not go to war. But Honeyghan continued to snap punches at Starling like a petulant child at a parent. By the eighth round, Honeyghan's mouth had become grotesquely swollen.

The end came in the following round. An exhausted Honeyghan dropped to his knees while retreating to the corner of the ring. To stay upright he tried to grab Starling, but his legs had given way. The sight of Honeyghan on his knees, arms around Starling's waist, told the story of the fight. Honeyghan rose, nose bleeding, face swollen and worn out, but still swinging wild punches. After Starling backed him into the corner again and landed more unanswered blows, referee Mills Lane had no choice but to stop the fight. Honeyghan would not give up. So, it was fortunate Lane came in when he did. Honeyghan had lost his world title and paid the price for what ringside commentator Harry Carpenter described as his 'insane determination'.

Starling remained contemptuous to the end. When Carpenter congratulated him, Starling replied abruptly, 'Thanks, I told you I was the best welterweight in the world, I think I proved it.' Honeyghan was more gracious, recognising the ills of his game plan. 'I let my aggression get the better of me, 'arry [Harry]. I wanted to beat the guy so much, I wasn't thinking tonight and aggression got the better of me.' Asked whether he respected Starling, Honeyghan said yes, but added, '[He] don't act like a man, he act like a kid.' Then Carpenter commended Honeyghan for 'going down fighting'. Honeyghan answered, 'Well, you know how us British are, we have to give it our all, you know what I mean?'

As Honeyghan said, 'you know how us British are', I laughed and thought Churchill must have been turning in his grave. I wasn't sure whether Honeyghan had been joking in the face of defeat. He wasn't. Honeyghan was serious, not one to lie. I thought that this must have been Britain's worst nightmare.

On the surface, Honeyghan's language, his colour, his Jamaican roots did not make him a natural native son. Yet he had many of the attributes associated with Britishness – heart, dignity, bulldog spirit, cheeky humour. Few British athletes had been as successful as or as charismatic as Honeyghan. Yet unlike Paul Gascoigne, another cocky, wisecracking working-class hero, he did not become a national treasure.

Honeyghan's statement made me feel uneasy. I would later have the same feeling watching Linford Christie drape the Union Jack around his shoulders after winning Olympic gold in 1992. Couldn't understand how they could pledge allegiance to England when they had never been fully or rightfully recognised as native sons. Didn't mean I disliked England, Linford or living in England. Yet I had never been sure whether England fundamentally liked me, or liked me living in England.

Such active displays of loyalty to England felt to me as if these athletes were selling out the black community. But you couldn't say that about Honeyghan. This had been a guy who threw his world welterweight title belt in the bin rather than face white South African boxer Harold Volbrecht. 'I would not fight Volbrecht for a million pounds – either here or in South Africa. How could I look myself in the mirror each morning or face my own people on the streets if I agreed?'[1] Honeyghan also displayed many of the characteristics considered important to be a strong black male in English society. I called these the 'Codes'.

The Codes of blackness were the behaviours and attributes required to negotiate your way in England. You don't go to school to learn it. There had been no manual or mentoring programme to guide you through it. No graduation ceremony, no rites of passage to indicate you've reached enlightenment. You had some idea of what those behaviours were because of the public figures commonly admired by the people who exemplified the Codes. But how do you create a Code job description from a combination of Malcolm X, Ice Cube, Mike Tyson, Chuck D, Alex Higgins (the white Northern Irish snooker player who was always admired by many people I knew in the black community for his carefree style of play) and Viv Richards?

The Codes existed in silence. Like the Spotlight. Like the Shadow. Dictating. Passing judgement. Only this time, judgement is coming from your own black community, not white society.

The problem was that these behaviours tended to emerge as a response to our social conditions, but without a clear vision of our own conception of Black-Britishness or Englishness. The Codes were susceptible then. Responsive to history, to crisis, to racial politics, to environment, to positive and negative stereotypes, to the Spotlight. Not always defined by us, but definitely a response by us.

The Codes tended to tell you more about what you couldn't do; describing what you couldn't be, more than what you could be. It could best be described as living in a 'can't, don't, never'[2] culture. You can't be soft, don't turn the other cheek, you should never compromise. Suffocating. Narrow. These rules had been far clearer than your 'cans' and your 'dos'. These rules were reinforced everywhere: in the playground, in the classrooms, on the bus going home. Can't, don't, never. Break them and you could find yourself marginalised as much by your black male peers as white folks. Gotta be tough. Can't be vulnerable. Cannot respond to being told off in a class by crying. You can't lose in any area considered a 'positive' stereotype of black masculinity. You can't be crap at sport, you can't lose a fight, you can't turn the other cheek when confronted, no matter the odds or who confronted you; you can't be weak or too emotional in front of girls. You. Just. Can't. Lose. Much of our status, our ranking, our credibility as kids and as young men had been based on the following:

1) *Prowess with girls*
2) *Ability to fight*
3) *Excelling as a dancer*
4) *Your dress sense*
5) *Sporting prowess*

And if you'd made it, made some money, made it 'out of the hood', made a name for yourself, by God you cannot change that behaviour. Be as you are on television as you are 'in the hood'. Be more Malcolm X than Martin Luther King. Be like Mike Tyson more than Frank Bruno. Be more Ice Cube than De La Soul. In or out. You were either cool and uncompromising or not black enough.

These 'can'ts' were clear to me from a young age, but my 'could bes' not so clear. I started to see the more positive side of the Codes through the West Indies, by learning about Malcolm X, through listening to Chuck D. But being cool. How, exactly? You had to have an attitude, to carry yourself with self-confidence, to show folks that no situation was unmanageable. You had to display these attributes in the way you walked, the way you talked, the way you dressed. The symbols of the Codes had to be on full display. But it's not like you get training in this. Being a success with girls was another symbol of black manhood. But how? Where's the blueprint?

Restrictive. Claustrophobic. Black. White. Yet British society had also defined me by what they thought I couldn't do, what I couldn't be. As much as I couldn't consider myself English through the lens of the English, I wasn't exactly a shining beacon for the Codes either. You tend to get your first lessons in the Codes, the first lessons in manhood, from your father. But as tough as my father could be with me, his approach had been more protective. My father tried to absorb the pain, absorb my pain, absorb any pain I might feel on my behalf. He wasn't preparing me to face a hostile world by teaching me how to be super tough, super bad, emotionally impenetrable. He wanted me to be better. 'Twice as good as your white counterparts.' A line used by many black parents across the UK. This he thought would level the playing field, although it rarely did.

He didn't apply adult rules to my childhood. My mistakes would not be met with damning or critical comments; the type that would make a boy question his toughness. As I got older, I understood why some of my friends' fathers were harsh and

critical with their sons. Any father put in a position of disem-
powerment would want to equip their sons with the toughness
to cope with being an adult. Many fathers who I observed
preached fighting back as a solution. At times, I wished my
father had preached the same. It would have been easier to fit in
with the Codes. I would have been more open in the way I dealt
with confrontation, not hemmed everything in so much.
However, it appeared that while these fathers were administering tough love, their motives had more to do with their
own insecurities, manhood and self-image than the good of
their boys.

My father appeared less willing to dispense such harsh lessons
in manhood. I didn't feel any pressure to be hard. When I made
a mistake, I could feel his frustration. I'd get that quizzical, questioning stare. But equally he was loving and affectionate. I appreciated this.

Still, it was hard not to be seduced by the Codes. And in Lloyd
Honeyghan you saw an athlete who had many of these characteristics. He was raw. Street. Tough. Brash. Cocky. Confident. He
didn't minimise. He could at times break away from the cool
posturing. But he was superbad. Had high levels of loyalty to
Britain too. Yet Honeyghan had been far more attractive than the
alternative.

The older I got the friendlier white folks became, and the fewer
times they invited me round to their houses. Our politics, black–
white politics, appeared to be closer. But our understanding of
each other, on a fundamental level, appeared to widen. Unease.
Not quite like the unease during my school days, when white
kids – those that would listen to rap music, come over to my

house, eat my mum's food – would also call a black kid a wog in anger on the playground. It wasn't right. It wasn't okay. But I knew where I stood. Who to befriend. Who to avoid. Clearer lines. There had been an openness and honesty to those relationships, and a few arguments.

When I entered Middlesex University in 1991, I met more liberal students, more middle-class students. They would say the right things; rarely would they offend. When they did offend, they didn't realise it. They had a theoretical understanding of black people. They had a better knowledge of black political figures like Martin Luther King than my friends at school. This seemed to give them licence to speak more openly about black issues. But I never really knew where they stood, what their 'understanding' really meant. Blurred lines. When the lines had been crossed, I never knew. But it was always there, always looming, always defining and dictating those relationships without ever being clear.

I remember one time, when I was with a white female friend and Public Enemy came up in conversation.

'I don't like them,' she said, 'they're racist.'

'No, they're not, they're just sticking up for black issues,' I replied.

'They're racist, they hate white people.'

The conversation didn't go much further. I was too angry. In no frame of mind to respond coherently. But conversations like this became more frequent. I noticed whenever I would talk about 'race', my white peers would either flinch in fascination (silence) or in fear (defensiveness). There would be looks of discomfort. Conversations would veer away from white racism towards blacks being the cause of our own problems. It was as if racism did not exist and was little more than a conception in black people's minds. Blatantly racist statements or actions by white folks wouldn't be acknowledged by my white peers as racist. They would make every excuse under the sun to say that a statement by a white person had not been racist. Yet they were swift to call out black people if they happened to say anything controversial about white people. The perpetrators had become the victims, the victims had become the perpetrators. Unease. Tension.

My friend struggled to understand black people's need for a 'black CNN', self-determination, self-governance, black newspapers and other services that catered strictly for our own community. 'What if whites had their own whites-only papers?' she once said to me. 'You do,' I replied. 'It's called the *Daily Mail,* the *Guardian*, the *Sun*, the *Mirror, The Times.*'

They covered the world from her perspective. They covered issues about the black community from her perspective. If they didn't, there would be a mainstream outlet where she could find validation in her views. And if not through the media, then through other institutions like the education system or one of the political parties. Black folks needed our own media, our own networks and charities as much as we needed to infiltrate and change mainstream institutions because we remained on the periphery, an afterthought, a conception through a white lens.

I felt like a massive experiment to those students. A taste of chocolate. A test of liberal values. Proof of their comfort with black culture, black politics, black men, while they too concealed their insecurities, their true beliefs. Couldn't bridge the fundamental unease between us. Black, white. Working class, middle class. I understood enough about my roots to know why I felt so uncomfortable with the class divide, their confidence, their education, their overwhelming sense of entitlement. I understood a lot more about their history, their heritage, their side of the story to know why I felt uncomfortable. Vice. No versa.

History and the media seemed to say so much about me, for me, before anyone had the chance to even meet me, or get to know me. Wanted to tell you my side. You wouldn't believe me, not unless you'd grown up with me, tasted my mum's food, played 'it' with me. My truths about you came through institutions, but also through experience. Your truths about me seemed to come through institutions, like school and the media. Maybe if we'd met a little earlier, at eight instead of eighteen, then you'd understand enough to trump history, trump your parents' understanding of our history, trump the media's interpretation of our history, trump the education system's editing of our history.

I wanted to know one thing. I wanted to know what it would be like to be your son. England's son. At least a conception of your son. Only then could I be in a place where I'd belong, where I'd feel at ease, where I could feel that if I did my best, I would be judged by my efforts and not by my skin. A fundamental right, right? But I didn't feel like a child of England. Was never made to feel like a child of England. Couldn't understand why. Could understand why. I was born here. I grew up here. Appreciated being here. But the reality had been: 'We are here because you were there.'[3] Yet my colour and the perception of my history, your version of my history, a history perpetuated within every institution I encountered, meant I was never really a true part of the family.

To cope, I minimised, of course. Smiled a lot. Avoided black and white conversations about black. Never entered a shop with an item purchased at another store. Never looked a copper in the eye. Never tried to show any form of anger in public. Crossed the street a lot. Away from older people and white women when it was dark. Away from anyone who could accuse me of stuff, because I'd been accused of a lot of stuff.

At university, I found myself trying to put white students at ease. Or had I been trying to ease their fears? Not sure. But kind of tiring. It was tiring worrying about your feelings, being responsible for your feelings, trying to rewrite history with politeness and humour with people who had little conception about how I had been feeling. I was not only in the minority because of the colour of my skin, I was also in the minority because of my class. Could never be your son. Could only be a conception of blackness that would be comfortable for you. And to be comfortable for you, I'd have to compromise my heritage and the Codes.

Through much of Lloyd Honeyghan's peak years as a fighter, the alternative, the compromise, the antithesis of the Codes had been Frank Bruno, the acceptable face of Black-Britain. He made every white person I knew, from my working-class peers at school to the middle-class students at university, feel comfortable. The closest black person I had seen to being considered a native son. Bruno was a nice guy out of the ring and an overachiever in it. He turned professional in 1982 and proceeded to knock out every opponent put in front of him. Britain had never had a heavy-weight like this before. The full package. He was physically imposing with sculpted good looks and could knock you out with one punch. Out of the ring, he spoke in a deep, nasal urban London drawl. He did not come across as being too sharp. It wasn't just his speech. Bruno was quick to play the fool in interviews and his remarks consisted of little more than clichés. This made him non-threatening.

Like the Harlem Globetrotters, to me his self-deprecating humour stank of a black man trying to please white folks. He grinned at any opportune moment. His catchphrase, 'you know what I mean, 'arry' to commentator Harry Carpenter, was a bit like a 'yes, sir' from a black butler in one of those old black and white movies. Often, Bruno represented everything most black folks rejected. A sell-out. Not black enough. He had a naughty giggle and wide-eyed rueful expressions which often made me and my peers cringe.

But the British public loved him more than any black celebrity. Perfection. A man whose physical prowess fascinated but whose subservience publicly and politically made everyone comfortable. A perfect stereotype. He had been a national treasure, the first black national treasure I knew of. A man who knew his place, a man who was courageous and noble in defeat. If Honeyghan had been emblematic of the Codes of blackness, I saw Bruno as symbolic of the 'Tiers' of a white society; basically, how a black man must behave to gain acceptance and integrate successfully in society. This meant being fully compliant to Britain's conception of blackness. The Tiers were born from and dictated by the structures, the history, the institutions of Britain, Britishness as whiteness, blackness as the other. Blackness as deviant. Blackness as inferior. Blackness as less than human. Blackness as non-British, never-be-British. Bruno had not represented all of these things. But he had been symbolic of elements of the Tiers.

You didn't really hear Bruno speak out about black issues. In fact, most black athletes in the eighties had been silent on racial tensions during this time, like the police shooting and paralysing of Cherry Groce in 1985 which led to disturbances in Brixton, or the death from heart failure of Cynthia Jarrett after a raid on her home, which led to the Broadwater Farm riots a week later.

Either they had no rage, hid their rage through fear of losing popularity or repressed it because, like me, it was often too painful to confront. American athletes like the boxer Mike Tyson had not been political. But he never appeared to bow to anyone either. At a time when N.W.A. were enabling the world to 'witness the strength of street knowledge', Tyson was swiftly becoming the personification of the nihilistic side of hip-hop culture and indeed the Codes.

He had become the youngest heavyweight champion in history in 1986 and wiped out opposition in the heavyweight division in such a brutal manner, many thought he was unbeatable. He was the antithesis of Ali. Where Ali had been pretty, graceful, radical and showy, Tyson was raw, menacing, street and unfussy. Like Ali, however, Tyson had been a dominant fighter while also being charismatic and uncompromising out of the ring. But where Ali and Public Enemy had been political, Tyson, like N.W.A., had been gangsta.

Tyson won the hearts of black folks because he did not change who or what he was once he became a mainstream star. He was an anti-hero, fearless, never bowing to convention, never silent or silenced. Tyson didn't conform and yet he continued to bank money.

But Black-America had a head start on blacks in Britain. The British may have become the largest transatlantic slave traders from Africa by the late eighteenth century, but they were primarily transporting enforced labour to the Americas and the Caribbean. While the earliest recorded black people dates back to Roman Britain, they had not been present in Britain en masse. Those numbers would not increase until the rise of the Empire and slavery, and during periods when Britain sought cheap workers from colonial states to fill gaps in the labour market. But the numbers of people from Africa had not been as great as they were in other parts of the globe. After the 'official' end of slavery through the nineteenth century, the United States, Brazil and the Caribbean were now populated with freed slaves in numbers not seen on these shores.

The common experience of slavery, majority-black regions, the longer-established communities of freed slaves, created a connectedness that had not been a big factor over here. Black-Britain's appreciation for our homegrown heroes was not as strong as it was in America. We still had strong connections to our Caribbean and African roots. But for African-Americans, they seemed to have a greater sense of nationalism.

So, when Bruno fought Tyson for the first time in 1989, I was conflicted. I didn't have blind loyalty to Bruno because of his nationality, as he represented the Tiers. Tyson came out swinging, knocking Bruno down within a minute of the fight. But near the end of the round, Bruno caught Tyson with a left hook, rocking and hurting the champion for the first time in his career. It had been a wild first round, one of the best and most underrated in heavyweight boxing. It was the first time people thought Tyson could be beaten. In the end, Tyson overwhelmed Bruno in five rounds and stopped the gallant Brit. But Bruno had had his Henry Cooper moment. Cooper famously knocked down Muhammad Ali, also with a left hook, in their first fight in 1963. Ali was hurt and needed his corner man Angelo Dundee to pull apart a split in Ali's glove to buy his fighter a little more time to recover. Ali recovered and finished Cooper off in the following round. If Cooper had been the British public's darling, Bruno's left hook ensured that he too would be as close to a native son as any black man would ever be in England.

Bruno took a break after the Tyson fight, but two years on he embarked on a comeback to win that elusive world title. Honeyghan's career faded swiftly after the loss to Starling. But another fighter had come along to replace Honeyghan as the great fighter the English public struggled to embrace.

Like Honeyghan, Lennox Lewis had been born in Jamaica. Lewis grew up in West Ham in east London until the age of 12 before moving with his mother to Kitchener, Ontario in Canada. Where Honeyghan's accent, his culture, his image had been distinctly Jamaican-English, which perhaps contributed to a slight distance between himself and your typical English fan, Lewis had represented Canada at the 1988 Olympics, winning the super-heavyweight title by defeating future heavyweight champion Riddick Bowe. When Lewis turned professional in 1989, he moved to and started representing England. Little about Lewis' English heritage had been evident. He had a soft Canadian accent, which veered at times into a Jamaican twang; you were more likely to see him at Reggae Sunsplash than a Britpop gig. Lewis was also laid back, self-assured and unruffled. Not quite as brash as Honeyghan but you wouldn't classify him as modest. Very un-British.

Lewis was, however, a heavyweight. Which meant that he was on a collision course with Frank Bruno. So, when it was announced that Bruno would meet Lewis for the world heavyweight title in 1993, what had been called the 'Battle of Britain' swiftly became for me a battle between the Codes and the Tiers. The fight took place on 1 October 1993 at Cardiff Arms Park. In Lewis, Bruno would be fighting a 'foreign' Englishman who did not outwardly comply to typically 'British' traits.

The public viewed Lewis' new-found Britishness with skepticism. Clearly England offered Lewis a more lucrative pathway to boxing riches than Canada. But I liked the way Lewis carried himself. He had been polite, quietly confident. At six feet five with a thick body frame, he was imposing but rarely bowed his body to look smaller or to fit in. When he began his professional career, he had a Cameo haircut (short back and sides) and looked more like an American swingbeat or R&B crooner than a fighter. Lewis could be curt; at times his eyes glazed over when under question and he wasn't a natural in front of the microphone. But he rarely showed vulnerability despite his gentle face. He had an air of dignity about him, something quietly combative but gentlemanly. Here, I thought, was a class act, a man who represented the Codes, not to Tyson extremes, but could infiltrate, influence, redefine the Tiers.

It was not difficult for me to view sport though the lens of keeping it real (the Codes) versus not selling out (the Tiers), as it had been symbolic of the choices I was facing day to day. Uber masculinity verses minimising. Not that black and white. But at times it had felt as if they were the only two choices.

I had been searching for another way, for this alternative. I just couldn't find a major Black-British figure who provided another option to the Codes and the Tiers. There was no one person, like Ali, like Richards, who completely ruptured that blueprint. As said, I personally swayed towards the Codes. Shared experiences over shared birthplace. There were many positives about the Codes. I couldn't find any positives about the Tiers. I liked the core Code principle of not compromising. I liked having a sense of belonging to something, feeling 'normal' when all around me – from the media to the education system – reinforced negative stereotypes of black manhood. But we also felt fully justified channelling the negative traits given the lowly perception of us in society. Canaries in the mine. An excuse. The Codes gave us power in a world that felt narrow without us quite realising that we had been narrowing our world even further. This attitude extended to our relationships with women, our preoccupation with sex, our objectification of women; another mechanism to conceal our fears, our insecurities. We felt demonised. Yet none of my peers challenged these perceptions, these actions, these ways in which we defined ourselves as young men. That said, there had been little to challenge the social conditions we faced either.

The differences between Lewis and Bruno emerged during the build-up to the fight. Bruno accused Lewis of not being a true Brit. Indeed, when Bruno entered the ring that night to fight Lewis, he did so with a massive Union Jack flag and 'Land of

Hope and Glory' accompanying him. The words 'True Brit' were stitched to the beltline of his shorts. Bruno said, 'Nobody cares about Lennox Lewis in Britain.' In response, Lewis allegedly called Bruno an 'Uncle Tom', meaning a black person who is subservient to white folks. Bruno would later try to sue for defamation.

It had been an uncomfortable conflict. Two black men fighting each other for the affection of the British public. This was a sport with historic ties to slavery. Black men from rival plantations were allegedly pitted against each other for the entertainment of their owners. Now, you had these two fighters scrapping over who was more British, a fight for belonging and acceptance.

Black people have historically been viewed by Europeans as being subhuman. Indeed, the image of the savage, devilish black pre-dates slavery. The association of the colour black with evil goes back centuries. It is, of course, prevalent in our language today, with terms such as 'black mark', 'black sheep' and 'blackmail'.[4]

Peter Fryer's *Staying Power: The History of Black People in Britain* had been like a Bible to me as a teenager. It had been the first book I read that acknowledged black people's existence and history in Britain. Not American blackness. Not the Empire's conception of blackness.

In this book, I learnt that early racial prejudice and bigotry had been born from folklore and reinforced by people's insecurities of physical difference. This turned into more systemic racism that justified slavery through the veneer of science, education, the arts and religion. I read about the early depictions of black people. In the seventeenth century, many European travellers fuelled these myths with their accounts of activities in Africa. Travel writer Sir Thomas Herbert described blacks as 'fearfull blacke ... Deuillish Sauages' and 'divels incarnate' after travelling to parts of the continent from 1627 to 1629. Herbert would later suggest that blacks had sex with apes and were 'addicted to rapine and theeury'. This had not been new. As early as the sixteenth century, French lawyer Jean Bodin suggested that 'promiscuous coition of men and animals took place wherefore the regions of Africa produce for us so many monsters'.

By the seventeenth century, scientists began to construct racial divisions; developing hierarchical orders based on skin colour. As such, blacks, the lowest in these racial categories, were lazy, limited in speech, unintelligent, incapable of being civilised, ugly and without arts or science. Polygenist François Bernier had been at the forefront of this thinking, although views on Africans remained essentially based on myth with little or no scientific reasoning whatsoever. The racial divisions devised proclaimed whites to be intellectually superior to blacks.

By 1677, Sir William Perry, one of the founders of the Royal Society, had already written in *The Scale of Creatures* of how 'They [Africans] differ also in their Natural Manners, & in the Internal Qualities of their minds.' In his essay *Of National Characters*, empiricist David Hume thought whites were naturally superior. These views were widespread and rooted in the establishment. One of the most influential pseudo-scientific books had been historian Edward Long's *History of Jamaica* (1774), which contained vile descriptions of blacks ('bestial manners' and 'stupidity' among his observations), which served as a prominent and widely read historical piece. Swedish botanist Carl Linnaeus' views were equally influential. A man responsible for the modern classification of plants and animals described Africans in 1758 (translated to English in 1792) as 'crafty, indolent, negligent ... governed by caprice' and declared fair-skinned Europeans as 'gentle, acute, inventive ... governed by laws'. United States President Thomas Jefferson added his weight to the subject in 1781, when he said, 'I advance it ... as a suspicion only, that the blacks, whether originally a distinct race, or made distinct by time and circumstances are inferior to the whites in the endowments both of body and mind.'

It had been clear that black people were not considered the equal of a Brit. It had been clear that this was so deeply rooted in the psyche of the British, reinforced in so much of its history, its literature, its science, its religion, that I wouldn't and couldn't, for years, grasp that sport would be another extension of this fundamental inequality.

It has been alleged that it was common for plantation owners in America to force slaves to fight or race against each other for gambling purposes and entertainment. Slaves could win their freedom if they performed well for their owners. Boxer Tom Molineaux had been one of the most famous sporting escapees.

I first learnt about Molineaux in *Staying Power*. Born in 1784, raised as a slave in a plantation in Richmond, Virginia, Molineaux won his freedom and $500 by defeating another slave called Abe in a bare-knuckled contest. Molineaux was around five foot nine and between one-eighty-five and one-ninety-six pounds. He travelled to England penniless in 1803 and soon came under the tutelage of American-born Bill Richmond, the first famous black prize-fighter. Richmond's fists had become so famous, he had broken the colour barriers of the time by owning the Horse and Dolphin pub near Leicester Square, where he also ran a boxing school.

Richmond turned the crude but powerful Molineaux into a better technical fighter. Molineaux's subsequent victories in the ring made him a celebrity. Around 100 years before Jack Johnson incurred the wrath of white America by beating up their fighters and sleeping with their women, Molineaux had been doing the same in England. At times, he would walk down the street with two white women on his arms. But then Molineaux had not been viewed as your average black. He could get away with it. He was beyond black. Superman. The English were as fascinated and compelled by Molineaux as much as they were disparaging, disinterested and dismissive of black people in their neighbourhoods.

Molineaux had become such a celebrity and performed so well, there were calls for him to fight the English champion Tom Cribb. An ex-slave versus a noble man from England.

Cribb versus Molineaux took place in Copthall Common in East Grinstead on 18 December 1810. On a cold, rainy day, the two bare-knuckled fighters met for what had been billed as 'The World Prize-fighting Championship'. Over 10,000 people witnessed the two fighters punching, wrestling and brawling on equal grounds for 19 rounds.

Molineaux started to dominate the fight and had been on the verge of knocking Cribb out when 200 people rushed towards the ring and attacked the former slave. The invading spectators tried to pull Molineaux away from Cribb, which resulted in the American breaking at least one of his fingers. The crowd were successful in pulling Molineaux away. Cribb sank to the ground, out cold, once Molineaux let go.

By the time the spectators left the ring and the ringside ropes had been put back into place, Cribb was ready to fight again. When the fight resumed, Molineaux knocked Cribb down almost immediately. Molineaux was winning the fight, prompting Sir Thomas Price in the 23rd round to say, 'Now, Tom, now; for God's sake don't let the n****r win. Remember the honour of Old England. Go for him; go for him!'[5]

In the 28th round, Molineaux knocked Cribb to the ground. Cribb's corner men dragged their man to the corner. The referee called the two fighters for the 29th round. Cribb rose to his feet only to fall face first to the canvas. His corner men could not revive their man. Molineaux and Richmond jumped for joy in the soaking rain. Molineaux was the first world prize-fighting champion. However, before they could officially announce his coronation, Jem Ward, one of Cribb's corner men, ran over to Molineaux's corner, grabbed Richmond and accused him of planting bullets in his fighter's fists. The referee checked Molineaux's fists but there were no bullets. Richmond and Ward and others brawled in the middle of the ring. It took 15 minutes to clear, by which time Cribb, propped up with brandy and blankets, recovered. Molineaux and Cribb staggered for a few more rounds when, in the 40th round, Molineaux, damp, face swollen and with broken fingers, said, 'I can fight no more.'[6] [7]

'The Black had to contend against a prejudiced multitude; the pugilistic honour of the country was at stake, and the attempts of

Molineaux were viewed with jealousy, envy and disgust!' wrote journalist Pierce Egan.[8]

In the return fight in 1811, Cribb knocked Molineaux out in 11 rounds. Cribb is regarded as the first world champion because of his victories over Molineaux. As for Molineaux, he never again fought at championship level. He split from Richmond, lost his money, became an alcoholic, contracted numerous STDs and by his thirties he was jaundiced, his body meagre and weak. In 1818, aged 34, he was found dead in a storage cupboard in Dublin, Ireland. He died of liver failure.[9]

The end of slavery did not herald the start of equality. Sport remained, alongside entertainment, the most feasible route to some level of parity for blacks. The alternative, of course, was for blacks to become 'Uncle Toms' or 'House Negroes' by ingratiating themselves to white society at the expense of their dignity and indeed fellow black folks. Many blacks in America and England gravitated towards sport, in part because in every other aspect of society – education, work and decent homes – they were denied access and equality. Success had been easy to measure in sport, particularly in boxing. You win. Or you lose. You win? Everybody profits. If you win and you're entertaining, even more profit. The combination of this and Europeans' morbid fascination and exoticisation of the black physique meant that boxing was desegregated way before most sports.

White society gleefully accepted blacks performing for them on this basis. However, they still wanted blacks to sit at the back of the bus, sleep in separate hotels, eat in different restaurants and work for, instead of alongside, them. Unfortunately, for the many blacks who rose above the system to become lawyers, educators and doctors, they had to face both the Tiers and the scrutiny of some folk in the black community who did not feel such heights were attainable without selling out.

Lewis–Bruno's fight took place on a cold rainy night in Cardiff. Lewis, in red shorts, and visibly lengthier than the stockier Bruno, came out swiftly, popping out his left jab, moving round the ring and generally posturing as if the fight would be easy. Playground posturing. Bruno didn't do much. But he applied steady pressure, closing the ring with minimal effort, covering up effectively and moving away from Lewis' vaunted right hand. Lewis was active, bouncy and energetic but Bruno appeared more focused.

By the second round it had become clear that Lewis was more concerned with looking good than trying to slowly work his way to victory. Lewis was throwing telegraphed right hands, holding his hands low, posing not imposing. Bruno stuck to his game plan, commanding the centre of the ring and coolly working his way into the fight.

In round three, Bruno caught Lewis with the best punch of the fight to that point, an overhand right that wobbled his foe. Bruno went to finish the fight, but Lewis held on and recovered. The fight followed the same pattern, Lewis bouncing, off balance and throwing punches wildly. Bruno composed, stalking and out-jabbing Lewis. Then something strange happened, something that would become a feature throughout Lewis' career. When under intense pressure, Lewis could fight with the best of them. Challenge him and he'd fight back with fury. But he had been prone to being tentative and reluctant to express himself in the ring. Not what you'd expect from a big puncher. Not what you'd expect from the heavyweight champion of the world. Not necessarily what the black community would want from its champion either. You wouldn't see Honeyghan be so tentative.

Lennox Lewis at this point in his career could not stand with Lancelot and Galahad, Ali or Marciano. Something was missing. Upon entering the ring, Lewis appeared almost unconscious to all that surrounded him, although at the same time completely aware of what was going on. He appeared too alert to what had been happening without acknowledging it. It was almost as if he had got himself into a mindset that he did not wish to leave at any point during the evening's proceedings. It may be focus. But at times it appeared as if he just wasn't present, as if the moment had been passing him by.

For the cerebral Lewis, nothing changes. He rarely blinks upon entering the ring, and when he does, it's as if someone has pressed a pause button on his face before, his eye lids open again. His doleful and glazed expression belies the alertness in his mind and underlines the fact that, unlike the true greats, he did not appear to think instinctively. He could not dwell within the two realms of cutting loose and expressing himself creatively in the ring while under some semblance of mental, fighting control.

Lewis is almost like a third person looking at himself and instructing himself in what is about to happen. Like he doesn't want to let go, to be *in* the moment. Perhaps Lewis cannot concede to his fears, and as such cannot overcome them.[10]

Against Bruno, he looked comfortable to the point of being complacent. He started dropping his hands playfully as if mocking the danger of the situation. He appeared confident without fully committing to expressing that confidence with positive action. The only thing that could raise him out of that funk would be a hard shot, something that hurts him, something that disrupts his fighting pattern. In this state, he fights suggestively. He throws a suggestive jab and progresses forward suggestively.

Against Bruno, he showed flashes of brilliance. At one point he threw a double jab followed by an overhand right. Beautiful. There were moments when I felt that the combination of Lewis' size, mobility, technique and quickness could make him stand with the Lancelots and Galahads.

Entering the seventh round, Bruno had been in front. Early in the round, Bruno gained the upper hand. Lewis had been off balance and doubled over when Bruno caught him with an overhand right. Lewis stumbled back clumsily, more through poor balance than genuine hurt. He found himself pinned to the corner of the ring by Bruno who, by this point, was holding Lewis behind the head with one hand and clipping him with uppercuts with the other. As Bruno pulled back slightly, Lewis hit Bruno with a vicious left hook, the best punch of the fight. We had seen this before in Bruno's previous losses to James 'Bonecrusher' Smith, 'Terrible' Tim Witherspoon and 'Iron' Mike Tyson. In each case, Bruno had been fighting well when a single shot changed the momentum of the fight. Lewis seized the moment, hitting Bruno with uppercuts and overhand rights. The overly fussy referee Mickey Vann, whose demeaning verbals were often over the top, stopped the slaughter temporarily to warn Lewis for holding and hitting. But Lewis launched straight back at Bruno who could no longer defend himself, could no longer fight back and no longer had the senses to know how to respond sensibly. As Bruno's trainer George Francis was about to enter the ring, Mickey Vann called a halt to the fight. Bruno's title dreams were over. Lewis retained his championship. But like Larry Holmes, he lost all hope of winning over the public by defeating a national treasure.

Was it a victory for Black-Britain? I didn't think so.

Even though Lewis represented the Codes, he too struggled to gain acceptance from the black community. Lewis did not personify black people's struggles in the way that, say, Mike Tyson did. Lewis didn't crush Bruno in the same way Tyson had.

Money and fame could not fundamentally change the dilemma faced by black folks, many black sports people; how do you live up to the lofty expectations of the Codes while negotiating the Tiers without selling your soul, without losing your soul? Athletes like Ali, who completely rewrote the rule-book and completely broke through the conceptions of Codes and Tiers, had been rare. For most black athletes, they would have to negotiate with both if they were to succeed with any level of credibility.

A week after the Lewis–Bruno contest, Nigel Benn would fight Chris Eubank for a second time. Eubank had won the first fight and their bitter rivalry had revived boxing in the UK. Twenty million people watched the second fight. In many ways, they were bigger characters than Lewis and Bruno. Extremes. So extreme, in fact, that they were almost like caricatures. Not real.

In Benn, you had a British bulldog type; he was an ex-army guy with a Cockney accent, easy for your typical working-class fan to embrace. Eubank had been the opposite. He had been a mimic man. Eubank embraced an almost comical English gentleman image, complete with a monocle, jodhpurs, riding boots and a cane. He'd strut around with his nose up in the air and appeared to enjoy pissing everybody off. Like Benn, however, he had been a warrior in the ring. Their powerful images and their guts in the ring masked any racial undertones. If there had been any under-currents between the two, besides personal hatred, it was likely based more on class than anything else.

Those fights capped a great year for the profile of Black-Britain in sport. Paul Ince became the first black captain of an England football team that now regularly featured black players such as John Barnes, Ian Wright, Des Walker and Les Ferdinand. During the World Athletics Championships, there had been gold medals for Linford Christie, who set a British record for the 100 metres, and Colin Jackson, who set a world record for the 110 metres hurdles.

In 1993, the 'Let's Kick Racism Out of Football' campaign had also started. Herman Ouseley founded the campaign in his role as Chairman for the Commission for Racial Equality (CRE). Ouseley, the first black chief executive in a local authority in England, would emerge as the most powerful public figure on anti-racism in elite sport. He was knighted in 1997 and made a life peer in 2001.

If ever there was a year when the prominence and presence of the black athlete had been established, then 1993 was significant. But progression on the field of play had not been matched by advancements off the field.

On 22 April, while walking home with his friend Duwayne Brooks, Stephen Lawrence was murdered in an unprovoked racist attack by a gang of white youths in Eltham. Through tireless campaigning from Stephen's parents, Doreen and Neville Lawrence, the case not only exposed the brutality of individual racism, but through the failures of the police it also exposed the constant reality of institutional racism. This would come out in the following years. However, in 1993 little had changed in terms of the public's perception of racism.

This was a period when there had been other 'race'-related killings. In 1991, 15-year-old Rolan Adams was stabbed to death in Thamesmead, when confronted by 15 white youths shouting racial abuse. Only one perpetrator was convicted of Adams' murder. The deaths of black people in police custody remained a major issue that few people outside the black community liked to discuss. Racism in society continued to be a major problem, yet fewer people in the mainstream media wanted to talk about it.

Neither Lewis nor Bruno had ever been a villain. Misunderstood, perhaps, but never villains. Bruno finally won a world title on his fourth attempt against Oliver McCall in 1995. McCall had previously defeated Lewis to win the title. During the post-fight interview, Bruno insisted, through bruises and tears, that he was not an Uncle Tom.

'I'm not an Uncle Tom, I'm not a sell-out, I love my people,' said Bruno.

Academic Ben Carrington would later call it 'a significant moment in the cultural history of race and nation in Britain'. In declaring his love for black people during the most significant moment of his sporting career, Britain's favourite black son had finally loosened the grip of the Tiers and revealed how reductive the Codes could be. Yet no one, outside of the black community, had anything to say about this moment.

Lewis, the nice guy, the great fighter but, for many, the not-so-English guy, continued to struggle to gain the adoration of the British public. He remained clean cut and single. Not what anyone would expect of a heavyweight champion. So much so, it seemed as if in every interview the journalist would ask him about his relationship status. He was later quoted in *New Nation* as saying, 'Nuff guys can sleep with a woman but I have slept with four belts.' Lewis, the noble, gentlemanly warrior, had proven to be more of a true conception of Britishness than his accent would imply.

As the years passed, the animosity between the two simmered. Bruno would later tell *New Nation* (9 December 1996): 'I always wonder why Lennox Lewis said I'd sold out. Is it because I'm married to a white lady? Or because I'm more popular than him? I'm not having people say that about me, that's why I sued him.'

Soon after, in *Total Sport* (1997), Lewis would say that he 'never resented the fact that Frank Bruno had the popularity here that I didn't'. Lewis felt that Bruno resented him because he was 'stealing his sunshine'. In the same article, he also refutes calling Bruno an Uncle Tom. 'I don't speak like that. I don't use those words.'

Yet the enduring memory of the two had not been the fight. It had not been the animosity. It had been the way in which the two met in the ring in 2010, prior to the David Haye *v.* Audley Harrison world heavyweight title fight. This occurred many years after they had both retired. Many years after the world title fights.

Many years after the adulation and the glory. It had come many years after Bruno had been diagnosed with bipolar.

They both looked physically well, in retirement. Both looked sharp, dapper in their dark suits. They gave each other a pound (hug), well, a half-pound, before Lewis lifted Bruno's arm in the air. The crowd went crazy with appreciation. I shed a tear.

Lewis could not be a Lancelot for the Codes or the Tiers because he wouldn't adhere to the stereotypes or behaviours within each. Neither he nor Bruno took the easy road. Both were heroes, in their own way. The two men Battled for Britain. Yet when the dust settled, I was still unclear about whose Britain they had been fighting for.

CHAPTER 5

NEW NATION

UNLIKE LEWIS AND BRUNO, it had been clear who the Black-British footballers I grew up watching in the eighties had been fighting for. They had a dual purpose. To represent the black community with pride and win the respect of the British public with dignity. But this too had been problematic for me.

Through the eighties, I couldn't support the English national football team. I'd only watch England games in the hope that the black players would perform well. I supported them as individuals, not the team. But then I'd also question how they could represent a nation that didn't seem to value them.

England has always appeared to have a superiority complex, in sport as in most things. Always felt as if this nation had a God-given right to be the best and if they were not the best, then the opposition must have cheated or England's own players were not true patriots or something. Victory expected. Victory symbolising superiority over England's opponents, which went beyond sport. Black players in the eighties were not considered 'true' Englishmen. We somehow diluted or compromised England's ability to maintain its natural place at the top.

We knew these Black-British footballers by their first names. Cyrille, Viv, Laurie and Justin. We knew them by their first names because we didn't know any Cyrilles or Lauries. We knew them by their first names because we felt every layer of abuse levelled at them from the terraces. We knew them by their first names because we knew the crowds were not cursing them because of the team they played for; they cursed them because of the colour of their skin.

Cyrille Regis received a bullet in the post when first selected to play for England in 1982. Threatened by English fans for representing England. Fans would greet black players with monkey chants delivered with greater harmony than they would the national anthem. These fans resorted to some of the oldest stereotypes of black people, likening us to apes, implying that Viv and Justin were less than human. These fans were equal opportunity racists. African, Caribbean, dark-skinned, light-skinned, British-born, England international, it didn't matter, they all got the same treatment. We knew them by their first names because, in England, they were you. You were they.

I used to approach *Match of the Day* with dread. It was the same feeling I had when I'd notice a policeman staring at me, the same feeling I had when walking down a side road and seeing a group of white boys, the same feeling I had when going into a shop with an item purchased in another store. Something bad is likely to happen. In such situations, my body tightened, and my mind sharpened in preparation of the inevitable. I became a pre-emptive person from a young age. Had to know what was coming next. Prepare your response. I cannot remember a time when I'd walked freely without thinking about what might happen next. Tried to walk freely as a kid and ended up being accused of too many things. I had to tighten, to sharpen, to pre-empt. Problem was, those scenarios had been so common, so frequent, I ended up in a perpetual state of numbness to avoid succumbing to anger, frustration, despair.

Until the early eighties when I had been in primary school, it remained odd to see a plethora of black athletes competing at an elite level in England in sports outside of boxing and athletics. Black-English athletes hadn't yet infiltrated football, cricket and rugby in the way African-Americans had basketball, baseball and American football. So, watching *Match of the Day* had been more like viewing a horror flick.

You're scared. You're young. You don't want to watch anymore. But you don't want anyone to know you're scared. You don't want anyone to know why you're so afraid of something so simple, so predictable. So, you keep it in. Tell no one. Stick it out. And you end up questioning yourself. *What have I done?* The questioning, that's the worst. The most unreasonable part of growing up as a minority is that you constantly stand on trial, condemned, indicted. You become what you are trying to avoid, because if you did not become what you are avoiding, then you wouldn't exist. I didn't really exist. Couldn't see myself. I was a middle man. Sitting between the Codes and the Tiers. But even in a state of non-existence, you still cannot avoid the monkey chants, the stares from the police, the hostility from those white boys.

As a kid, whatever pride I felt watching black footballers on *Match of the Day* quickly soured once the abuse from the crowds rained down. Every match was Minter–Hagler. A hostile environment. A heavy cloud would engulf the pitch when a black player touched the ball. I only saw this in snippets. Black players had been facing this week in, week out.

Viv would later recall a bottle being hurled at him at Upton Park. When he notified the referee, nothing was done. Couldn't avoid *Match of the Day* though. Before hip-hop, football ruled my school playground. To be a part of the conversations, to be picked in the football games, you had to know what had happened over the weekend. Had to know the scores, who scored, who had been the hero, so you could imitate them, so you could be a part of the 'cool' crowd. Rush, Dalglish, Keegan, Brooking. To be like them, you had to watch them. To watch them you had to face the thing you hated the most. The crowds. Their fears. Their hatred. Their racism. Yourself.

You couldn't trust the commentators. They said nothing. They were outraged by hooliganism. Violent play on the field swiftly condemned. Any form of cheating by non-English teams caused outrage. But the poor treatment of black players was somehow acceptable. Ignored. They justified the crowd's racism with their silence. Reinforced the feeling that it was acceptable for black people to be treated less than.

It should have been different by the time I had started watching football around the late seventies. There had been black footballers in the UK as far back as the 1870s, when Andrew Watson and Robert Walker played in Scotland. Watson would go on to represent the Scottish national team in 1881. The first black professional footballer had been Ghanaian-born Arthur Wharton, a goalkeeper and winger who once equalled the world amateur record for the 100 yards dash. He had been followed by Walter Tull, a second lieutenant in the British Army who played for

Tottenham among other teams but died while on duty in France, aged 29, in 1918.

The first major wave of black players came into mainstream football in the seventies. Most were scattered across England. Rare to see more than one black player in a team, although West Ham once fielded three black players in a game. By the late seventies, race relations had changed in society and in football. Regressed in society. Progressed a little on the football pitch.

Turning point: In 1978, Margaret Thatcher, then the opposition leader for the Conservative Party, warned that Britain feared they might be 'rather swamped from people with a different culture' and that 'people are going to react and be rather hostile to those coming in'. Softened National Front's lines. Made those racist lines more palatable, more acceptable, gave it a hook and a snare. The National Front had been on the rise, feeding off people's fears and their poverty, turning vulnerability into votes by turning vulnerability into hatred. Thatcher appealed to the covert racists, to the people who had a problem with immigration, to the disenfranchised indigenous, to those who had become sick of mainstream politics. It solidified her popularity, gave racism a popular face, it condemned Labour to failure. It had been like a call to arms against immigrants of colour. Culture a proxy for 'race'. This had been the most directly racist mainstream call to arms since Enoch Powell's 'Rivers of Blood' speech in 1968. Another tone-setter for 'race' relations in the UK. Another statement legitimising racism. The disenfranchised and the coverts joined typical National Front supporters in taking their fears and what little power they had out on black folks, including the players we knew by their first names. I didn't quite grasp it at the time, but if ever there had been a symbol of swamping, then the influx of black players in football had been it.[1]

Viv Anderson became the first black player to represent England on 29 November 1978. West Bromwich Albion regularly fielded three black players in a single team. Cyrille Regis, Laurie Cunningham and Brendon Batson were known as the Three Degrees, after the black female soul group. Justin Fashanu became Britain's most expensive black footballer, transferring from Norwich to Nottingham Forest for £1 million in 1981. The value of black talent and the success and profit that came with it had started to outweigh prejudice. Trophies to be won. Money to be made.

Off the pitch, black players had been subjected to racism from their own teammates, fans, managers, coaches and the media. There were negative assertions about black players' intelligence, toughness, leadership and discipline. Professional teams fielded black players in positions where pace and 'natural athleticism' would be an asset. Rarely in central roles. The managers of these teams did not trust them to lead, to be in charge, to be at the centre of play. Black players spent their time on the margins. On the right. On the left. Full-backs. Wingers. Black players were cast as lazy and naïve. *Naïve.* That seemed to be a term specially designated for black players. A term that for me and my peers had been as offensive as being called a wog or coon.

The only respite came when I watched Brazil for the first time at the 1982 World Cup in Spain. Brazil's victory at the 1970 World Cup in Mexico had almost been as important to my father as an Ali or West Indian victory.

Brazil often featured black players. Black players in central roles. They always played with flair, technique and passion, making them the 'must see' team in every football tournament they entered. But the 1970 World Cup had been different. These finals were the first to be televised in colour. What the world would see was arguably the greatest football team in the history of the sport, led by black and brown players. In living colour.

Pelé had been the star. Ali's only rival as the greatest sportsman of the time. A black superhero, an icon. Such was that team's influence on black folks, two of my school friends were named Pelé and Jairzinho, another of Brazil's top performers in 1970.

The 1982 side played a brand of creative, one-touch football that drew comparisons to the 1970 team. They teased, flicked, circled, stroked, moved swiftly, then slowly; a bunch of hairy men in tight golden shirts suspending you for 90 minutes seemingly with a philosophy of *you score four, we'll score more*. Brazil played to entertain, to elevate, to expand, to try and take you beyond Hendrix, beyond Jilly from Philly.

I had no conception that the brown players on that Brazilian team would have been considered 'white' in their native country. To me, Brazil comprised black and brown players, their equivalent of Black-British and Asians, in one team. To see this team perform with such audacity, such passion, to expose themselves so willingly to scrutiny in front of predominantly white audiences was a thrill. With the exception of Ali and, at times, the boxer Sugar Ray Leonard, I just hadn't seen any athletes of colour be so bold and so playful and yet win. They won games, they won hearts and they showed me that the narrow conceptions of blackness and brownness, symbolised in English football, needn't be my reality.

Like all great teams, 1982 Brazil had a distinct set of characters. They were captained by Socrates, full name Socrates Brasileiro Sampaio de Souza Vieira de Oliveira. A Che Guevara-type who smoked 60 fags a day, had a bachelor's degree in medicine and founded Corinthians Democracy, which directly opposed Brazil's military government in the eighties.

Their best player had been Zico, who looked too slight to play sport. Mousy-type. Rarely touched the ball. You'd barely see him during a game. But if he only touched the ball five times, each touch would lead to something. A goal. An assist. A through-ball. Like a Notorious B.I.G. track where every line had an impact, was a potential punchline or sample, with Zico, his every touch was a moment to savour. Something you'd remember. Something you couldn't see coming until he'd conjured it. Zico went to where the ball would be going, not where it had been. He would pass the ball into spaces where his teammates would be going, not where they were.

The team also featured Cerezo, gangly with a thick moustache and Afro, who treated every game as if a series of 100-metre races. Roberto Falcao had the cheeky but mildly haggard face of actor Robin Nedwell. But he could turn defence into attack like Magic Johnson in basketball and later Kaká in football, even if his long, thinning golden hair looked to be receding every time he ran. Eder had sharp features, thighs like Naseem Hamed and a shot like thunder. And full-back Junior was an architect, a risk-taker, a defender who rarely defended. Every goal they scored was a thing of beauty: complex, unexpected, memorable. Every goal celebrated wildly, veins popping with ecstasy. Brazilian football was beyond hate. Beyond nationalism. Beyond football's tribal base. No boos. For black kids like myself, a yellow jersey had nothing to do with the Tour de France but everything to do with black and brown power.

In the Black-British footballers, I saw dignity and nobility, not a vision of power I had observed in the Brazilian team. Black British footballers provided a lens into what black folks had been facing in workplaces across the country, what black kids were experiencing in schools, what black families had been experiencing in their neighbourhoods. But I didn't always want a reminder of my everyday struggles when I was watching sport.

Black footballers in Britain often survived by minimising. Walking soft. They knew it wouldn't be productive to fight all the time. They minimised but remained honorable. Remained silent. Silenced. Business psychologist Binna Kandola describes it as: 'What you're worried about if you react to something on the pitch, it will be seen [as] a characteristic of you and your group. Having to be careful to manage yourself. Moderate [your] own behaviour. Not say what I [am] truly feeling.'

They were the pioneers. Without them, there would not be so many black footballers in England. But I wanted more. I wanted to see athletes that fought back like the black and Asian elders in my neighbourhood, like the West Indies, like the Topcats.

This was not the complete story. Players like George Berry and Bob Hazell at times physically fought back. Cyrille Regis refused to go on a tour of South Africa soon after the Soweto Uprising in 1976, when some 20,000 black students protested in response to the introduction of Afrikaans in schools. South

African police had opened fire, reportedly killing at least 150 black children and young people and leaving close to 700 injured. The football tour that Cyrille refused to go on had been billed as some sort of peace-building trip, when in fact it had been little more than a stunt to mask the harsh realities of apartheid. Laurie Cunningham allegedly did the Black Power salute during a game early in his career to combat racism on the terraces.[2] Wish I'd known more about these incidents as a kid. Seen the fuller picture. My view of black footballers at the time may have been different.

The one player that provided hope, that had some potential to change the narrative of black players, had been John Barnes. Symbolically, that goal, in '84, at the Maracana Stadium, against Brazil, had been one of the most significant moments for me as a child. Barnes weaved past five Brazilians and their goalkeeper and then casually rolled the ball into the net with such ease, it was like he had been playing against schoolkids. *Hope.* Not sure there had been a moment by a Black-British athlete that offered as much promise, as much power, as that goal. To some England fans they had found a saviour, a Maradona, a world-beater who could take them back to the glory days of '66, England's one and only World Cup victory. To me and many within the black community, we had found our saviour, our Pelé, a world-beater who would become the first black player to be the main man in the English national team. So good, his voice could not be suppressed.

On the school playground, kids wanted to be Barnes in a way they wanted to be Gascoigne in the nineties and Rooney in the noughties. The first black English player I can remember being mentioned in the same breath as a Rush or Dalglish. We're all attracted to the players who can glide past two or three opponents and then score or supply a killer pass that leads to a goal. It's what we tried to do in the playground. It's what we tried to do in video games. It's what we recognise as dominance on a football pitch. That was Gascoigne. That was Rooney. That was Barnes.

When Barnes moved to Liverpool in 1987, he replicated the Maracana performance regularly, but rarely produced similar levels of dominance internationally. Barnes had been a great player, twice voted the player of the season in England. But John Barnes just couldn't win. The Maracana goal and the expectations that came with it, combined with the racial tensions of the time cast an oppressive shadow.

England football fans booed him unmercifully. Not just on *Match of the Day*. Live matches. Wembley Stadium. The biggest stages. On national television. Prime time. Booed and jeered every time he touched the ball. By his own fans.

While on England duty on a flight to Santiago, Chile, he had been travelling with two other black players, Viv Anderson and Mark Chamberlain. Four National Front members were on that flight and spent the journey abusing the black players.

To anyone who could hear, they said: 'England won only 1–0 because a n****r's goal doesn't count.'[3]

To the white English players, they asked: 'How can you mix with blacks?'[4]

To the FA Secretary Ted Croker, they said: 'You f**king w**ker, you prefer sambos to us.'[5]

Fans across the country disliked Barnes. When he went to Liverpool, a club that had not previously bought a black player, he had been greeted with slogans such as 'White Power' and 'There's No Black in the Union Jack'.[6] Barnes' performances and community work won Liverpool fans over. But he continued to receive vile treatment from fans at other football grounds, his fame making him even more of a target.

Despite the abuse Barnes endured, I was cruel to him too. Barnes had never been a rose that grew from the concrete. Middle-class background. Not quite one of us. Didn't speak like one of us either. Didn't appear to adhere to any of the Codes. When my friends and I first saw that famous picture of Barnes backheeling a banana off the pitch in a game against Liverpool's Merseyside rivals Everton, we didn't comment about the racism he faced, but the patchy nature of his haircut.

Through all the racist chants, Barnes remained noble, often laughing it off while recognising that ignorance should not be met with ignorance. The media would later applaud Barnes for the dignified way he dealt with racism. But this did not ingratiate him to some in the black community who felt that he should be more vocal, more militant. He was often juxtaposed against more vocal (read: to the media more threatening) black players. A media trick. Good black, bad black. Playing the two camps off against each other. They used Barnes (the good black) to under-mine his more outspoken peers, therefore making Barnes appear more like a 'sell-out' than strategic.

'My philosophy is to treat racists with the contempt they deserve,' said Barnes, 'to ignore them or laugh about the situation. Neither of these approaches endears me to the black community, who still call me an Uncle Tom.'[7]

The media were hardly understanding either. He didn't perform as well for England as he did for Liverpool. That made some commentators question his Englishness. Could a Jamaican-born player really give his all for England? He's not a true patriot? Commentators appeared to be more critical of Barnes too, almost as if a spotlight highlighted his every mistake, amplified for the viewers to see.

Barnes couldn't win. But he opened the door for black players to play a more central role for England. He had been the key reason why Merseyside clubs started openly courting black talent. He had been among the most dominant players ever to grace the English First Division (now the Premier League). He had been the first black player to be considered a regular for the England national team. Ashley Cole (107 caps) and Rio Ferdinand (81 caps) are the only black male footballers to have played more times for England than Barnes, who won 79 caps. He had also been that rare player who could disarm an audience, whatever their political beliefs, whatever side they supported. If, for just a moment, he could erase media conception, he could erase history; he could make white folks scream, scream in a way that you would only see them do so at a Michael Jackson concert or a Muhammad Ali fight. Barnes, in flashes, could achieve those moments that made every black kid up and down the country proud.

In her Northern Lights blog, Ruth Ibegbuna, the founder of youth leadership charity Reclaim and the Roots Programme, told the story of how much Barnes had meant to her as a primary school kid who endured racist bullying with 'endless cruel nicknames' like B A Baracus (Mr T's character in *The A-Team*) and Rustic Lee (an eighties' TV cook).

'He was Black Excellence personified,' she said in the blog. 'JB faced racism. If Adam … in my class could be rude about my looks, surely I could stand tall when John Barnes could win matches single-handedly, whilst opposition fans rained bananas down on him. Actual bananas. They bought and brought fruit to a game to unleash on a grown-up man and he still persisted in showing them up, scoring wonder goals that made grown racists cry.'

Barnes opened the doors in many ways. Little did he know that he would be a bridge for what was to follow: a more confident and outspoken generation of black footballers, who would build on what the pioneers had started and that stake Barnes had implanted in the national game.

By the mid-nineties, many things had changed. There had been more black players in the national team and there had been a greater presence of black people in British society. Black people, black culture, black politics had infiltrated the mainstream. The late Bernie Grant, Diane Abbott and Paul Boateng were major figures in British politics, Soul II Soul and Maxi Priest had been selling millions of records across the globe, pirate station Kiss FM was legal, comedy sketch series *The Real McCoy* was giving the nation a slice of Black-British life on terrestrial television, and, the Let's Kick Racism Out of Football campaign would be in full swing. And Thatcher was no longer in power. Underneath the surface, however, not everything had been different from Barnes' day, as I discovered once I'd entered the job market after university.

I had my graduate suit on. Olive green. Slightly oversized in the shoulder, my arms lost in the sleeve. Still shiny. Rarely worn. I arrived at the building, where I would be interviewed for a job, about 45 minutes early. Circled the multi-story building a few times. I went to reception about 20 minutes before the interview. I was sweaty. Maintained the glazed smile of a politician who'd just lost their seat.

The PA called me up. I took a deep breath and smiled. But not too much. I lightened the tone in my voice. I had been as non-threatening as possible. I made sure that my physique could not intimidate. I hunched a little.

As I entered the room for the interview, the man sitting behind the table was writing. He was white and balding, in a grey suit. I walked towards the desk. As I approached, he looked up and a startled expression covered his face. Hastily he said, 'It's all right, we're no longer hiring, thanks for coming.'

'Sorry?' I replied.

'There's no longer a job, thank you for coming,' he said.

'But I'm here for the interview. The advertised sales job?'

'There's no longer a job. Goodbye,' he said.

'Then why are you seeing me?'

'Look, there's no job, now if you can leave?'

'I'm not gonna leave,' I said. 'You advertised a job here, as far as I know there is a job. I want an interview.'

He interviewed me. Briefly. I didn't get the job. I had been angry to the point of tears.

I graduated in 1994 with a 2:1 degree in sociology and communication studies and spent the following eight years unemployed. Felt cheated. After a poor start at a poor school, I had slowly improved academically. I worked through my final year at university and felt I had done everything society had asked of me. Work experience. Check. Managerial experience. Check. Qualifications.

Check. Didn't think I had made it, but on entering the job market I quickly realised that I was still at a disadvantage. For many of my white university peers, they walked into jobs related to the careers they wanted to pursue. They knew people, connections. Others played around after graduation, darting between activities with little or no direction but seemingly ample money to see them through more years of indecision. For me, I just could not get a job through regular channels. Some of it was my fault. Bad interviews. Poor preparation. But there had also been too many occasions when I had seen that look from horrified white men behind desks. This ranged from the subtle (interviewers showing little interest in me to the point of clock-watching from the outset of the interview) to the blatant (interviewers essentially deterring me from doing interviews before starting them).

Through the eight years of 'unemployment' it had been black businesses that had kept me sane, kept me employed, put me on the game, diluted my rage. As a student, I worked at the Electric Cinema on Portobello Road in Notting Hill. It had for a brief time been part-black owned, primarily exhibiting the best of black cinema. You will not know this unless you had been there at the time, because this has been all but erased from its history. My friend Errol alerted me to the cinema and the two us went up there while it was still being refurbished. We were given jobs on the spot.

I started writing because I couldn't find work. My entry into the world of journalism came from an agency called Power Moves, run by Justin Onyeka, Lee Pinkerton and Paul 'Rapscallion' Ryan. It enabled me to build my portfolio. After a recommendation, I worked as a part-time press officer for a record company called Jet Star, the largest black-owned distributor in

Europe. I eventually ended up as the music editor at the black newspaper *The Voice*, this time due to reputation. For eight years, this is how I earned a living, which led to gigs at the BBC, MTV, *NME*, *Time Out* and other mainstream media.

Meanwhile in sport, there had still been an absence of a public figure akin to a Soul II Soul. Someone that gave a slice of Black-British life. Someone that would not dilute, someone that would be very much of the Codes, but could somehow win mainstream acceptance on our terms, therefore cracking the Tiers in a way Lennox Lewis couldn't. That athlete, for me, wouldn't arrive until the nineties, and by the latter part of the decade he had created a whole new blueprint for the Black-British athlete.

There he was, strutting up the football pitch, physically smaller than most but owning the field, owning the moment, owning the cameras, puffy cheeked, shirt always looking a little too big, never hiding his emotions. There he was, after scoring a goal, celebrating wildly, showing off, bogling (a Jamaican dance) as if in Moonlighting, Granaries, Night Moves or any one of the famous night spots frequented by black celebrities through the nineties. The sort of night spots I craved to go to, to get into (more so than Ministry of Sound or Hacienda); to be a part of the black underground scene, our scene, our music (the soundtrack for the Codes), our marginalised selves, back in the day before black was pop, before black was commercially cool (and profitable), before black was urban. There he was, shouting, demonstrating, remonstrating, cursing, eyeballing, gesticulating at the referee, at opposing players, not giving a damn about what people thought. There he was.

He did not achieve as much in his career as Linford Christie in athletics or Lennox Lewis in boxing. He did not win an Olympic title or a world heavyweight championship. He did not break barriers like Tessa Sanderson. He was not considered the greatest athlete in the world like Daley Thompson. He would not be mentioned in the same breath as the all-time greats in football in the way Ellery Hanley would be considered among the best in rugby league history.

Ian Wright won a Premier League title, the FA Cup (twice) and the European Cup Winners' Cup with Arsenal and played 33 times for England (scoring nine goals). I had never seen a mainstream athlete adhere to the Codes and yet be so universally popular. He had been among the first black English athletes to personify our existence in this country.

I was first aware of Wright when he played for Crystal Palace in the 1990 FA Cup final at Wembley. The game had been historic, although few knew it at the time. Palace was the last team comprising all-English players to compete in an FA Cup final. It had also been a team that featured five black players, the shape of future England teams. Back then, five black players in a single team had been unusual. Palace faced the might of Manchester United who featured great players like England captain Bryan Robson and Welsh forward Mark Hughes.

United had been expected to win but the first game at Wembley Stadium ended in a 3–3 draw. Wright twice cracked his shin bone during the 1989–90 season, causing him to miss Palace's semi-final victory over Liverpool and most of the matches leading up to the final. Given his lack of fitness, Palace manager Steve Coppell started Wright on the bench in the final, before putting him on after 69 minutes, with United leading 2–1. Within three minutes, Wright skipped past one United player then cut inside another and scored past the outstretched arms of keeper Jim Leighton to level the score. Two minutes into extra-time, Wright volleyed in a John Salako cross from close range to put Palace ahead. United would later equalise, forcing the replay. In the return match, United defeated Palace 1–0 to lift the FA Cup. However, Wright became an immediate name brand player after his heroics.

By the time Wright had scored two goals in the final, he was already 26 years of age, a time when most players would be approaching their peak, not just starting out. It had been his back story that had first attracted so many to him. Before he signed for Palace in 1985, Wright had been playing Sunday League football while working as a labourer. He'd had run-ins with the law and once spent two weeks in Chelmsford Prison. His career had been going nowhere. Wright doggedly pursued his dream and played every match as if it would be his last. This endeared him to fans. An everyday man, a working-class hero, the underdog, a trier who appreciated every opportunity he had and grabbed it with both hands. Physically he didn't look like Linford or Bruno. At five feet nine, he couldn't be accused of making it through natural ability. It helped that he had a strong southeast London accent, so he couldn't be accused of being a 'foreigner'. It helped that he pledged his undying devotion to England, so he couldn't be accused of having split loyalties.

When Wright moved to Arsenal in 1991, my allegiance to West Ham started to switch. Not long before Wright's move, I had gone to a few West Ham games at Upton Park. The home of

Brooking, Allen, Best, Cottee, McAvennie, Dicks. It had been wonderful and frightening.

Wonderful. No seats in stadiums back then. When West Ham scored, a complete thrill. Dangerous too. The momentum of the crowd would carry you forward as if being scooped up by a tidal wave. No control. I suddenly moved from being midway in the stands to being close to the pitchside barriers. Before I could find my feet again, I had been scooped back to where I had been originally standing.

Frightening. I had been sunk into a sea of white faces. Constant racist chants. Not reserved for the opposition. The West Ham fans abused their own player George Parris. Parris had been a marauding midfielder, who came up through West Ham's junior ranks. He was an East Ender, one of their own. One of our own. Yet every time he touched the ball, sections of the crowd where I had been standing would boo or make derogatory remarks. After a while, I dreaded Parris touching the ball. Just wanted him to be anonymous. Yet for all the hostility towards Parris and the racist abuse, and despite being completely outnumbered, I didn't feel as if I would come to any harm. I did not feel under threat. But they could do as they pleased without fear of repercussion. I kept my mouth shut, celebrated every West Ham goal, so I didn't have to worry. But it didn't make me feel any better knowing that in order to support my home team, I would have to endure this abuse to be part of the gang.

Ian Wright's Arsenal represented black London, Joel Moore in football boots, the Topcats on telly. Crystal Palace may have featured many black players, but Arsenal had been an elite club.

Wright joined his old friend David Rocastle in a team that included black south Londoners Paul Davis, Michael Thomas (although he would move to Liverpool soon after Wright's arrival) and Kevin Campbell. English football was now in the process of sweeping up its eighties mess; the boggy pitches, hooliganism, all-standing stadiums, dour television presentations and racism on the terraces. In 1993 the Premier League was formed, with the First Division separating itself from the other divisions, creating an elite league in England. But to be successful, English football needed to rid itself of the debris from its murky past.

Wright did not moderate his behaviour like other black athletes. He didn't appear to worry about other people's worries. The media, fans, managers or opponents that considered him brash, wild and chippy didn't seem to bother him. Wright played with the heart of a lion and, while not necessarily flashy like the Brazilians, he performed with similar levels of theatrical verve.

He had shown black players who would follow that they didn't need to strictly play to the media and fans' agendas to attain popularity and acceptance. He didn't minimise. He wasn't marginalised. This had not been my reality in adult life. Whenever Wright featured in any publication I bought, he reinforced his uncompromising ethos. 'I won't sell myself out. I'm true to myself.' In the February 1997 edition of *Total Sport*, he spoke of getting a Rosa Parks tattoo, in homage to the civil rights activist who in 1955 in Montgomery, Alabama refused to give up her seat to a white passenger on a bus, for which she had been promptly arrested. This led to the Montgomery Bus Boycott, a significant moment in the civil rights movement.

Wright had been playing for a side in Arsenal that became my side. Paul, David, Kevin. Sorry, West Ham. Still my favourite club. Always will be. But, see, those guys, the ones you sometime refer to disparagingly. I love those guys. Get more from them than I do you. You may know me, relate to my East End past, you may defend me. But at some point, when you get angry with me, when we fall out, have a disagreement, when you see something you don't like in a black person, you're going to call me a black something. Not a something. A black something. Black as much an insult as an identifier. Precursor of your curse. I have never called anyone a white something. Not even in the height of anger, not even in a rage, not even when I had been insulted because of my 'race'. There had not been a resentment so deep, so ingrained, that – naturally – it would come out. But with you, I would always be waiting for that moment.

I remember going to a white friend's house as a teenager. Sat down eating chips, watching Saturday night television with him and his dad. Then a black person came on the screen, and the dad suddenly shouted 'wog' and let out a sharp piercing laugh, 'HA-HA.' Why was that okay? Why was it okay to say that in front of me? Because I am a friend of your son? Does that make it, make me, acceptable? Would I be acceptable then if I dated your daughter? Would it be okay if I got a better job than your son? Or moved out of the neighbourhood, to a middle-class neighbourhood? Would I be acceptable if I started saying matter instead of mah-ugh or maths instead of maffs? Would I be acceptable if I said that I was offended by the word 'wog'?

Watching Wright screw up all those restrictions, my insecurities, and chuck those damn Tiers in the bin told me that, in a little way, I could be me, not perfect, not always correct, but just be me. That was important. Couldn't take that for granted. I had seen what had happened to John Barnes in the eighties; the man who should have shifted the paradigm for the black athlete in Britain, and in a way did, but instead fell victim to the Codes and the Tiers.

In the 18 November 1996 edition of *New Nation*, Wright was interviewed by broadcaster and journalist Brenda Emmanus. I had been writing for *New Nation* at the time, a newspaper that had for a short spell rivalled *The Voice* as Britain's leading black newspaper. *New Nation* had been progressive, a tabloid with high-quality journalism, informed columnists and decent design quality. It had been fitting that Wright had been among the first black celebrities featured in the newspaper.

In his interview with Emmanus, he said: 'I want to be recognised as someone who never sold out: as someone who made black people proud and was fearless in the same way Malcolm X was. I'm very conscious of the fact that my community perceive me as a role model.'

He added: 'I am more your community leader type or spokesperson type. I am not saying I want to be the new Malcolm X, but I would like to be the Ian Wright that people will listen to and be inspired by. My priority is to see the black community start caring about itself, unify and stand proud. I want us to be constructive members of society and build for our future.'

In that same edition, *New Nation* released the results of a survey it had conducted. It declared that a black middle class had been created. There were more black home and car owners, more black people in higher-income brackets and more declaring themselves as Black-British than any other racialised category. Wright had been voted the most popular sportsman. Jazzie B from Soul II Soul had been voted the most popular musician.

Wright had been a leader of this new nation. Symbolic of a period when the distinctiveness of Black-Britishness appeared to be breaking through to the mainstream. Wright's success, Soul II Soul's success, the breakthrough of artists such as Chris Ofili and Steve McQueen, the scramble for black R&B singers by mainstream labels, the dominance of jungle music and later UK garage in the clubs and on the pop charts, Benn and Eubank could not mask the racial prejudice still prominent in society. This had also been highlighted by *New Nation*, when they reported on the 213 deaths in police custody between 1986 and 1995. But if *The Voice* newspaper had been created in the eighties to give black folks a voice, then *New Nation* had come to symbolise the dawn of Black-Britain. A Britain where someone, like myself, would become more visible.

The *Observer* once wrote the following about Wright's appearance on *This Is Your Life* in 2000: '[It was] just a big warm celebration featuring an awful lot of very un-white, un-middle class touchy-feeliness, Suddenly, in living colour, England looked like another country, and it was good.'[8]

What were white folks scared of? It had not been another country. It had been your country, your England. This *was* England. For you, perhaps, a new nation. For us, nothing new.

Wright spoke of being a community leader like Malcolm X. I am not sure Wright was ever really that. Yes, he lashed out. Yes, I enjoyed watching *Match of the Day* again because I knew he would not back down in the face of adversity. Never shrank.

Never diminished. But he didn't lead a revolution. When Manchester United goalkeeper Peter Schmeichel allegedly said to Wright 'you f**king black bastard' in a match in November 1996, he didn't mobilise black footballers, or create a collective voice. In his autobiography *A Life in Football*, Wright said: 'It turns out to be a blatant case of sweeping it under the carpet. Gordon Taylor, the PFA and whatever faction it was of Kick It Out … none of them did anything.'

In February 1997, Wright, according to some, responded with a two-footed tackle on Schmeichel that reignited the rivalry and brought Schmeichel's alleged comments back to life. The papers couldn't get enough. A perfect time for Wright to respond, a perfect time to let England know how they reverse situations of 'race'. A perfect time to point out how England was at pains to call white people racist, but quick to accuse black folks of being 'chippy', racists in reverse and playing the 'race' card. Wright said little. I'm sure he had his reasons.

Later, sociologist Ben Carrington would argue in his book *Race, Sport and Politics* that Wright was 'outspoken with no agenda, a threat to mono-cultural nationalism, but an uncritical endorser of populist nationalism'.

I was never quite sure what Wright stood for. In truth, I didn't care. He had been our contradictions and our assertiveness. For me, more than anything, Wright was how we could be if we didn't edit ourselves as a minority, how we could be if we ignored the Spotlight, how we could be more than the Codes or the Tiers. The honest part of us. He demonstrated that it was possible, even if we were not sure what the possibility could be. Shared experience and a shared birthplace could be compatible after all. Black and British. That's why he had been such a pivotal figure – my favourite footballer. The only major footballer to came close in later years would be Rio Ferdinand.

Ian Wright provided a lens into black lives. He may not have been as globally revered as some homegrown athletes, but he was one of the most significant sportsmen from these shores. Wright's presence indicated that the Black-British athlete was starting to find his/her voice.

CHAPTER 6

BEYOND SPORT

My opponent's confidence weighed heavily on my arms, my legs and any thoughts of success I may have had. He was a shade under six feet in height, three inches shorter than I was. His profile was shaped like the side of a spoon, his chin sagging into his chest as if he had no neck. The man did not look like an athlete, but he carried himself with an elite sportsman's confidence.

I had seen him many times before. I would pass 'Spoon' on my way to the badminton courts at Kensington Sports Centre every Friday evening. A huge green net sliced the main hall in two; basketball was played on the entrance side, badminton on the other. There were vociferous, whooping youngsters on the basketball side and thirty-somethings trying to work off some life-fat on the other. On this occasion, as I waited for the badminton courts to be free, Spoon asked whether I'd like to play a game of two-on-two basketball with his colleague. I accepted without hesitation.

I hadn't played basketball since a Comic Relief charity game in 1989 when I was 16. That game ended in disaster. Frustrated by a teammate showing off in front of the female-heavy audience, I tossed the ball at his head as if trying to break a window and stormed out of the gym. It was now the noughties and I was in my thirties. What made me think I could pick up where I left off, I didn't know. However, no one was watching, so I thought 'what the hell'.

Spoon handed me the ball. His smooth, chiselled face and arms glistened with sweat. Mine didn't. I hadn't warmed up or taken any practice shots. My arms and legs looked as dry and thin as a Matchmaker. However, I immediately assumed the triple threat stance. Body crouched, legs spread (left slightly in front of the right) with the ball cupped in both hands, which were next to my right hip. It's called the triple threat because it puts you in an ideal position to either dribble (or drive) past an opponent, pull up for a shot or pass to a teammate. I was ready to make my move. My teammate, my brother-in-law, had been jockeying for position to my right while Spoon crouched down so low in front of me, it was almost as if his drooping arms were sweeping the floor every time he moved.

I pretended as if I was going to drive past Spoon. This, I hoped, would move him out of position. Once he'd react to my fake move, I would stop and shoot the ball. But he didn't flinch. I faked again. This time I acted as if I was about to shoot (once he'd responded to this fake move, I would drive past him). Again, his body remained still; although his eyes followed the ball's every move. *Move, goddamn it.* I was running out of ideas. It suddenly dawned on me. I couldn't dribble well with my left hand and while I had been sure I could effectively dribble a ball through my legs given ample time and no opponent, in this situation a move like that would probably be as effective as a one-year-old trying to bounce a tennis ball.

Maybe I should pass it. Every time I thought about it, Spoon raised his arm to prevent any possibility of this happening. I felt ridiculous and paralysed. Three or so seconds had elapsed and Spoon seemed seven feet tall and seven feet wide.

I faked one last time, a kind of axe-wielding motion with the ball. This time he bumped my chest with his forearm. I think he was bored. I leaned back, pivoted off my right leg, leapt and swiftly lifted my hands above my head to launch a shot about 18 feet from the basket. Spoon challenged the shot but wasn't quick enough to block it. Images of Michael Jordan were in my head as I held the follow-through pose (right arm pointing skywards) after the ball had departed, although my posture probably looked less like the Statue of Liberty and more like an old watering can. The ball moved hurriedly in the air. Too hurried. Too flat. The ball barely touched the front of the rim before it sank to the floor as if punctured in flight.

I cannot remember much after that, except the one time Spoon didn't even bother trying to defend my shot. He let me shoot without contesting, telling his teammate, 'Don't worry, he ain't gonna hit it.' My team lost badly. We made two baskets. Well, my brother-in-law did. But Spoon and his friend raced to ten without much effort. By the end of the game, my chest was burning. I felt sick; every breath felt like sandpaper had been scraping my air passage. Yet despite the pain of my tiredness, my overwhelming feeling of humiliation had been more hurtful. It had nothing to do with my ineptitude on court. I wasn't suddenly experiencing an early mid-life crisis, realising that I was no longer as young as I thought. I had not been an old sports star who clearly couldn't compete anymore. The experience hadn't brought back memories of being picked last for football at school. At the moment Spoon sank that final shot and then at the point we exchanged hand-shakes, I felt as though my mediocre performance had been a violation of the Codes.

It was illogical. Stupid. It's not like being good at basketball is an inherent black trait. Couldn't shake the negative feelings though. Had any black person seen my performance, they would have laughed, cursed, shook their heads in disappointment. Had white people seen me play, I would have singlehandedly broken a 'positive' myth about black men. As I said, stupid. But the feelings were real and symbolic of a problem far deeper and broader than this five-minute game.

As I trudged off the court, I felt the burden of being trapped between the Codes and the Tiers, and the expectations and pressures that came with them. The negatives caused overwhelming tension in my head like sinusitis. The Codes: Don't be weak. Don't sell out. Don't be crap at sport. The Tiers: Accept Eurocentric conceptions of race. Be tolerant. Be quiet. Accept the fact that we black folks, to quote the Reverend Jesse Jackson, are 'free but not equal'.

This moment did not leave me. This feeling did not leave me. Always returned every time I played sport. It had been the same when I started Muay Thai at a dojo in London Bridge in the mid-noughties. I had been sparring against a stocky white dude who looked a little bit like actor Stephen Graham in *This Is England '86*.

This guy didn't look in great shape. But he had been training for many years. For some reason, I expected to be as good as him. Not consciously. Not like I thought I had the right to be good.

But looks can be deceiving, and my opponent looked more like a beer-drinking brawler than a martial artist. So, I moved, flicked out my jab, floated around on the mats like Ali. He threw nothing back. He didn't try any kicks. Barely moved. My jabs had been landing just short of his face. Every time I closed in, he took small steps back. I'd edge forward, he'd edge back, never in a straight line though. He'd always edge back at an angle, a little step to his left. When he could see me throw an overhand right, he'd edge back to his right.

It didn't take long for me to become frustrated, impatient and fatigued. I started crouching lower when I was throwing my jab, lessening my size to match his. As I threw a stringy jab, in one motion he shifted his upper body to avoid my punch and *BOOM!* cracked me with a left hook on the chin. It didn't hurt. I didn't go down. But I blacked out for a second. Couldn't gather my thoughts. I had been in shock. Shook. Instinctively I kept punching. I'd throw four or five shots, all missing or glancing blows, and he'd counter *BOOM!* with flush single shots. He couldn't miss. At the time, I couldn't comprehend what he had been doing to avoid my shots and counter so effectively. The pain of those shots had not been a problem. It had been the embarrassment of failing at something everyone thought I would be good at.

I thought such unsettling feelings had long passed. I was a grown man. I had been a relatively successful music and sports journalist. Through my twenties, I had travelled from New York to the Bahamas, allegedly given pop stars All Saints their first major magazine cover story, hung out with Jay-Z, talked about shopping in Camden with Beyoncé, shared a bed with Mel B (while interviewing her), dined with Afrobeat legend Fela Kuti's most famous son, Femi, annually met the top reggae artists Buju Banton, Bounty Killer and Beenie Man, immersed myself in the English basketball scene, been threatened by rappers and questioned by the police, attended press conferences for Will Smith, P Diddy, Al Pacino, Jamie Foxx and Lauryn Hill, argued with the Wu-Tang Clan, interviewed Aaliyah not long before her death, met the godfathers of hip-hop like Kool DJ Herc and Grandmaster Flash, had my most enjoyable interviews with Chuck D, Jill Scott, the Geto Boys' Bushwick Bill and Sizzla, and interviewed Mary J Blige, Allen Iverson, Lennox Lewis and Denise Lewis.

Through this period, I had only just scraped a living financially, but I felt secure in myself, or so I thought. I had cultivated a laid-back façade, one that rendered me friendly to a fault, assertive when required, but non-confrontational. How I felt rarely saw the light of day. I had battled to find a balance between my blackness and Britishness which, for so long, appeared at odds. I thought I'd nailed it. But it was clear that my work had provided the ideal veil to cover how I really felt about lying between the two without truly finding my own comfort zone or fully committing to either. I had been constantly changing my behaviour to fit in with the expectations of each crowd, each scenario. I could talk about the clash between black and white culture, the conflicts, the contradictions. I didn't realise, until these sporting moments, however, that I was still a victim of it. These seemingly irrelevant moments had exposed a deep and surprising truth. But then sport tends to do that.

As popular and inspirational as sport could be, equally it could also be extremely problematic.

While sport amplified my struggle between the Codes and the Tiers, for others sport had been more damaging. For me, the expectation that I would be good at sport had meant that, from an early age, my school had pushed me more in a sporting direction than an academic one. Through years of involvement in sport – writing about it, participating in it – most of my experiences had reinforced a kind of toxic masculinity and some negative aspects of the Codes.

Sport can bring out the worst in you, and it is often the case that poor early childhood experiences can stick in adulthood. That had been the case with me. During this period, elite sport did not speak to my experiences.

If the nineties had been a breakthrough period for Black-British athletes in finding their voice, this did not seem to progress much in the noughties. I thought we would be flooded by more Ian Wrights, more political Ian Wrights, more outspoken Ian Wrights, more Ian Wright-types playing more central roles for England. I thought that hyphenated style would help put the black in the Union Jack through excellence on the field and by breaking away from the narrowness of the Codes and the Tiers which had, for many years restricted, afflicted my generation.

Black athletes during this period appeared to be veering further away from politics, from identity, from a clear sense of Black-Britishness defined from within the community, and not by the mainstream. Part of this I put down to the continuing influence of American culture on British sport. Black-America, and the Codes that came with it, were more influential than the British Codes.

For the black male athlete, you still had to be like Mike. Either Jordan or Tyson. Jordan, through the eighties and nineties, had created the model for black commercial success. Black as in apolitical, black as in fashionable, black as in colour-blind. This had been the safe route.

The other route that emerged had been to be like Mike Tyson. If rap music provided the soundtrack to Jordan's moves, Tyson personified elements of the genre's post-Public Enemy, no sell-out, gangsta era. By the early noughties, Tyson was no longer a force, his demise well documented. We knew about trainer/father figure Cus D'Amato saving him from a life of crime, the impact of D'Amato's death, becoming the youngest heavyweight champion, his turbulent marriage to actress Robin Givens, the 91 seconds wipeout of boxing legend Michael Spinks, his difficult relationship with promoter Don King, losing the heavyweight title to 42–1 underdog Buster Douglas in Tokyo, being found guilty and sentenced to six years in prison for raping beauty queen Desiree Washington, coming out of prison and regaining the world title, losing it to/with Evander Holyfield, biting a chunk off Holyfield's ear, losing badly to Lennox Lewis (a man of whom he once said he wanted to 'eat his children') and declaring bankruptcy, despite making an estimated $700 million during his career.

In 2000, Tyson came to the UK twice, to fight Julius Francis in Manchester and Lou Savarese in Glasgow. While in the UK, he said, 'I'm a totally different entity to what most people think. I'm Tyson here – Mike and daddy to my children and my wife. Tyson is nothing. Tyson is a freak. The fans don't know why they cheer me. I'm the guy who makes the freak show happen. People come to watch me kill somebody, beat somebody up and knock somebody out.'

When it had been announced that Tyson would be fighting in Britain, one British publication carried the cover story headline 'Lock Up Your Daughters'. When Tyson arrived, he generally played the nice guy, something which had not been expected by the press. Tyson brought Brixton to a standstill. His adoring black community had forgiven him for past sins. Instead, their wrath appeared to be directed at the media, which generally attempted to pick on every negative aspect of Tyson's visit.

As the *Sunday Times* journalist Nick Pitt reflected: 'The *Daily Express* produced a classic: "Repellent spectacle, foul man, despicable entourage, sick insult, revolting quagmire of shame," with the names of Tyson, Warren and Straw interspersed among the hyperbole. (Despite their sensibilities, the *Express* covered the fight and took paid advertisements for Sky's TV coverage.)'

Tyson, it seemed, knew the role he had to play. He could be the stereotype, not give a damn, be raw, unfiltered and still get paid. But this attitude did not necessarily signal the end of his career. Like many other black athletes, Tyson generated money for television networks, franchise owners, promoters, sports clothing companies and all the power brokers in sport. He was widely condemned, fined, banned and often reviled, but as long as he had the ability to make people money, as long as people were paying money to watch him, there had always been an encore.

If golfer Tiger Woods ended up being the heir to Jordan, then boxer Floyd Mayweather had been the heir to Tyson. When Mayweather shifted from 'Pretty Boy Floyd' to 'Money Mayweather', he became a visionary businessman, boxing's ultimate pay-per-view king and, along with Woods and Jordan, the only black sporting billionaire. He did so by trading the boyish looks and wide smile for playing the role of a hip-hop generation bad guy, 'The N***a you Love to Hate'.*

Mayweather's rise had been remarkable, unprecedented, unpredictable. Unlike Tyson, he wasn't a source of fascination as he didn't reinforce stereotypes of black men being savage or physically superhuman. Unlike a Joe Louis, George Foreman (during the second phase of his career) or a Sugar Ray Leonard, he wasn't openly patriotic and didn't have a palatable American Dream narrative. Unlike a Marvin Hagler or a Joe Frazier, he wasn't a blue-collar warrior, although much of 'Smoking Joe's' fame had a lot to do with America's hatred of Ali. These had been the common models for black popularity in boxing.

Mayweather was more like Jack Johnson. Unapologetic. Abrasive. A technically brilliant fighter but not necessarily exciting to watch. Mayweather flaunted his wealth and his extravagant lifestyle unashamedly. White folks paid to watch the uppity hip-hop kid lose. Being the bad guy had been more lucrative for Mayweather than towing the line. But it meant that for every black athlete who would follow – whether controversial like Mayweather or not – parading wealth of any kind would be met with coded racism from the media. For the black athlete in the twenty-first century, this was almost as much a sin as Johnson dating white women a century before.

Being like Mike, however, did not give the black athlete a political voice. As writer and activist Mike Marqusee once said

* The N***a you Love to Hate, a song by Ice Cube from his 1990 album *AmeriKKKa's Most Wanted* (Lench Mob/Priority).

back in 1999: 'Sports, which did so much to force whites to acknowledge the black presence in America, now contribute to the invisibility of both the real hardships suffered in black communities and the persistence of racism.'[1] That appeared all but gone by the early noughties. England had been no different.

The decade started with hope. Not just in sport, but politics, music, art, literature, theatre. Dawn of a new nation. Heptathlete Denise Lewis won gold at the 2000 Sydney Olympics. Through the late nineties Lewis had, like Wright, been symbolic of a more confident hyphenated Britain. After surprisingly winning Commonwealth gold in 1994, Lewis made the heptathlon – an event with early morning starts, where endurance, versatility and consistency were core attributes – hip. She inspired future stars like Jessica Ennis-Hill and Katarina Johnson-Thompson. Lewis was cool, credible and successful; a rare British athlete who featured in cult black music magazine *Touch* and the lads' sports mag *Total Sport*. She never let fame distract her from remaining an elite athlete, she never shied away from questions about the black community. She was fiercely proud of her muscular body and quietly outspoken about various issues, from funding for athletes to the double standards faced by female athletes. She could also laugh at herself.

It remained unusual for most Black-British athletes to have that level of confidence and poise on and off the field of play. But then it wouldn't have really paid off to be an outspoken athlete at the beginning of the noughties.

Dawn of a new nation quickly became fear of a new nation when in 2001, a spate of riots and disturbances occurred in northern towns in England. The battles in Oldham, Leeds, Burnley and

Bradford between Asian and white communities heightened racial tensions in towns that had been deeply segregated. On 11 September 2001, the terrorist attack on the Twin Towers, orchestrated by Osama bin Laden, killed almost 3,000 people. The debate would shift. Popular narrative in England centred on whites being the victims and multiculturalism being one of the causes of divisions in society. A common view was that multiculturalism had not worked and it had been responsible for creating extremist, anti-white behaviour.

There did not seem to be much resistance in the mainstream media to the negative views of multiculturalism. Anyone who defended multiculturalism was swiftly attacked for being extremists or anti-British. There did not appear to be much of a constructive debate.

It swiftly became the case that to bring up racism against black and brown communities had been to highlight something that did not exist. We had a chip on our shoulder, we were playing the race card, we were responsible for keeping racism alive, racism against white folks was worst. Can't tell you when this happened or how it happened. But once racism went mainstream and multiculturalism had become the root of social division, it felt as if Britain had been let off the hook for decades of racism. A couple of decades of multiculturalism, and black and brown folks had somehow mislaid the trust given to us despite the several centuries of exploitation we had endured. Britain had found redemption, had solved their ills, had learnt to live (read: put up) with us, and had created some institutions to tackle inequality, yet we had somehow let them down. Couldn't be trusted.

As had been the case in the late seventies, the extreme right re-emerged, re-surfaced, gained confidence, and the mainstream media and politicians fuelled and adopted their rhetoric, made it passable, and packaged it as some form of democratic debate.

Most elite athletes stayed quiet. They were tied to contracts, tied to sponsorship, tied to grant funding, tied to the reality that an already short sporting career would be shortened. Much of the resistance came from people on the periphery of sport. They were former athletes, athletes that did not quite make it, professionals and volunteers who loved sport, people who believed that sport could be more than just entertainment or a recreational activity.

By 2002, I had moved from journalism to community work. I retrained as a youth worker and finally found employment for the first time through a formal channel. It was a mentoring scheme, catering for the needs of young people facing disadvantage; this included runaways, those caught up in youth violence, some with drug-induced psychosis, others on the verge of gang involvement, some with poor mental health, others displaying risky sexual behaviours, some who would never leave the house. I followed this by working with young offenders, and designing and delivering journalism courses for a variety of schools, charities, housing associations, youth centres and estates.

I worked with hundreds of young people across London. I was attacked. Had to avert riots. Was the responsible adult when the police came knocking. Stopped a youth from attempting to stab a fellow youth worker. Helped runaways find food and shelter. The work was more '5 pm to 9 am' than '9 am to 5 pm'. The times when young people really needed help.

I worked for those young people. Laughed with those young people. Admired their confidence. Questioned how confident they really were. Was startled at how quickly the most vocal would flinch in moments of vulnerability. Wondered why they felt more comfortable working in JD Sports than in more corporate settings. I worried that their routes, their daily routines rarely moved them more than a mile from their houses. I worried about the relationships they had with non-parental adult figures who seemed to loom in their houses. I tried to provide a bridge between often difficult home, peer and environmental circumstances and the services and opportunities that could help them progress, seek help or escape their situations. I saw how these young people, from different backgrounds, were bonded through music, fashion, schooling, environment, poverty, trauma. I saw how they were divided by limited opportunities, limited routes and competition.

I also started to see how different interventions could be effective in tackling racism, helping young people move out of poverty, bridge divides, access opportunities, cope with trauma, deal with conflict and mistrust. Sport was one of the tools I had seen that could contribute to helping young people.

It had been at the inaugural Laureus World Sports Awards in Monaco on 25 May 2000 that Nelson Mandela said, 'Sport has the power to change the world. It has the power to inspire. It has the power to unite people in a way that little else does. It speaks to youth in a language they understand. Sport can create hope where once there was only despair.'

Mandela's speech resonated with world leaders, elite athletes and non-governmental organisations (NGOs) across the globe.

He understood the impact sport could have in addressing or highlighting some of the world's major problems. Mandela often said that the boycott of South Africa in sport during the years of apartheid contributed to breaking down the racist regime. In 1995, when South Africa hosted the Rugby World Cup, Mandela, dressed in a Springboks rugby shirt and cap, presented South Africa's winning captain François Pienaar with the cup. As John Carlin, author of *Playing the Enemy*, said, 'The thing about rugby was that it was really a powerful symbol of a deep racial division. For the white population as a whole, a symbol of their pride and identity … For the black population, the Springboks were a symbol of apartheid.' Mandela's gesture symbolised sport's ability to unite black and white and his speech became the driving force behind the sport for development movement.

Throughout the noughties, the importance of sport as a tool for addressing world development problems had been furthered under the leadership of United Nations (UN) Secretary-General Kofi Annan. Following a meeting among world leaders at the Millennium Summit in 2000 at the UN's headquarters in New York City, the 191 UN members signed up to the eight Millennium Development Goals (MDGs). The MDGs provided specific targets and globally became the foremost way of measuring progress against the world's biggest problems, from child poverty and gender inequality to environmental sustainability and HIV/AIDS. Annan recognised the power of sport and, through the noughties, encouraged governments to take it seriously as a way of tackling the MDGs. If Mandela had provided the inspiration, then Annan supplied the policy framework for sport to try and combat major disparities in society.

At a time when athlete activism seemed non-existent, there was a proliferation of people, organisations and initiatives using sport to tackle major issues. This included Fight for Peace, started by ex-English boxer Luke Dowdney in 2000 after seeing a friend killed in a favela in Brazil. He used boxing and education programming to develop young people on the edge of youth violence and street crime. The Homeless World Cup Foundation started organising an annual world football tournament for homeless people, while Street Games, Street League, Connie Henry's Track Academy and Active Communities Network among others used sport constructively to engage young people who had otherwise been isolated from mainstream activities.

In England, the fight against racism in sport (and by default society) was also being tackled on the sidelines. While I rarely heard racist chants on football terraces anymore, black and brown people continued to face barriers in accessing sport due to exclusionary environments, culturally inappropriate coaching, stereotyping and racist experiences (from coaches or local crowds).

I had never been that kid – less able than others – who had been excluded from physical activities. I had never been prevented from participating in sport for cultural reasons. I had never been afraid to make mistakes on the field of play through fear of being insulted by a teammate. I never feared playing sport or doing PE because of my body shape or the uniform. While I had experienced racism on terraces of Upton Park, my love of football had not been such that I had to endure this every week for the love of my team.

For many, sport had not been an inspiration but a hindrance. It had reinforced gender, ability and racial stereotypes and put young people on a weekly basis into winner–loser, hero–villain situations. There had been little in education or in most children's first experiences of sport to encourage them to do much more than observe. The virtues of sport, often illustrated when you watch it on an elite level, rarely translated to increased participation at a school or grassroots level unless you were incredibly good or extremely resilient.

It always felt as if people within sport tried to divorce what had been happening in society from what occurred on the pitch, on the court and in the boardrooms. It always felt as if bringing up racism in sport was akin to mentioning the time you cheated at the height of romance. A deep pain you do not want to revisit, a deep pain you think you've overcome, just a deep pain. It had been former athletes such as Michelle Moore and Rimla Akhtar who were not afraid to confront deep pain, and indeed find solutions to it, on all levels.

It had been her love of sport, a passion for education and the belief that sport could tackle racism, that led Moore to the Charlton Athletic Race Equality (CARE) partnership. CARE had been created as a direct response to the racist murders of Rolan Adams and Stephen Lawrence in southeast London. Moore, a former athlete, took over the running of the programme in 1999.

Moore focused on three core components at CARE: 1) diversifying coaching staff, mentoring and equipping them to get qualifications; 2) getting those coaches to go into local communities as advocates to use sport as a way of bonding communities; and 3) going into schools and using sport to teach anti-racism. The programme also featured international exchanges and footballers like Paul Elliott, Chris Powell and Mark Fish talking to pupils about their experiences.

At its heart, Moore's work used diverse and quality coaching to engage those boys who had been picked last at school, those girls who hated physical activity because of the uniform they had been forced to wear, those kids who had been exposed to unhealthy relationships from coaches, those young men who wanted to find a sense of belonging outside of unhealthy peer groups, those young people for whom English was a second language but found ways to communicate with other communities through the language of sport, and the many others who previously didn't like sport but discovered that it could be a good way to learn life skills.

Through Moore and her coaches, young people discovered healthy peer relationships, they found a safe environment, they enjoyed physical activity without competition (but with great coaching), they had clear goals and educational support, they had positive youth development from coaches, they had adults who treated them as individuals and they had pathways to use their learning to progress into other areas of their lives.

For initiatives like CARE, there would be no bright lights. No magic moments shared with a global audience. No one would be in awe of participants' bodies: neither the body of their work on the field of play, nor the ability of their bodies to do what normal people's bodies couldn't achieve. The magic. The writer's metaphors. Comparisons to Galahad. But there was a different kind of magic. The magic in these young people finding a purpose in life through sport, which had been every bit as thrilling and significant as watching Zinedine Zidane's trickery on a football field.

When Rimla Akhtar was growing up, she had difficulty fitting in and belonging. She had been one of the few brown people in

Edgware in the eighties. Before her teenage years, Akhtar didn't understand that what was happening around her was not right. She had two older brothers and they introduced her to sport. It became a vehicle that made her feel included and accepted. She had been pretty much in every sports team at school; however, she decided to play cricket, lacrosse and football at a higher level. Her enjoyment of sport wasn't just about her talent or her identity. Sport helped to prepare her for wider battles in society.

Akhtar started her own lunchtime football club in sixth form and continued to play lacrosse to a high level. She had been the odd one out. Brown girl with a hijab surrounded by white middle-class girls. Akhtar had been a goalie for her county side Hertfordshire. When Hertfordshire defeated Kent 24–3, she was sure she'd be selected for the East of England team over her rival, who had conceded 24 goals. She didn't think about discrimination. Too much on her mind. Excelling at and enjoying her sport, her studies, her family. But she knew she had been challenging her peers' perceptions: the hijab, taking a break for prayers, wearing a tracksuit top and bottoms instead of standard vests and skirts. She also knew she was unique. While she had been a Liverpool fan, admiring the likes of Ian Rush and John Barnes, and an athletics fan, appreciating hurdlers Colin Jackson and Sally Gunnell, she had no role models, no one that spoke directly to her experience.

Then, with the additional pressure of taking some of her GCSE exams earlier than usual, her mother counselled her to focus on her studies that year. It was only when sport was taken away from her that she realised how much it meant to her.

Akhtar continued to play sports but she also started going to sporting events, her first a Pakistan versus England cricket match.

Among her own community, she did not feel any fear. She did not feel any fear when she attended her first football match at Anfield. For safety, her brothers advised her not to wear her hijab in case of a violent reaction from fans. She wore a baseball cap and scarf. She heard sexist and homophobic chanting but didn't hear any racist comments. It wasn't until 2005, sick and tired of covering her identity, hiding something that was important to her, that she decided to ditch the baseball cap and scarf. She got stares. Some used colourful language to question whether she belonged. Nothing she couldn't deal with. This was Liverpool. Her team. A team she followed here and abroad. She didn't question her presence. So, she was not about to be deterred by anyone else questioning her presence.

The Muslim Women's Games, which began in the early nineties, had been an event that encouraged Muslim women to take part in Olympic-style games. In 2001, with the support of Ahmed Versi, publisher and editor of *The Muslim News*, a Great Britain Muslim women's team was created. There was a trial for a British Muslim Women's futsal team. Akhtar didn't feel confident to try out, but with the encouragement of her mum, she made and captained the team. 'Suddenly I found a group of women who looked like me and felt like me.'

Akhtar became the chair of the Muslim Women's Sports Foundation in 2005 and set about increasing the participation and presence of Muslim women in sport. She also wanted to challenge the narrative around Muslim women. When she was growing up, nobody in sport looked like her or experienced life as she had experienced it. She wanted to create more role models that looked like the diverse group that Muslim women are.

Through the Foundation she helped create more role models, increase access and change the narrative, helping overturn FIFA's ban on the hijab. 'It was a decision made by old white men who had no idea of the impact it would have on women wanting to play the game,' she said.

She now has these role models going into communities telling their stories while she is creating pathways for elite athletes from her community to navigate their way through an industry that is still ill prepared to support them appropriately.

The Foundation's work provided an inclusive environment, tackled structural discrimination and challenged the old boys' network – the conscious and unconscious biases. It tackled the issue of 'race' and faith and sporting authorities' general diffidence to this concern while continually making sporting bodies aware of the women on the margins, the women who fall through the cracks, the women on the intersection, who face challenges based on gender, 'race' and faith.

By the mid-noughties, there were plenty of reasons to feel optimistic about sport's role in tackling racism on and off the field of play. In addition to Moore and Akhtar's work, you had mainstream bodies like Kick It Out and Show Racism the Red Card, which used footballers to create awareness about racism in schools; Sporting Equals, promoting 'greater involvement in sport and physical activity by disadvantaged communities, particularly the Black and Minority Ethnic (BAME) population'; and Football Against Racism in Europe (FARE), campaigning against discrimination in football.

The UN declared 2005 as the International Year for Sport and Physical Education, the same year that the winning bid to host the

2012 Olympic games would be revealed. London's bid to host the Games would in time become central to creating hope during a time of racial divides in British society. The Games had not been hosted in London since 1948. If London won, it would be the biggest sporting event in the history of the UK.

On 6 July 2005, thousands of people gathered in Trafalgar Square to watch as Britain's sporting elite gathered in Singapore to find out the result of the bid. In Singapore, the likes of David Beckham and Daley Thompson were accompanied by 30 children and young people of different shades from the East End. Sebastian Coe, chairman of the bid, had pulled a masterstroke. During a period when the US and the UK had been questioning multiculturalism, London's rush to the finish line centred around the power of diversity. Harmony. Ebony and ivory. Side by side. It became one of the most powerful images of multiculturalism in sport.

International Olympic Committee (IOC) President Jacques Rogge took to the stage and slowly opened the large envelope. 'The International Olympic Committee has the honour of announcing that the games of the thirtieth Olympiad in twenty twelve are awarded to the city of … London.'

As the dignitaries in Singapore and the people in Trafalgar Square erupted, the commentator shouted, 'The games are coming to London, absolutely brilliant!'

I remember watching Denise Lewis, dressed in a shiny tanned suit jacket and skirt with a blue blouse, jumping manically as if she'd won another Olympic title. There were lots of shots of Beckham. Politicians such as the late Tessa Jowell, MP for Dulwich and West Norwood, and the London Mayor Ken

Livingstone were celebrating too. Even though I knew tons of money had been spent on the bid and even though I knew a false narrative had been created around a cohesive multicultural Britain, it was difficult not to be emotional and excited at the announcement. London had won. And it had done so with people of colour as a core asset.

The following day, I was on my way to work. I lived in Ladbroke Grove and worked at the Volunteer Centre Westminster on Praed Street, not far from Edgware Road. I ended up walking to work. Traffic had been slow. There did not seem to be many people walking on the streets. Everything, from the walk down Praed Street to entering my office, vague. I just remember the Centre manager informing me that something had happened at Edgware Road station and that we could go home. The Centre would stay open to provide refreshments and support the efforts of the services.

I, like most, had no idea what had been going on. Through the day, a picture had started to emerge. One that had been far worse, far bigger than any of us could comprehend. On a day when the UK should have been celebrating the Olympic victory, its attention turned to terrorism as four coordinated suicide bombings took place across London, on a double-decker bus in Tavistock Square, on the Piccadilly Line near Russell Square and on the Circle Line at Edgware Road and Aldgate.

Fifty-two innocent people died and more than 700 were injured in the attack. It was a sick and brutal act. One that would cause fear among all communities across Britain. The fact that the four bombers were born or raised in England reignited the anti-multiculturalism narrative that emerged post-2001 riots. It highlighted that Britain had become increasingly segregated. It also provided impetus to the far-right movement again.

'Once it became clear that the four bombers were in fact British and that these were so called "homegrown" terrorists, the public debate shifted towards examining the role of multiculturalism in "fanning the flames" of terrorism,' said academic Ben Carrington. 'Many right-wing, as well as some liberal, commentators suggested that multiculturalism had "gone too far" in promoting separate segregated communities. Rather than assimilating into British values and mores "ethnic communities" had been allowed, if not actively encouraged, to celebrate their difference from the rest of "mainstream society".'[2]

'Thus, in *less than twenty-four hours*, "multiculturalism" had shifted from a signifier that embodied all that was great and strong about Britain, to all that was wrong and weak with contemporary British society,' said Carrington.[3]

Race relations would never be the same. The tone of the narrative would switch from one of progression or denial to one of conflict and fear. No middle ground. Not even sport could mask these problems.

Unfortunately, those with the power in sport had little interest in using their wealth to try and use sport to firmly tackle issues such as racism. Maybe not sport's responsibility. Not their responsibility if there's abuse on the terraces, exclusionary practices, abusive coaches, systematic preference for the privileged because the important decisions are made by the privileged, biased reporting by the media because there are few who are versed enough in race relations to have a sensible conversation about the issue.

Problem is, when so many of your sports people are black, more prominent in this field than in other fields, then ignoring the issue is not an option.

While there were many mainstream bodies like Kick It Out tackling racism and delivering great work, the fact they were supported and funded by major sporting bodies such as the FA, UEFA and FIFA more than likely limited their power to tackle some of the more systemic racial tensions that existed within sport. Difficult to bite the hand that feeds you.

Much of the challenge came on the periphery of sport. Perhaps if some of these voices had been more central in leadership or governance, then decision-making at the top would look different, PE would look different across the country, development would be central to all sporting activities, sport itself would be more diverse at all levels and racism in sport would carry real penalties. Perhaps if more of these interventions had been adopted, elite athlete development would better prepare youngsters for life in the limelight and how to manage their careers. Maybe the more inclusive or culturally appropriate approaches used by Moore or Akhtar could have opened more pathways, connected grassroots, elite sport and national teams in a way that would enable more funding to go to a broader cross-section of the population. We will never know just how much better Great Britain could have been at sport. I am not sure we will ever realise how much better Great Britain could be.

I did not see sport as a meritocracy. All things had not been equal. Success in sport did not mean that the disparities in society had changed. Particularly when there had been so many disparities within sport. If society could follow sport's lead, then things could be better. That had been the story, the spirit of the

Olympics. But this had been a mask. For every black athlete that succeeded, there were plenty more who had been marginalised. For every gold medal we won at a sport that had traditionally been the preserve of the wealthy, there were plenty more inner-city sports that had been neglected. Sport did not mean equal pay. Even though you may not have experienced racism on the terraces, it did not mean you escaped the unfavourable press coverage, lack of access to the boardroom and bad treatment in the changing rooms. Sport didn't just mask society's problems, it reflected it.

For all of Ian Wright's popularity, Denise Lewis' achievements and the array of talent produced by Jimmy Rogers, there remained a frightening absence of black people in power positions. Despite the likes of Ashley Cole and Sol Campbell being regulars in the England squad, black footballers remained among the most unpopular. Despite the likes of Ian Wright and to a lesser degree Paul Ince showing that you can have a strong black and white fan base, I started to see more black athletes adopting a posture akin to their African-American counterparts. Not quite as outlandish. But with seemingly a greater loyalty to their brand than to the black community.

This was different to the '81 uprisings, when the black athlete had very much been on the margins. This was also different to '93 when Stephen Lawrence had been murdered, when the black athlete had just started to break through. We were now in the noughties, a period when black athletes were mainstream, where they made the news for good reasons, where they were integral to the success of the country, yet we had no voice in positions that mattered and expressed little or no opinion on social issues that counted. It was easy to see that, despite progression, the goalposts had moved systemically to prevent blacks from converting popularity on the field of play to greater power off it. Lack of diversity off the field of play did not even register with the sporting authorities, so there had been no impetus to change. Indeed, it had not been until Ashley Cole and Shaun Wright-Phillips faced a torrent of boos and racist abuse while playing for England in Madrid in 2004 that racism was thought to be relevant again. The message seemed to be, shut up and play.

The most significant voices for change in sport during the noughties had likely been Nelson Mandela and Kofi Annan. The most significant voices in sport in Britain also seemed to come from those who were off the field of play. If the presence of Ali, baseball player Jackie Robinson, tennis player Arthur Ashe, basketball player Bill Russell and athletes Tommie Smith and John Carlos had set the tone for the African-American athlete to use their platform to highlight the plight of black people, then Mandela and Annan seemed to set the tone for Black-African athletes to use their platform politically.

Congolese basketball star Dikembe Mutombo donated over $15 million to build the 12-acre Biamba Marie Mutombo Hospital in Kinshasa, which opened in 2007; Kenyan long-distance runner Tegla Loroupe, the first African to win the New York marathon, established a 10 km Peace Race in 2003 to promote peace between warring tribes while her Peace Academy and orphanage served children in northwest Kenya; Ivorian footballer Didier Drogba helped with a ceasefire during the civil war in the Ivory Coast; while former world footballer of the year George Weah would later become the Liberian president. Guadeloupe-born, French World Cup winner Lilian Thuram not only opposed then Minister of the Interior Nicolas Sarkozy's stance against young people during the 2005 French riots, he invited 80 people – expelled from a flat in which they had been living illegally by Sarkozy – to a football game. He also campaigned for same-sex marriage and spoke out against racism.

These were all elite athletes who had been using their voice and power to change their communities. There seemed to be a clear history of protest among African-American, Caribbean and African athletes. But this did not seem to be the way for Black-British athletes. As Kevin Hylton, a Professor of Equality and Diversity in Sport, Leisure and Education at Leeds Beckett University, said to me, maybe the legacy of the Black-British athlete is one of dignity and perseverance. No shame in that. But as the Black-British athlete in the noughties had been starting to find his/her voice, I had started to question whether it would remain, like Ian Wright, distinctly British or continue to be imported heavily from abroad. This tension was not only confined to the playing field.

Anti-black and anti-Muslim racism continued to be a problem in British society. But no one wanted to talk about it anymore. Black people couldn't mention it through fear of being called reverse racists or extremist; while extreme right rhetoric found its way into mainstream dialogue, unopposed. Attending a Met Police event when I worked at the Stephen Lawrence Trust, I found it interesting that the police would declare that they were no longer institutionally racist.[4] In a society whose wealth had been built on slavery and had systematically, for hundreds of years, justified slavery through pseudo-scientific racism; and in a society where the racist hierarchies it created still existed – miraculously, institutional racism within the police force had been defeated within a decade. And within two decades, multi-culturalism had fundamentally been responsible for all of society's divisions. During this crucial time, during this crucial period, there had not been much resistance from sport.

CHAPTER 7

THE GREATEST WEEK EVER IN BLACK HISTORY?

Got a son of my own, look him right in his eyes,
I ain't living in fear, but I'm holding him tight.

'Animals' by Dr. Dre (featuring Anderson
Paak & DJ Premier)

LIFE HAD NOT BECOME US. Not any of us. Not at this moment. Not through much of the decade. Not the men in different shades of dark suits, legs sprawled, dominating the seats on the upper deck of the bus, not the construction students of all ages and colours lost in music, shutting out the world; not the young mums with hastily thrown-on clothing trying to appease fidgety children, not the night-workers, their heads leaning against the windows nor the girls in school uniforms at the back, giggling, not finishing sentences, each with three or four styles in their hair, playing tinny grime music.

It was now 2008. The bus turned into Brookmill Road around 8.30 am, and crawled down a street as grey, hushed and unhopeful as Nurse Ratched's corridors in *One Flew Over the Cuckoo's Nest*. A road congested with silence and insane in its normality. Curiosity on the upper deck turned to agitation. This had been the era before the prominence of the smartphone. No one Googling. No one could find out why we had been crawling, what had happened before people closest to the situation knew what had happened. No one making calls to say that they may be running late or placing themselves at the centre of whatever had been causing the bus to move so slow. Just loads of people, some waking up, some taking off their headphones, practically all mumbling ill-informed theories about what may have happened.

Some folks started to stand up, hoping to get a look, a little peek, all hoping to find out what was going on. Not many of them concerned about the incident causing the delay. Most used it as an excuse to huff. To puff. To openly display dismay. Others more curious, I think wanting to be the first to say something that influences the behaviour of others on the bus. Others just wanted to know whether to stick or twist. Stay and be delayed or run off the bus and find an alternative. What I didn't hear, what I didn't see, was anyone with legitimate concern for what may have occurred. You know it's not going to be good. It could only be a tragedy that has caused this disruption, this stop in this corridor.

There was nothing to see, but cars. People stood but couldn't see anything. Another reason to huff, to turn one's head and shake it. Funny how communal irritation can help people align. Should be a community cohesion or integration strategy. Create disruption, watch us unite in misery. But the lack of concern for what might have happened, an incident that may have changed someone's life forever, stuck with me. Brookmill Road was my place of work. For most, this had been a road you passed through, not one where you'd stop. The hidden park the only thing of natural beauty. There was also a greasy spoon café, a rarely used train station labouring down a side road, a run-down corner pub with a permanent stench of cigarettes and the River Quaggy, hidden, murky with household goods floating along.

I had a sinking feeling. As people stood, theorised, tapped their phones, glared out the window, wound each other up, shuffled their feet anxiously, woke up, slept more, attempted to escape, turned their headphones up, I felt punctured. Facial features melting, forehead knotting, a feeling like you will never dream again.

As the bus crept further, we could see the police. The bus stopped. I ran down the stairs and off the bus and walked hastily to the police barriers. They let me through, I was one of the few. I had reason.

A week earlier, almost to the day, we had opened the Stephen Lawrence Centre. I had worked there for around 18 months, furiously developing programmes that would celebrate Stephen's life and his aspirations. It had been decided that the Centre would honour Stephen's ambition of becoming an architect by supporting young people facing disadvantage into careers in the built environment.

By the time the Centre opened, Doreen Lawrence had already spent close to 15 years trying to find justice for a young black man, his life taken away by five white men who stabbed him to death while shouting racist abuse. The five men escaped jail despite witnesses, due to the ineptitude of the botched police investigation. There were cover-ups, the Lawrence family were seemingly policed more than the suspects, Doreen and Neville tirelessly campaigned, there were trials, little justice, and then the Macpherson Report that in 1999 deemed the police institutionally racist. There had been many other racist murders of black and brown people. But this would be the permanent stain on any claim Britain had to being a racially just society. There were no excuses. Individual racism. Institutional racism. Married as one. Stephen became one of the most famous teenagers in British history.

There had not been one black male in my peer group that didn't feel Stephen's death profoundly. At a time when black males had been represented in the extremes, ghetto or bourgeoisie, activists or politicians, the one time I had seen someone who didn't reflect the extremes, he had died. We were only present in Stephen's death. Present in the mind of Britain's guilty conscience.

As Doreen's campaign continued, the Centre aimed to inspire a new generation of young people who wanted to reinvent their environments. Roughly six months before opening, we decided to trial a few programmes in the new Centre. It was not open to the public. Snagging, threats, security, equipment failure, staffing issues, getting used to the neighbourhood all meant that we were cautious in opening, but ambitious in programming. We went into partnership with Imperial College and entered local pupils into the FIRST Robotics Competition at NASA, we had an exchange programme with Central Saint Martins, we taught literacy and numeracy to year six pupils through game design, as ever we offered bursaries for architecture students, we supported the careers of young construction workers, we had worked with RIBA (Royal Institute of British Architects) and secured placements with some of the best architecture firms.

We dreamt big. Worked hard. Provided tough love to young people. We worked with schools and local charities to give their young people top-class programming that built into the school curriculum. But we didn't try to keep young people at the Centre. We inspired, developed and tried to prepare them for the next stage of their careers. We let them go while always keeping an open door for them to come back if they needed support.

During the opening, all the guests were taken round the building where they would see displays, observe workshops and generally see the building in action. The tour had been compulsory for any young person entering the Centre. We wanted them to know about Stephen's story, about architect David Adjaye who had designed the building, about artist Chris Ofili whose moiré-styled drawing on the glass window façade made Brookmill Road, from the inside of the building, dance to the waves of the pattern. It was the Stephen Lawrence Centre matriculation, something we hoped would give young people a sense of belonging while making it clear that the building represented the intersection of art, social justice and hope. Some cried. Some walked slowly as if entering a church service. No one who entered the building did it any physical harm.

Harm. That's what I had seen once I had passed the police barriers. One week after opening, after demonstrating six months' worth of discreet programming, after hosting politicians, after watching the Centre featured on television, there it was, vandalised. It was widely reported as a racist attack. An obvious assumption given the case, given the fact that Stephen's memorial plaque had been frequently vandalised and defaced. It had allegedly been a group of young men. One allegedly of mixed heritage. Ofili's windows no longer danced. Three had been smashed and were lying, shattered, on the ground.

We knew an attack on the building could happen. There had been threats. Some had said that we would never open the building. Others threatened arson. But we had delivered programmes for six months with little or no incidents.

The Stephen Lawrence Centre, this delicate experiment aimed at creating beauty in the face of hostility and providing aspiration in the face of a guilty conscience, had been damaged. Ofili's waves had been boarded up. The boards looked ugly. Ruined the building. Three used large plasters on the cheek of a pretty face. We couldn't raise enough money to replace the windows immediately. So, we embraced them. On future tours, the boards became a feature. It had been a reminder to us not to become complacent, a reminder that justice had not yet been done. I called the boards the Centre's teardrops.

Little had changed. Everything had changed. The Macpherson Report labelled the police as institutionally racist in 1999 and in 2000 the Race Relations Bill was amended, seeking more proactive approaches to eliminating race discrimination in public bodies. Lots of policies written. Little in the way of progressive implementation. A bit more accountability though. In the early noughties, there were riots, terrorist acts, the rise of the extreme right, radicalisation, moral panics about multiculturalism and general indifference, disdain even, to the fact that racism continued to be a major problem; that racism had been a root cause of these problems. There were lots of debates about what institutional racism meant. Lots of fear about being classified as institutionally racist. Action, accountability and impact swiftly lost in bureaucracy. Action, accountability and impact swiftly lost in a narrative where whites had been the only victims.

You're once more reduced to worrying more about what white people think than what you've done, because you know what they think will dictate your fate more so than what you've done. You're reduced to a reactive state of mind because you've been, as Malcolm X once said, indicted before birth, knowing that you're living in a country that did not seem to value your brown-ness. You're reduced because, as much as you may try to comply, try to integrate, try to fit in, your brown-ness never quite allows you to blend, and you know that you will be blamed for not being able to blend. You're reduced because they just don't know, never been conditioned to know; they cannot conceive that what they know and how they got to know it is a lie, or an incredibly distorted version of the truth, or just half the story. Not my story.

I started to realise, sometime in the mid-noughties, that my life choices – work, where to live, nursery provision for my daughter – were becoming increasingly narrow at a time when access to opportunities should have been improving. My father had been working near Ladbroke Grove station, not too far from where I had been living at the time. He had been painting a basement flat, I think, on Blenheim Crescent, not far from Dub Vendor, the famous but now deceased reggae record shop. I had been freelancing at the time as a journalist and youth worker. I met him for lunch and a chat. My father had been described, by a previous employer, as a 'paragon of patience'. He had always been diligent in his work, working all hours to complete jobs, doing so on time, and leaving each room, house or hall he'd completed spotless afterwards. But he also treated it like an art and was a perfectionist in it. His attention to detail was incredible. Every job was something more than just a task to be completed.

The ease in which he carried himself remained. That easy smile and that kind, stoic face that hid a million stories, stories of his early years in Jamaica, stories about how he made his way to England. That easy smile. Those stories. Those hidden truths. That willingness to absorb on behalf of his loved ones. His kindness, plain for everyone to see, which is why my friends were so fond of him. The love, the overwhelming love and the half-truths, the many things that were not said, not said to protect, not said because it may hurt, not said because it would inflict an abrasion on his parenting, not a black manhood perfection, not a Code perfection, but a parenting perfection, where he could not show vulnerability, where he could not show pain.

He had been approaching retirement. I was happy for him. As for him, not sure. I returned the easy smiles and it was only around this time when I had started to reveal certain things in my life that I had previously avoided telling him. The police stops, the conflicts at school, my frustration at my inability to find work. I told him these things because I knew he wouldn't need to absorb them on my behalf. Not resolved. Never resolved. Work in progress. But these stories were far enough in the past for me to reveal without anger, but with an easy smile.

My smile still hid rage. My father likely mistook this smile for contentment. I mistook his easy smile for contentment. I, too, had thought I had escaped the burden of the Codes and the Tiers, when all I had been doing was hiding behind a smile. The smile did not mean contentment. It meant mobilisation, negotiating between the Codes and Tiers. A middle man. A neither here nor there man. Never belonging to one, never being the other. A good thing. My own thing. A hard to equate thing. An invisible thing.

I sat one day in this basement flat and I could see what lurked beneath that smile of his. Discontentment. Age. The swiftness of life and how quickly it passes you by. But something more. My father had been more. More than a husband, a father, a hard-working citizen of Jamaica and England. What lurked beneath had not been a resentment towards his life in England. He had regrets. Regret maybe too strong a word. But a cousin of regret, for what he wanted to be, could have been. He had been big, great, broad and bold as a husband, a father, as a hard-working citizen. But I think he wanted more. A boxer. A writer. An interior designer. He dreamed. Dreamed big. Perhaps. I don't know because he smiled. We smiled.

'You have it much tougher now than I had at your age,' he told me.

'You're kidding,' I replied, surprised. 'With all the racism you guys faced in the sixties?'

'I didn't let that bother me. But there was a freedom to make your own way.'

I can't remember much more of the conversation, because I had still been shocked by my father's revelation.

There you had it. Hope. The element of surprise. Hip-hop. The West Indies. Winning by not revealing. The game, the race on how to mobilise in Britain, had not been invented for black folks to win. The more we revealed of ourselves, the more the rules of the game adjusted to control and inhibit our black and brown progressive selves. I started to understand why my elders had been so nervous about telling our stories. Now I had been witnessing it, living through it. I had seen blackness main-streamed, in sport and in civil society. I had seen blackness diluted, blackness misappropriated, blackness given a new narrative. The opportunities had widened, but the barriers had become more discreet. Chris Grant, former chief executive of Sported!, would later say to me, 'In the 80s the systems hadn't worked out how to block you. There were young black men much brighter than me that followed, [but a] whole generation has been blocked, haven't made it to the top level.'

The more open you are, the easier it is for the system to put up barriers. You're reduced to the Codes and the Tiers, either activist and marginalised, or mainstreamed and diluted. It had become even tougher for the marginalised to mobilise because the centre, where decisions were made, where black had been mainstreamed, had become gentrified.

Hope is important. Disrupts the norm. Makes people strive, be peaceful, have faith. Not about playing for the Lakers or getting a deal with Def Jam, conceptions of hope and accept-ance crafted for us, not by us, not on our own terms. They were routes, not hope. Routes out of oppressive systems, ways in which we could use our bodies – the threat, the desired – to make our way through the world. These were routes we remod-elled, reinvented, reimagined, redefined, but not *our* roots. We didn't know our roots. Didn't know our roots well enough to know that the only routes that had been offered to us were the ones that had not been crafted by us.

I had rarely felt at ease in this country since Minter–Hagler. Ease would give me hope. Hope would give me ease. Those moments when I truly felt at ease were unforgettable. Never having to explain my existence, why I'm here, how I got here, why I'm still here, whether I had been born here. I'd give anything for my son to feel at ease through his life. To win or to lose because of his deeds not because of his skin, not because of someone else's narrow routes.

Ease. Hope. I felt it when I went to Jamaica for the first time as an 18-year-old in 1991. My colour the majority. You don't know what unease feels like until you've been living as a minority, treated like a minority and othered in your place of birth.

Hope. Ease. I felt it that week beginning 3 November 2008. Barack Obama would become the first black president of the United States of America. He had been victorious because of the audacity of hope.

I didn't think of Obama as a Messiah type. I knew Obama's blackness – however symbolically meaningful – would be limited within the operating context of America's political and corporate system. But his rise to the presidency had been a monumental achievement. I had hope. Faith. I thought that people would no longer sweep the issue of 'race' so easily under the carpet. I thought the dialogue would open up. I didn't think I would live to see the day. A cliché. But true.

The day after Barack Obama's election was a truly utopian moment. We all stayed up through the night to watch the elections. Those of us who didn't watch, couldn't, because we were too nervous. The following day, every black person I came across acknowledged me, or I acknowledged them. Maybe a nod of the head, a smile. It had been magical and reminded me of earlier days when that brief acknowledgement from black strangers had been a regular occurrence.

My white colleagues I met the day after the election didn't quite get why I had been so happy. Often, they didn't say anything, but I understood that look. Others said he wasn't black but mixed race. Lots of people claimed he wasn't a black president because he was of mixed heritage. Although it was also true that Obama had unprecedented levels of security, despite being one of the least controversial and highly qualified elected officials in the United States. Others hated the way we celebrated after he had won. They perceived our euphoria as gloating. There were some who implicitly expressed fears that Obama would do unto white folks what white folks had traditionally done to blacks. I listened. I ignored. Didn't want anything to take away from the ease I felt. By the time I arrived home that evening, I decided I would throw a party over the weekend. Black, brown and white folks, like-minded folks, came around. Felt a bit like a secret club. A place where we could be without being questioned. A place where we could feel at ease in each other's company. A place where we were not being reduced. A safe space. A space where we could all just be.

That same week, Lewis Hamilton became the youngest and first black Formula 1 world motor racing champion. Hamilton's victory not nearly as important. But it was game-changing, nonetheless. For a young black Englishman to win the biggest prize in motorsports – a sport not associated with a high participation of black athletes, a sport that requires a vast amount of money to participate in and a sport that was not stereotypically physical in the requirements of its protagonists, the customary allowed routes for athletes of colour – had also been unexpected.

Obama and Hamilton would change the narrative on 'race' and, more than anything, provide some positive headlines at a time when upbeat stories about black folks had been at a premium.

On 4 November, the *Guardian* didn't quite capture how epic the week would be. The headline read, 'A great week in black history?', based on what Dotun Adebayo had said on his BBC London radio show that weekend. Adebayo, with his usual swagger, asked whether it was 'the beginning of the greatest week ever in black history?'

It wasn't. And I'm not sure Adebayo meant it literally. He did, however, want to emphasise the importance of this moment to the African diaspora. I am not sure he wanted the moment to be lost in some conservative, over-analysed, well-rehearsed statement. He made it big. He made it bold. This was no time to minimise.

Journalist Aida Edemariam, who penned the *Guardian* article, would go on to emphasise the importance of the week, quoting Simon Woolley, Co-founder and Director of Operation Black Vote, who had been on Adebayo's show. Woolley said of Hamilton, 'It's like watching your child race. It's about winning against adversity.' Earlier in the season, Hamilton had to deal with racism during the Spanish Grand Prix. Hamilton had been lauded by many, including the press, for handling adversity with dignity. In other words, he didn't shout too loud about it. 'Our journey to success is always peppered by obstacles of racism,' Woolley would add.

Woolley had, in a couple of sentences, stressed just how important the black athlete had been for the black community. Shared experiences. Athletes of colour, whether they liked it or not, whether it was right or wrong, ended up representing other people of colour in their endeavours. Their actions, their performances, their deeds would reflect on other people of colour. For black folks, the black athlete becomes more like an extended family member. For the rest of Britain, the black athlete provides a lens into a world they knew little about.

Journalist Mike Bianchi once suggested that Obama's election had in part been a result of black athletes like Tiger Woods and Michael Jordan. They had, according to Bianchi, conditioned whiter America to accept black accomplishment and even find it desirable. This, he felt, opened doors for blacks in other spheres.

Indeed, after Woods won his first major championship (the US Masters) in 1997, setting an American television ratings record for golf, Oprah Winfrey called him 'America's son'. She also said that he was 'just what the world needs right now'.

Woods' father, Earl Woods, once said, 'He will transcend this game ... and bring to the world ... a humanitarianism ... Which has never been known before. The world will be a better place to live in ... by virtue of his existence ... and his presence.'[1]

Woods was a phenomenon. A man of colour redefining one of the most traditionally segregated sports in America. He infiltrated the preserve. But he did so without rocking the boat. In many ways, he had been more powerful than Jordan because of golf's privileged history.

C L Cole and David L Andrews in their essay *America's New Son* said: 'Winfrey identifies Woods as an "antidote" to the anxieties weighing down America ("the world") at the end of the century. Although the anxieties remain unnamed, Woods enters a context defined by the regular fanning of apprehensions about and celebrations of America's multi-cultural racial future: racially-coded celebrations which deny social problems and promote the idea that America has achieved its multicultural ideal.'[2]

It became common for commentators to compare Hamilton to Woods. The narrative was simple. Too simplistic. Hamilton, a person of colour in a sport traditionally dominated by white men, would impact on Formula 1 and society like Woods. But there were prominent black golfers before Woods. There was no one before Hamilton. I thought of Hamilton's victory as being the closest thing that British sport had to a Jackie Robinson moment. Robinson broke the colour line in baseball, America's national sport, in 1947. He opened the doors to blacks integrating in sport and, symbolically, in society.

In winning the Formula 1 world championship, Hamilton's victory had been more symbolic than Viv's England debut, Barnsey's Maracana goal, Linford's 100 metres Olympic gold, Lennox wiping out Tyson, Tessa Sanderson becoming Britain's first female field gold medallist, Daley's and Dame Kelly's Olympic doubles or Paul Ince's England captaincy in '93. I didn't think black athletes would start 'swamping' motor racing, but Hamilton's victory with his back story felt more universally transcendental.

Here was this 23-year-old of mixed (a white mother and a black father) parents, who'd divorced when he had been a child, with a disabled brother, who grew up on a council estate in Stevenage. His grandparents were immigrants from Grenada and while his parents were no longer together, they worked their arses off to fund Hamilton's dreams, interests and racing talent. This was not your usual Formula 1 back story. He had in no way an entitled background, except for the fact that he had been so good at such a young age that sponsors clamoured to get a piece of motor racing's potential Tiger Woods. The Hamilton story was less about entitlement and more about the resilience required to be the odd kid out on the racing track, to be the kid that excelled on the racing track, to be the kid that got special treatment because of talent, determination and earning potential.

Hamilton debuted in 2007 as an understudy on the McLaren team to reigning world champion Fernando Alonso from Spain. He came within one point of becoming the world champion in his debut season, winning four races. 'Single-handedly he has restored public interest in a sport that had sunk up to the axles in its own cynicism,' said Richard Williams in the *Guardian*. Hamilton ended the year as runner-up in the Sports Personality of the Year (SPOTY). As footballer David Beckham's career had been winding down, British sport had found a new major star.

I didn't think it was a Jackie Robinson moment strictly because he had become the first athlete of colour to win a Formula 1 world championship. He also became the first person of colour to poll in the top three for SPOTY who had not been a boxer or a track and field athlete. These were sports in which black people were expected to excel because of the age-old stereotypes of black physical superiority.

Hamilton broke the mould. He set a precedent. Made people aware that access and exposure, resource, good coaching, clear development pathways, intelligence and determination were important factors in an athlete's success, not just natural athleticism. He made people aware that lazy stereotypes about physical advantages went both ways; what about the disadvantages, what about the advantages other 'races' hold, what about context and conditions, what is it that we don't know, how much of this is theory, pseudo-scientific theory, racist theory or just what we see on TV, or how we perceive what we see on TV?

Hamilton was potentially changing the paradigm.

'The thing about Lewis Hamilton, and to a big extent Barack Obama is that they are running counter to stereotype,' said Diane Abbott in the *Guardian*. 'They're not sportsmen – obviously formula one motor racing is a sport, but it's not a stereotypical physical or muscular sport. There's this idea that black men have physical prowess, which is not, in itself unremarkable. Where it's about how fast you can run and how strong you are, you will get black champions. What is interesting about Hamilton and to a lesser extent Tiger Woods, is that we're talking now about very cerebral sports.'

By his second season in 2008, I didn't know what to make of Hamilton. He had been a safe public figure. Not at all controversial. But he didn't bow to the mainstream media either. Nor did he seem overtly connected to the black community in the same way that Ian Wright or Lennox Lewis had been.

Lewis Hamilton was light skinned, well spoken, gentle in many ways although extremely driven and competitive with no Caribbean lilt to his accent. He had been apolitical, with no major black cultural identifiers of note. Not just a colour thing, though. Hamilton didn't really look much like a sportsman. To me, he looked more like a junior accountant than an athlete or a racing car driver.

'Their Englishness,' remarked sociologist Ben Carrington of Hamilton and cricketer Monty Panesar, 'is simply an unremarkable, uncontestable given.'[3]

Carrington would add: 'There is, to put it simply, no script at this historical conjuncture for understanding how we are to read the political and symbolic significance of a black English Formula One driver.'[4]

The post-racial narrative had really started to advance at pace after Barack Obama became president. If a black man can become the most powerful leader in the world, then racism must have died. Vindication. Black, white. America would not have voted a black man into office if they were racist.

Hamilton became an important part of that post-racial narrative; he became a symbol of equality and progression. Proof that things must be better. Proof that things can only get better. Proof that we have now entered a new era. Proof that racism was not a major factor anymore. Sport always provides the perfect antidote to society's ills and Hamilton's victory and later the London 2012 Olympics would provide the perfect narratives to illustrate how a good, tolerant and multicultural society could be.

What I liked about Hamilton is that he didn't seem to play ball. I never got the impression that he bought into the narratives being written about him, written for him. He didn't seem to be overly concerned about trying to re-write them. He raced. He won. He partied. He was outspoken, but often within the context of the motor-racing world. He showed great resilience, confidence and calm in the face of Formula 1 politics, intense rivalries and media criticisms. And when things fell apart, he seemed to recover swiftly, with little or no fuss.

I was never a great Formula 1 fan. Admittedly when Hamilton came on the scene, I started following the sport in the back pages of the newspapers and online. I wanted him to win. Wanted him to do well. To me, he had been an underdog. But the best type of underdog, one you expected to win. In every aspect of his life he had been different to, say, Lloyd Honeyghan. He had the same pit-bull attitude, an attitude I recognised when I was growing up in Newham. But I couldn't quite relate to him in the same way. My Newham elders, the Windies, the hyphenated 'ballers, their attitude, their style, their urban-ness, had all been more familiar as part of the Codes I grew up with. Hamilton came across as more mainstream, less of a rebel. I didn't think this was a bad thing. Perhaps this would be a sign of progression. Yet, somehow, Hamilton became a symbol of a post-racial Britain without ever being fully embraced by the British public.

Hamilton didn't become the new Becks, even though he too had a celebrity girlfriend in Nicole Scherzinger, formerly of the Pussycat Dolls. Hamilton remained successful. Not particularly controversial. Apolitical. Brash at times. A sore loser at times. He had been a master at his sport, able to generate speed like no other, always daring to take risks for victory; a man who respected the sport, respected its history and was obsessed with winning. Hamilton wouldn't win another world title until 2014, at which point he had moved from McLaren to Mercedes. But he remained the biggest name in the sport after the 2008 victory.

Despite this, it seemed that every single article I read about Hamilton would mention that he's not very popular with the British public. His notoriety had been as a much a source of fascination as his driving skills. It was not too long after winning his first world title that the theories started.

'Lewis moved to Switzerland in 2007 and later to Monaco, both well-known tax havens.'

'Lewis has a playboy lifestyle, a pop-singer girlfriend and spends most of his time hanging out at celebrity parties, all of which was terribly un-British.'

'Lewis is too bling. The way he dresses, he's more like an American rapper, like his pals Kanye West and Pharrell, than a British sports star.'

'Lewis is a brat. Too entitled. Lacks humility, particularly when he loses. Sore loser. Arrogant. He never gets on with his teammates.'

'Lewis is too good, too dominant. How is it that he can party so hard, hang with celebrities and yet win so many races? How can he really be focused on the task at hand?'

I struggled to understand why the British public could not embrace him. Why would he get a bad rap for his tax arrangements when other racing drivers, who also lived in Monaco, did not receive the same treatment? David Beckham had a pop-star girlfriend in Posh Spice. Former Formula 1 world champion James Hunt had become an icon in part because of his playboy lifestyle. It was not unusual for the likes of LeBron James and Cristiano Ronaldo to be splashed on celebrity pages, and Hamilton being a bit of a sore loser was hardly an unprecedented response in motor racing. As for him partying too hard, as one publication put it, he just had a good work–life balance.

Hamilton himself offered little in the way of explaining why he had not been embraced by the public. 'The way I live my life,' he once said. 'And maybe where I live. Who knows?'

Racing legend Stirling Moss once said, 'He was one of the racing crowd before, and now he's whatever you call those super-stars. And that's not really the way we English go. We're more reserved.'[5]

I always felt that the British public acknowledged Hamilton's brilliance. I also felt they bought into the post-racial narrative. If he can, any black can. He had become a symbol that we are now living in a society of equal opportunities. But I also felt that his lack of popularity had been racialised, without ever being explicit. Lewis was not going to be what anyone wanted him to be, and I think that caused resentment. He was not going to play the Frank Bruno role for the camera or express his Britishness in a way that an Ian Wright or Paul Ince had displayed. I think there was a feeling that Hamilton's colour had meant he'd received preferential treatment, from his teams, from team orders, from sponsors. Almost a suggestion that he had not been as good as billed. That his colour, the novelty, was a major part of his success, the reason why he had been pushed to the fore-front. Positive discrimination. The British public had been checking Hamilton's privilege while ignoring the fact that he had been the superior driver to most of his teammates and acknowledged by most as the best driver on the circuit, even in seasons when he did not have a strong enough car to win the championship.

Hamilton's growing links to black culture was also hard to ignore, particularly his relationship with American rappers. He was more bling than bulldog. I think this caused resentment. He had become a twenty-first-century uppity urban negro who did not know his place. Hamilton's Englishness tinged with

African-American culture and swag had not been quintessentially British. There was a highly racialised narrative at play without anyone really saying it. Not the writers. Not Lewis. Not anyone in Formula 1. It went unsaid and the implicit digs from the media continued.

What had become clear was that the post-racial narrative did not reflect what had been happening in British society.

A year after Hamilton's Formula 1 victory in 2008, I moved from delivering programming at the Stephen Lawrence Trust to funding charities. Through many years of delivering projects to young people, I had exceeded the targets (the number of young people we worked with, how many hours we engaged them in activities, progression to employment or education, things like that) set in our funding agreements. But I had spent more time filling out endless funding reports, being treated as if our success was indeed a failure (too much success often meant that we wouldn't be re-funded – a bit like winning a medal and then having your funding pulled) and missing out on funding because a nicely written application had been favoured over the quality of delivery. I had also spent too many years speaking to faceless and condescending people in positions of power who treated work with vulnerable people as an act of compliance not compassion. I wanted to know what it would be like on the other side, where more of the power lay.

Having spoken with many institutions and individuals, I found that in this new world, the narrative about what could be funded and what was unlikely to be funded around 'race' equality followed a distinct anti-multicultural narrative. Not that this had been expressed explicitly. But it appeared that funding for single-identity causes was frowned upon, while funding for 'race' equality needed community cohesion or integration outcomes to be considered seriously.

This pattern continued through the early years of the coalition government. 'Race' was off the political agenda. It remains off the political agenda. Multiculturalism a dirty word. 'Black' made white folks feel uncomfortable. Whenever I'd talk about high unemployment of black boys or in Pakistani communities, the typical response would be 'but what about the white working class?' '... that discourse of the white working class "un-classes" black people, as if we have no class.'[6]

The Equality Act of 2010 may have been the key to legislating multiculturalism out, diminishing the influence and impact of single-equality organisations by reducing funding and, critically, condensing all people with protected characteristics ('race', gender, age, ability, sexual preference, etc.) almost into one group. It failed to recognise that different people within these protected groupings were positioned differently and should have services that met them where they are, often a major failing of public and private services. Someone who is white and working class may face many disadvantages, just like someone who is black and working class will face some similar disadvantages. These mutual disadvantages may be related to poverty, poor schooling, low job prospects, debt and other issues. However, if you are black and working class, you will likely face more barriers, given the mass of evidence related to racially prejudiced practices in employment, health, housing, schooling and policing.

The Department for Work and Pensions (DWP) report in 2009, *A Test for Racial Discrimination in Recruitment Practice in British Cities*, found that applicants with ethnic-sounding names had to apply almost twice as many times to get a job interview as their white counterparts with similar or the same qualifications. Black people were being stopped and searched by the police 28 times more than whites. Improved educational attainment among young black men in London had done little to advance their job prospects. Black people were more likely to be referred to mental health services, more likely to be excluded from schools, more likely to be in the criminal justice system than in university, more likely to be identified with behavioural problems at school. Black women had to access domestic violence services more times before they received appropriate help than white women.

Poverty may have been the root cause, but when poverty intersects with 'race', ability and/or sexuality, this produces multiple barriers and multiple layers of discrimination. But we had entered an era of de-racialisation. Little or no money to support services tackling or analysing these 'race' disparities despite reams of evidence suggesting that the negative impacts in mental health, policing, employment, etc. were highly racialised.

Two thousand and eight had been a golden year for sport. Hamilton had become the Formula 1 world champion; Usain Bolt won three Olympic gold medals in Beijing in three world records, swiftly becoming one of the biggest names in sport; and Amir Khan, a young British Muslim who would quickly become a symbol of racial harmony, won a silver medal at the Olympics. It was also a year when a then record 28 youngsters had died in gun, knife or gang-related crimes in London, most of them young men of colour. Black-on-black crime became a thing. Little was mentioned about this 'epidemic' being severe in other places in the UK, where the term white-on-white crime had not been applied. Little was mentioned of the backgrounds of the criminals and the victims. Yes, many were young people of colour, but many had come from wildly different background and cultures. Much had been mentioned about the motives behind the crime and none, or very few, were racially motivated. Gang related, perhaps. Territorial, maybe. Stupid and violent, absolutely. But not racially motivated. But once more, black people had been presented as a problem to society.

A pattern emerged. I'd attend conferences or roundtables and I'd see the latest report about crime, poverty, poor education. And there, on the cover, would be a black face, a black child. Black as a problem. Black as disadvantage. But there would be little or no analysis of the challenges faced by black communities. How could solutions be created when there had been no recognition of racial discrimination as a root cause of some of these problems?

'... just before Tony Blair came out of power, he ordered a report into equalities in Britain and the document was 120 pages and the word "race" was only mentioned once,' said one community activist in Birmingham.[7]

My dad's words about the sixties being easier than the noughties struck. Would the eighties be easier than the future?

In 2010, my son was born. Beauty and worry. I knew he would be cute in a hoodie at six but a threat in a hoodie at 11. I knew that in the future he would be racially profiled by the police. I knew he would be under extra scrutiny from security guards and shop owners. I knew he would get the looks of fear from children, from older people, once he became taller. I knew he would be a target for gangs and street kids wanting to make a name for themselves. I knew that on just about every level, he would have to be smarter and bolder than me, because negotiating the Codes and the Tiers had become more implicit, more insidious. I knew that he would have a greater sense of belonging to England than me but might not be accepted any more than I was.

As I held my baby son, I could feel myself saying sorry. Sorry that I may not have all the answers to how he should deal with this, because I'm still kind of trying to work it out myself. Sorry because I don't want to afflict him with my condition, yet I do not want to conceal the truths of growing up black in Britain. Sorry because I knew he'd be entering a society that will continually imply that he must be wrong about how he feels.

Panic set in. I lived in Sydenham and I wanted out. The reality of knife crime had been stark in his early years. I had little faith that much would be done to combat this growing problem. I had been aware of Strathclyde Police's Violence Reduction Unit and the early success it had in combating gang and knife crime in Scotland. I had read the Centre for Social Justice's *Dying to Belong* report, which made numerous recommendations on how to tackle gang crime. I had funded and worked with many initiatives, including those using sport, that had proven successful in steering young people away from a life of crime. I had seen interventions that were tackling the causes of knife crime, from fatherhood training and conflict resolution to new ways of safeguarding, and initiatives to reduce school exclusions. But there did not seem much urgency in tackling this epidemic. The value of black lives did not seem any greater 27 years on from the New Cross Fire.

I started looking on Rightmove and Find A Property to find out where we'd move to. Needed to reduce the odds. Unofficial specs:

- *There needs to be a black and brown presence. Not just people. But a presence. Some history. A pattie shop or two. Culture needs to have infiltrated the area enough for me to move there.*
- *But no single 'race' should be too dominant. Need a mix. Give me an even spread.*
- *Good schooling of course. But he can't be the only black kid in the school. Too easy to stereotype. School will make no effort to consider black history, his history, even in October. They'll make no effort to challenge their own stereotypes, be inclusive, check the type of books they have on the curriculum if there're not many black kids in the school.*
- *No chicken shops, bookies, McDonald's or any other place where kids would just hang out; not within 5 to 10 minutes.*
- *Need a garden as an alternative to playing out on the street.*

I wrote this all down, then ripped up the paper and continued to search online some more. My paranoia had been justified. On Tuesday evenings, I'd pick up my daughter from Brownies. The journey back by bus was only 10 minutes. Always drama. This included some girls throwing a bottle from a first-floor bedroom window at my daughter and me, as we waited at the bus stop. We witnessed constant conflict on the bus on the way home, including one incident where three teenage girls refused to pay their fares. The driver stopped the bus. Refused to move. They shouted. Screamed. Threatened. At one point, I intervened. Offered to pay the driver but one of the girls ended up shouting at me. At one point, she pulled up her jeans to show me her tag.

'I'm trying to help,' I said.

'I don't need your f**king help,' was her reply.

She continued shouting until, eventually, she and her friends left the bus. As the doors were shutting, the girl apologised for swearing in front of my daughter.

On another occasion, as I was coming home from work, roughly around 7 pm, I saw three young men kicking a teenager on the floor. In the middle had been this woman, maybe in her early forties, grappling to protect this young kid writhing around in pain on the floor. I jumped in and dragged the boy on the floor into an off licence. He had beautiful skin. Looked no older than 16. And a bump on his forehead the size of a squash ball. As I pushed the kid into the shop, one of the assailants swung at me with a broken bottle, barely missing my head before running off. The kid in the shop ran off too.

There was another occasion when half a dozen boys surrounded me as I walked down Sydenham High Road. When I slowed down, they didn't overtake me, so I figured I could be in trouble. So, I stopped, turned around and asked one of the boys for the time. When he mumbled a response, I started making light conversation with him. I made eye contact with him and his friends to engage them too. I thanked the boys and walked off, hoping I'd fractured their intentions. It worked.

These would turn out to be minor incidents. Five months before my son was born, 16-year-old Nick Pearton had been stabbed to death in Home Park, where I used to take my daughter to the library and to play on the swings on Saturday mornings. In 2015, an 18-year-old was stabbed to death by a 16-year-old girl at midday outside our local Co-op. In between these murders, there had been a kidnapping on our street, gunshots fired at 3.45 pm at the top of my road and another teenager had been stabbed near my local gym by around a dozen teenagers.

At a time when there had been cuts to services targeting specific communities, particularly in mental health and school exclusions – two root causes of teen youth crime – an epidemic, a moral panic had started, which located blackness as extremists or gang members, as a threat to harmony. At the same time, the far right had been gaining momentum and while their political power would extinguish as swiftly as its fire had been lit, the racist rhetoric of Nick Griffin and Nigel Farage had gained traction, been mainstreamed and was accepted almost as rational, not extreme.

This was not the London the members of the IOC had bought into. London's bid to host the Olympic Games had been sold on multiculturalism. Now anything deemed multicultural was seen as a threat.

By the time Hamilton had won his fifth world championship in 2018, joining Michael Schumacher and Juan Manuel Fangio as the only drivers to win that many crowns, his peers and critics had started calling him one of the greats. His 73 victories only trailed Schumacher's, his win percentage was fourth on the all-time list and he had the most pole positions of anyone in Formula 1 history.

How many mainstream British athletes would make an all-time top five in their sports? Andy Murray is a great tennis player, but his legacy cannot match the likes of Serena, Steffi, Federer, Martina, Sampras, McEnroe, Billie Jean or Nadal. George Best is the only British player who would be mentioned in an all-time list of greatest footballers. But even he would struggle to crack a top five against Maradona, Messi, Cristiano Ronaldo, Johan Cruyff and Pelé. In cricket, you could certainly make a case for W G Grace and Jack Hobbs being among the top five cricketers ever, although both I suspect would remain firmly behind Australians Don Bradman and Shane Warne, West Indian all-rounder Gary Sobers and India's little master Sachin Tendulkar.

When we talk of greatness, we're not just talking about dominance in sport, longevity, the titles you've won, the quality of your performances over quality opposition, the records you've set. We're talking about transcending the sport, shifting the paradigm, being the blueprint, doing things others couldn't, wouldn't dare to do, have never done. As great as Linford, Seb, Mo, Jess and Dame Kelly were, only Daley Thompson would potentially get a place on a Mount Rushmore for track and field athletes and even then he would struggle against Usain Bolt, Carl Lewis, Jesse Owens, Jackie Joyner-Kersee, Paavo Nurmi or Michael Johnson.

Only Chris Hoy in track cycling, Ellery Hanley in rugby league and Steve Redgrave in rowing would make an all-time list in their respective sports. Jonny Wilkinson and David Beckham may have been icons in rugby union and football respectively, but never among the half a dozen or so names mentioned as being among the very best.

Hamilton, for his part, has continued to do things his way, without ever getting caught up in the criticism. I remember reading Toure's *Who's Afraid of Post-Blackness?* where he looked at American academic and writer Michael Eric Dyson's 'three primary dimensions of Blackness … accidental, incidental, and extroverted'. Dyson had been referring to African-Americans. The accidental say, 'I'm an American, I'm a human being, I happen to be Black. By accident of my birth I am Black. It just happened that way.' The incidental are 'people who more completely embrace Blackness – they aren't trying to avoid it – but that ain't the whole of their existence. I love it but it doesn't exhaust me.' And the extrovert say, 'I be Black, that's what I do, that's what my struggles are about.'

No African-American or black person fits rigidly into these three characteristics. Depending on context, I have used/been all three dimensions. And if I think hard enough, there are probably more dimensions I have employed. My father had inadvertently taught me how to mobilise effectively with different audiences. When he had been trying to attain work from clients, his language would change. He'd become a little more English in tone, a bit more accidental. I had employed this to lessen the threat of my height in situations in which I could feel other people's fear. Incidental had been the realm in which my father probably sat most of the time. He did not have any major 'hang-ups' about the colour of his skin, likely born from growing up around black and brown people in Jamaica. He also had an ease about his relationship to England. He hated the English cricket team but liked the country. I, too, probably sat in the incidental realm, but growing up in a majority white country, and being othered as a result, exhausted me. My father's extrovert side emerged when he had been in safer spaces, around friends, at parties or watching cricket. I had more of the extrovert in me, again likely the result of growing up in England. The struggle against racism, overt or covert, had never been far from my day to day existence. I didn't have my father's ease to rely upon, so I had been more outspoken when stopped by the police, when followed by security guards, when accused of stealing. Yet I found ways of minimising in situations where I had been confronted by fear and power.

Hamilton likely sat more in the incidental bracket where Dyson would put the likes of Barack Obama and Will Smith. Widely accepted and popular black men who did not ignore their identities but also did not make an issue of it all the time. Whether Hamilton needed to have more of a Black-British, hyphenated identity to be more popular, I don't know. Ian Wright had been moderately extrovert but has mobilised across all three of Dyson's categories. Frank Bruno was distinctly accidental through his boxing career, although it had been clear that he also had an incidental side, which did not play much of a role in his public profile.

At a time when the post-racial narrative had been in full swing, Hamilton never attained the same level of popularity as Wright or Bruno, which remains a mystery. But then again, nor did Daley Thompson, arguably the greatest British athlete of the eighties and a man who wouldn't be what the black community or the mainstream public wanted him to be. All he wanted to be was the best and, like Hamilton, he succeeded in achieving that on his own terms. Thompson had also been perceived as brash and flash. Black privilege (contemporary uppity negro) probably played a role in the public's ambivalence towards Thompson and Hamilton. Perhaps the invisibility of being the middle man had been the reason because no one could quite define them, categorise them or stereotype them.

Hamilton's invisibility will only become visible, I suspect, if he does something wrong. It happened to Tiger Woods once his infidelities had been revealed. The black athlete's excellence is such that it stops racists being racist, if only for a short time. They can support a Lewis Hamilton on a Sunday afternoon while being abusive to a black person at a train station the following day. Racism will not rear its ugly head unless Hamilton mentions it or if he does something wrong. But you just couldn't talk openly about whether 'race' played a part in Hamilton's notoriety because you would be accused of having a chip on your shoulder, playing the race card or creating problems when there were none. Britain can – I think – acknowledge that 'race' is a social construct while ignoring a British history that had produced unfair outcomes for the black community. It had become impossible to have a conversation about 'race' and racism.

American political sociologist Eduardo Bonilla-Silva said in his book *Racism Without Racists* that, 'In the eyes of most whites, for instance, evidence of racial disparity in income, wealth, education, and other relevant matters becomes evidence that there is something wrong with minorities themselves; evidence of minorities' overrepresentation in the criminal justice system or on death row is interpreted as evidence of their overrepresentation in criminal activity; evidence of black and Latino underperformance in standardized tests is a confirmation that there is something wrong (maybe even genetically wrong) with them.'

Bonilla-Silva added: 'Today there is a sanitized, color-blind way of calling minorities n****rs, Spics, or Chinks.'

I could see this in the way the British public viewed Hamilton. The implicit had replaced the explicit. I could see it in the commentary of black athletes. 'Race' would rarely be mentioned. But black athletes would delicately be condemned or overscrutinised. Racist incidents would rarely make the headlines or be a topic of conversation in chatrooms or on talk radio. When it became the topic of conversation, it would either be reduced to political correctness gone mad or wide condemnation that would be swiftly resolved by absolving the perpetrator of being racist. Individual incidents of racism would make the headlines more so than any systemic analysis around the governance and coverage of sport. And through it all, much of the debate, much of the narrative had been controlled by wealthy white men in suits.

Racism without racists.

It had not been the greatest week ever in black history. A good week. Not the greatest week. The brilliance of Obama and Hamilton could not shift one simple fact, that it really didn't matter as a black athlete whether you adhered to the Tiers (selling out) or to the Codes (keeping it real). The system that created these reductive binaries had mobilised, switched the narrative, de-racialised 'race'. It had never been, as the press would always suggest, political correctness gone mad. We had entered a period where colour blindness had gone mad.

CHAPTER 8

POOR PEOPLE'S OLYMPICS

THAT HOME-STRAIGHT LOOK. THAT HOME-STRAIGHT facial expression during the final sprint to the line. That facial expression combined with running action. I'm not sure there's a moment in sport quite so thrilling, so disarming, so beautifully human.[1] I think of those other great sporting moments, the last-round knock-out, the penalty shoot-out, the buzzer beater, the perfect floor routine, the fourth-quarter comeback, and something is missing. Sometimes the thrill of the moment is too swift to fully grasp; at times the sport is so tribal the moment is lost because your team lost; the human connection in the moment is absent because of a helmet, a car or bike, or athletic perfection.

Can't explain it. Is it because it's a race against time as well as a race against other humans? Double whammy. Individual. System. We can all relate to that. Is it a question of nationality, the flag on their vest? Is it the athlete? Perhaps the colour of their skin? Some of it. All of it. None of it. As I said, I can't explain. But watching an athlete come around that final bend to end a race is at times like the intoxicating horns in Fela Kuti's song 'Water No Get Enemy', the searing vocals of Sharon Jones, the withering pain in Kurt Cobain's voice.

There are a few things I have come to realise through years of watching sport, in stadiums or arenas, in bars, on the couch, lying on the floor. First, I probably have more favourite home-straight moments than any other instants in sport. Second, for all that I've said previously about sport and 'race', it is normally the one moment where nothing matters, nothing comes into consideration, not 'race', gender, ability, nationality. Nothing. Thirdly, and this goes out to all the non-sporting people in my life – my exes, some of my friends, my kids (who prefer to play than watch) and all those who I've dragged to sporting events and invariably watched them fall asleep, read, eat ungodly amounts of popcorn, consume copious volumes of beer, play Lego and clock-watch – athletics, especially that home-straight moment, that race to the line, seems to be the one thing that keeps the non-sporting fan hooked. It's a moment that does not seem to lose its drama, even when you replay it. There are some moments that you can only truly feel live, be it watching on television or in a stadium. But that home-straight feeling as a viewer rarely fails to thrill, past or present.

Maybe it has something to do with track and field as a sport. Athletics had always appeared to be a little different to other mainstream sports. When I watched track and field, I tended to support individual athletes irrespective of their nationality. It mattered little that sprinter Calvin Smith was American. Tiny, with a running style full of contradictions – smooth but his head rolling from side to side, slight but an athlete who tended to come on strong late in the race – Smith always felt like an underdog against his more powerfully built opponents, which is why I always wanted him to win. I loved the cheekiness of middle-distance runner Steve Ovett, the way 400 metres runner Butch Reynolds would shift from last to first in the final 100 metres of a race and the grace and humour of high jumper Blanka Vlašić.

Supporting athletes from different countries had been kind of cool, reflective of what I liked, reflective of my identity, reflective of the multiple sides of me. This may have been a sport riddled in politics, corruption and drugs, yet no other sport offered a true melting pot in the same way as athletics. You had your favourite events, your favourite athletes, you watched the rivalries and would at times happily support no one if the race had been thrilling enough or a world record at stake. The athletes also came across as ordinary people. No entourages, no boozing. They raced, they acknowledged each other's performances, then they'd put on a rucksack and go on their way.

Each home-straight moment is different. I remember watching Mary Decker's home-straight moment in the 1500 metres during the inaugural World Athletics Championships in Helsinki in 1983. Decker would gain greater fame a year later at the Los Angeles Olympics when South African-Brit Zola Budd accidentally tripped her in the final of the 3000 metres. Going for her second gold at the World Championships, Decker was clad in a tangy red vest and short pants. Her mousy, shoulder-length perm had been bobbing. Her running posture looked so perfect, back upright, top half of her body barely moving, legs working. She controlled the pace of the race. Wouldn't let anyone go past her. Then, as the final bend approached, Soviet athlete Zamira Zaytseva overtook her and opened a significant gap. The race seemed to be over. Decker was chasing down Zaytseva while two other Soviet athletes were pursuing Decker. Decker looked round. Her face cracked, I think, for the first time in the race. Just a little. But her posture didn't change much. She kicked. She closed. Zaytseva flailed. Decker's face hardened. Posture dipped forward. A little. Zaytseva seemed to stop. Decker ran her down. Overtook her on the line. Decker won, by a vest. Against the odds. But her posture at the end suggested that she had no doubt she would win. Zaytseva collapsed over the line.

I remember the Kenyan 800 metres runner Paul Ereng at the 1988 Olympic final in Seoul. Entering the final lap, he had been in second-to-last position. No one had heard of Ereng. He had not been in the story of this race. Prior to the final, everyone wanted to know whether the Brazilian Joachim Cruz could retain his Olympic title. They wanted to know whether Moroccan Saïd Aouita, better known for breaking world records at longer distances, could prove himself to be the greatest middle-distance runner of all time. We wanted to know whether Brit Peter Elliott could maintain Britain's dominance of the middle distances, a legacy created by the likes of Coe, Ovett and Cram. Ereng looked more like a high jumper than a middle-distance runner. He was lean, springy, more likely to jump than run. But as the likes of Cruz, Aouita and others rounded the final bend, Ereng was still not in television shot. Then, suddenly he emerged, trapped in the middle of five bodies, looking as if there would be no escape, no route to victory. Those five bodies looked pained, desperate, faces a different shade to when they first started the race. A gap appeared, and Ereng cruised through. I cannot remember my allegiance switching so swiftly. I kind of wanted Cruz or Aouita to create history. I wanted Elliott to do well, because I'd always remembered how he'd beaten Coe during the 1500 metres Olympic trials in 1984, only for Coe to be selected ahead of him. Coe went on to win the 1500 metres Olympic title, justifying the selectors' decision, but

I always had a soft spot for Elliott. That all went out the window when Ereng coolly drifted past everyone as if play-racing with his children.

The ultimate home-straight moment probably came when Kelly Holmes won the 800 metres in the Athens Olympics in 2004. I didn't know then what I would find out later about Holmes' battle with depression or her self-harming. But I had been following Holmes for years and watched as she battled frequent injuries and bridesmaid moments in major championships. Like British long-distance runner Paula Radcliffe, you could feel every inch of pain, every early morning training session when she ran. Effort personified.

Holmes had suffered injuries going into the 2004 Olympics and while she was among the favourites, most critics favoured her training partner Maria Mutola from Mozambique to take gold. Holmes cruised through the first 400 metres at the back, way off the pace, moving through swiftly during the second half of the race. She picked off more runners and, as the final bend emerged, I thought she'd cruise past the two or three runners ahead of her. But then she was stuck. Didn't go past anyone else. Stuck behind Mutola. Two athletes faded, leaving Holmes and Mutola to battle it out. Holmes kicked. But she could not pass Mutola. Mutola edged ahead and it looked as if Holmes would lose. Then Kelly kicked again, head bobbing forwards and backwards, her slender self expanding with every stride, breaking Mutola, showing that Mutola could not break her. Holmes edged ahead, but behind her Moroccan Hasna Benhassi and Slovenian Jolanda Ceplak started to chase the Brit down. They closed in. They overtook Mutola. They looked like they were about to do the same to

Holmes. But the Brit kicked some more, held them off and won the race.

Then there was that look. A look of surprise. Astonishment. A look of a person who had gone beyond what they could have imagined. Steve Cram in the commentary box shouted, 'You've won it, Kelly, you've won it.'

It had been such a moment that capped the greatest day in British sport's history since England won the World Cup in 1966. Within 44 minutes, British athletes Jessica Ennis in the heptathlon, Greg Rutherford in the long jump and Mo Farah in the 10,000 metres won gold medals. It had been a day when Great Britain had already scooped golds in the women's cycling team pursuit, the men's rowing and women's double sculls. The 4 August 2012 would forever be known as 'Super Saturday'.

It started with Ennis, who had dominated the heptathlon. She had practically been secure of victory (barring a fall) by the final event, the 800 metres. Near the end of the race, Ennis was lost among far taller athletes, but emerged from the pack to win. She had been London 2012's 'golden girl' along with cyclist Victoria Pendleton. On the biggest stage of her career, she had such humility, determination and confidence, I never had any doubts she would win. I still remember that moment she crossed the line after winning the 800 metres and the heptathlon gold, with 80,000 people at the Olympic Stadium cheering her on. She collapsed to the floor near the finish line, laid on her back and covered her face. I was sure she must have started crying. She did. I think. Her face was contorted as if she had been crying. But she kind of swept away the tears, quickly; tearfulness turned to happiness as she went on her lap of honour. No emotional breakdown there. Like every great heptathlete, she had been brilliant at switching emotions, she had demonstrated that you did not need to growl and cry to show you cared, she had proven herself to be one of Britain's greatest competitors and she had won and then celebrated on her own terms.

While Ennis celebrated, Rutherford was in a battle for gold in the long jump. Rutherford would later confess to being happy that all the attention had been on Ennis and Farah. By the fourth round, Rutherford had leapt into the lead with a jump of eight metres and 31 inches. As the long-jump competition neared its conclusion, Rutherford congratulated Ennis, and then Mo Farah came out for the start of the 10,000 metres. The tension created by the events overlapping made it even more exhilarating and exhausting to watch. As Mo battled in the 10,000 metres, Rutherford, the ultimate good guy and an athlete who had himself suffered through numerous injuries in his career, won gold, although he and the crowd couldn't quite soak up the moment because the drama in Mo Farah's race was still unravelling.

Farah controlled the race, even when he didn't look in control. The actions of all his competitors had been geared towards defeating him and, through it all, he appeared calm and determined to watch, and wait for the final moment. Two laps from the end, there were 12 athletes bunched together, including Farah's teammate Galen Rupp, three Eritreans, three Ethiopians including the legendary Kenenisa Bekele and two Kenyans. At the bell for the final lap, Farah went to the front. The 12 started to stretch, but Farah couldn't shake three of his competitors. I had been thinking that they might take him as he went round the final bend. But Farah stretched away and had his home-straight moment. Farah has one of the great home-straight expressions. He runs as if he is being tracked down by hunters. He keeps his running form, but his eyes look fearful and tearful, his broad white teeth chomp on invisible gobstoppers, everything about him is exaggerated – the thinness of his body, the sharp beauty of his features, the glistening of his bald head, everything thinner, shinier, browner, whiter. Mo won. Team GB had exceeded expectations.

Ex-footballer turned broadcaster Gary Lineker said: 'I can honestly say that was the best day's sport I've ever seen.'

Lord Coe said: 'The greatest day of sport I have ever witnessed.'

The following day, the *Observer* ran with the headline: 'Britain's Greatest Day.'

When London won the bid to host the Olympic Games in 2005, with those 30 kids from the East End, this is what Coe and the Committee members must have envisioned. The Games had been won because London was this multicultural city and now, in one symbolic evening, Ennis, Rutherford and Farah had come to represent a victory for difference, united under the Union Jack. The pride I felt watching all three athletes succeed in the biggest moments of their lives had me jumping for joy.

Director and producer Danny Boyle had set the tone during an opening ceremony where, amid celebrations of Winston Churchill and the NHS, Windrush had been honoured while, at various points, Dizzee Rascal and Soul II Soul provided a soundtrack to the occasion. A bit later, Doreen Lawrence, Shami Chakrabarti, then director of human rights charity Liberty, and Muhammad

Ali were among the chosen few to represent the Olympic values. Black-Britain had not been an after-thought, invisible or a clumsy add-on. It was central.

A survey carried out by NatCen Social Research demonstrated that self-reported racial prejudice dipped to close to an all-time low in 2012, such had been the impact of sport and the London Games. But it had also been clear that not everyone felt so optimistic by these images.

A few years later, I attended a panel that featured historian, writer and filmmaker David Olusoga, the author of the book and docu-series *Black and British: A Forgotten History*. In reference to the Olympic opening ceremony, he said: 'Windrush, the ship that is symbolic of post-war migration from the Caribbean to Britain, and for that to be represented alongside those uncontested moments of obviously, clearly British history that no one would ever question as being British history, that was an amazing moment and arrival. And I and a lot of people wrote about it at the time. A lot of people thought that this was, if not the arrival of the Britain we wanted to live in, it was at least a vision of a possibility of reaching [this] in our lifetime. And we were wrong because four years later we woke up and realised two things; one is that millions of our fellow countrymen and women watched that Olympic ceremony red in the face with rage because it represents a vision of Britain that they hated and the other thing that was pointed out to me by a friend, [was] that [it] was the London Olympics, not the British Olympics. It represented London and it was an accurate reflection of where London had got to, but London's eight million people and the UK's 65 million people, 'and we got it wrong.'

It was not only the people who would later vote to Leave in the EU Referendum who had been in a rage.

On 4 August 2011, a year before 'Super Saturday', 29-year-old Mark Duggan died of a gunshot to the chest in Ferry Lane, Tottenham. Duggan, riding in a minicab, had been under surveillance by Operation Trident, a sub-division of the Metropolitan Police, set up to investigate crime in the African and Caribbean community. Trident officers had shot him in the belief he had been carrying a firearm.

Duggan's girlfriend was notified but his family had not been informed. They heard rumours, they tried to find out what had been happening, they didn't know whether their son was dead or alive. The family would find out about their son's death in the media. Controversy surrounded the shooting too. Was Duggan carrying a gun? Had it been an unlawful killing? No answers. No response. On Saturday 6 August, Duggan's family and friends, around 300 in all, marched peacefully to Tottenham police station. They wanted answers. They wanted a response. They wanted a little respect.

A peaceful protest turned into a disturbance. A disturbance between the police and young people. The disturbance escalated. The Duggan family appealed for calm. By mid-Sunday morning, Tottenham had been set alight, 49 fires that night. The disturbance turned to rioting and looting. The police cowered, the roofs erupted, there were shelled buildings, incessant sirens, rushing crowds, confusion. I had seen the night distorted this alarmingly before.

The riots continued through to Monday. I remember coming back from work to Sydenham that day. As I left Bellingham station, on my way to Lower Sydenham, shops were closed. Shutters down. The streets were empty, like a ghost town. Not many cars. Just the rustle of litter in the wind, the sound of a breeze. Silence on the streets. It was like a curfew had been enforced.

There had been rumours that the riots were going to hit Sydenham. There had been a couple of minor incidents reported on Sydenham Road, which had also been, it seemed, boarded up. There were young men strutting down the street confidently as if they owned it, as if they were warning folks that you could be next.

The riots spread. First across London: Croydon, Lewisham, East Ham, Enfield, Clapham, Hackney. Then across England: Nottingham, Birmingham, Liverpool. It didn't feel like it would stop. London felt out of control. Then the first death. A man was shot in Croydon. Then an elderly man was beaten up.

On the Wednesday, the fourth night of the riots, three young Asian men were killed in Birmingham, mowed down by a car while trying to protect their community, trying to protect their mosque. Revenge was in the air until Tariq Jahan, whose son Haroon had been among the three killed, said: 'Today we stand here to plead with all the youth to remain calm, for our communities to stand united. This is not a race issue. The family has received messages of sympathy and support from all parts of society.'[2]

The riots ended on Thursday 11 August, a week after Duggan's death. A week where there had been five more deaths. A week where there had been over 3,000 arrests. A week which had led to over £200 million worth of damage.

As frightened and upset as I had been, as inexcusable as the actions of the rioters had been, I couldn't help but feel frustrated by the media coverage. There had not been a shoot-out as originally reported between Duggan and the police, which led to his death. A police officer had not been shot first as reported in the press. The Independent Police Complaints Commission (IPCC) would eventually release a statement saying they may have 'inadvertently given misleading information to journalists'.

The media depicted Duggan as a gangster. A call by Bishop Kwaku Frimpong-Mason for mourners at Duggan's funeral to stretch their hands towards the coffin had been classified as a gangsta salute by the press. And who could forget the cropped picture of Duggan, eyebrows lowered close to a scowl, head tilted, eyes piercing, unsmiling. Not quite a gangster pose. No hand gestures in shot. Nothing too demonstrative. But a picture that seemed to confirm the narrative of Duggan the gunman, Duggan the shooter, Duggan the bad boy. The full picture would show Duggan holding a heart-shaped emblem as a tribute to his deceased daughter. Duggan may have had a criminal past. May have been up to no good that night. But the framing only served to devalue his life, to devalue his body, to devalue his right to fairness, his right to live. Good black. Bad black. Deserving. Undeserving.

The rioters were widely condemned as looters, opportunists, career criminals. No back story, no history, nothing to suggest that their actions may have had some explanation. Then the riots were being perceived as a black thing, a gang thing, the rivers of blood.

In his book *Out of the Ashes: Britain after the Riots*, David Lammy condemned the rioters, saying: 'There was no shame in their actions, just pride in their new possessions. This was not a protest; it was rampant materialism.'[3] But he too put the rioters' actions into context when he added: 'The tragedy is that the common experience of hard work and low pay, of cramped houses and overburdened services, is a source of division, not solidarity. The scramble for resources – homes, jobs and school places – drives a wedge between those who have the least. People who contribute through hard work see a system indifferent to their needs. People who should be friends and neighbours become rivals.'

Two hundred and seventy young people who were involved in the riots were confidentially interviewed for the subsequent *Reading the Riots* report by the *Guardian* and the London School of Economics. Everyday policing and the police's discriminatory practices as well as opportunism emerged as two of the core reasons for their participation in the riots. The war between gangs ceased during the disturbances; rioters were primarily white although in proportion to population, there had been a higher percentage of black participants.

I had been working at a grant-making foundation at the time of the riots. Naturally, the trustees of this charity were concerned about what underpinned the riots. So, I invited Ruth Ibegbuna, Founder and Director of Reclaim, and Tom Lawson, Chief Executive of Leap Confronting Conflict, to tell my trustees more about the riots, and to provide an alternative narrative to the ones they would have heard in the media. They listened. Intently. Never interrupted. Or passed judgement. They winced, at times. Shook their heads. But never questioned or scrutinised the empathetic stance of both speakers. Ibegbuna and Lawson didn't excuse the actions, but they provided a rare glimpse into the lifestyles, the motivations, the back stories of these young people; stories that rarely made the light of day.

At one point, Ibegbuna, buried in a thick scarf due to poor health, called the riots the 'poor people's Olympics'. The phrase never left me and some years later I asked her to revisit what she'd meant by the phrase.

'Some young people saw the riots as a possible "once in a life-time" opportunity to get involved in a movement bigger than themselves. A national moment of significance. A way of making a mark; of being seen and heard. Maybe some even felt respected – temporarily. Some treated it as a laugh. Better than staying in and watching it on the telly. Literally some young guys got prison sentences because their families failed to keep them at home, watching the drama unfold on the TV.

'Young people from poor communities had a moment when they dislodged power and disrupted the national narrative. They were the lead item on the news and more than just nicking trainers from shops, there was the exhilaration of important people being aware of your presence and seeing the media congregate, desperate to hear your opinions. At one stage in Manchester, there were more journalists than "rioters"; all the actors were in place and the stage was set. It just needed someone (literally) to strike a match.

'The rioters of 2011 had exactly the same things to say about the policing of their communities as in 1981, yet this time they were just dismissed as materialistic and there was little attention paid to their protestations of over-policing and Stop and Search. Bearing in mind a young black man had died at the hands of Police Officers, the ease at which the cause of the riots was reduced down to the desperate need to steal new trainers and widescreen TVs suited a tabloid narrative of thick hooligans out of control. I was contacted by a national broadcaster and asked if I could provide urban young people to be interviewed on the national news about the riots. I suggested two names. I was then told by the broadcaster that they were a little too "articulate and polished" and could I provide young people more "rough around the edges". They wanted to represent a certain kind of black young adult. Edgy, lacking vocabulary, easily recognisable.

'The riots definitely happened. We saw them. The media acted as an effective stage manager, ensuring we saw a version of the truth that made the most sense to the majority. Black feral teens with no respect for communities; stealing new sportswear. In hoodies.'

The riots were condemned by footballers Rio Ferdinand, Wayne Rooney and Michael Owen and cricketers Michael Vaughan and James Anderson. But it had been left to football bad boy Joey Barton, whose brother Michael had been part responsible for axeing black teenager Anthony Walker to death in 2005, to empathise with rioters when he said, 'Violence always comes from a place of misunderstanding and low to zero self-worth. Well mine did anyway ... #educatethem.'

The Olympics could not mask the racial tensions that had been prominent in society. Further incidents in football following the riots would highlight the link between racism in British society and sport.

On 15 October 2011, in the second half of a match between Manchester United and Liverpool at Anfield, a fiery exchange took place between United's Patrice Evra and Uruguayan star Luis Suárez. According to the FA report on the incident, the exchange, which took place in Spanish, reportedly went as follows:

Evra: 'F**king hell, why did you kick me?'
Suarez: 'Because you're black.'
Evra: 'Say it to me again, I'm going to kick you.'
Suarez: 'I don't speak to blacks.'
Evra: 'OK, now I think I'm going to punch you.'
Suarez: 'OK, blackie, blackie, blackie.'*

As the referee Andre Marriner stopped play, Suárez used the word 'negro' to which an incensed Evra responded by telling the referee he had been racially abused. When Suárez put his hand on the back of Evra's head, the United defender pushed it away, declaring to the referee that he didn't want the Uruguayan to touch him, to which Suárez replied, 'Why, black?'

Evra and Manchester United would report the incident. Suárez would claim that his use of the term referring to Evra's skin had not been meant to be offensive; he implied that it had been a cultural misunderstanding.

Gus Poyet, a former Uruguayan international and then manager of Brighton, came to Suárez's defence in the *Independent* (25 November 2011) by saying: 'You cannot accuse people without a proper investigation, especially when it's a foreigner who is coming from a different place where we treat people of colour in a different way. So it was very easy to accuse someone. Luis Suárez is 100%

* From the *Daily Telegraph* (12 February 2012): not direct FA report.

not a racist. Me, I'm not racist. I've lived with people of different colours in different countries and I adapted to every single situation. Suárez needs to adapt to England, and England needs to adapt to the players that come here. England needs to understand how the rest of the world lives. If we have that understanding, easy.'

Poyet would add: 'You are not racist when you go against one, but you are if you go against the whole world of different colour and nationalities. That is being racist, not saying one word in one moment.'

In December 2011, the FA's hearing panel reached its conclusion, disagreeing with Suárez's defence and stating that, 'Suárez's use of the term [negro] was not intended as an attempt at conciliation or to establish rapport; neither was it meant in a conciliatory and friendly way.'

Suárez was fined £40,000 and he received an eight-match ban.

After the ban and fine had been announced, Poyet said: 'The ban is incredible, shocking, disproportionate. I back Luis to death. Things have happened before with Evra. He is not a saint. He is a controversial player.

'I don't know in which world we are going to live from now on. People will accuse each other of anything. Suárez just arrived [in the Premier League] and there are things that he has to learn when you are in another country because they might be normal in your country but perhaps they are not considered that way in other parts of the world.

'I have tried to explain that we live with coloured people in Uruguay. We share different experiences with them. We play football, we share parties. We are born, we grow up and we die with them. We call them "blacks" in a natural way, even in an affectionate way. That is the way we were brought up. We are integrated and there are no problems from either side.'

Soon after the ban and fine, before a game against Wigan Athletic, the Liverpool team, including manager Kenny Dalglish, decided to wear T-shirts depicting the image of Suárez. Dalglish, once one of Britain's greatest footballers, would say: 'I think the boys showed their respect and admiration for Luis with wearing the T-shirts. It is a great reflection of the man as a character, a person and a footballer that the boys have been so supportive and so have the supporters. He has earned that, he deserves it and we will always stand beside him. They will not divide the football club, no matter how hard they try.'

Liverpool's show of solidarity for Suárez prompted then Black-burn Rovers forward Jason Roberts to tweet: 'The stance on the Suárez issue from LFC has bemused me ... are United going to print Evra shirts now? Some issues are bigger than football.'

Roberts would also say: 'Really? Here's a man who has just been found to have used racist terminology and they are backing him as if he were the victim. What kind of message is that sending out?'

Paul McGrath, the former Republic of Ireland defender, also tweeted: 'As an ex-footballer having experienced racist comments throughout my career I was saddened to see Liverpool players wear those t-shirts last nite.'[4]

When Suárez returned from the ban, it had been thought that a handshake with Evra in Liverpool's match against Manchester United on 11 February 2012 would silence this ugly incident. Suárez approached Evra for the customary pre-match handshake between teams. Evra held out his hand. Suárez appeared to blank him and shook the hand of United goalkeeper David De Gea instead. Evra tugged on Suárez's elbow only for the Uruguayan to brush the United player off.

This could have been a moment to have an honest conversation about racism. An honest conversation about cultural differences. What is acceptable, what isn't. Not a time to hide behind football, behind nationalism, behind a rivalry. But in football, nationalism and rivalry trumped morality. Once 'race' had been involved, all prospect of an honest conversation was gone. The debate unsophisticated. And through it all, with the fear of talking about 'race', the fear of being accused of racism permeating, accusations being tossed from Manchester to Liverpool, from the press to the public, the narrative had not at any point been controlled, dictated or led by anyone black. The most powerful voices in stirring the racism narrative had not been Evra, it had not been Kick It Out. The 'race' debate took a life of its own, played out in the media, selected by the media, antagonised by the media, and at no point had there been a sensible discussion about what was acceptable and what wasn't. The voices of the marginalised had not been heard while the debate had been dictated by people with little or no knowledge of how to conduct a sensible debate about the issue. This pattern of absent voices and unqualified authority would play out in future debates about 'race' in sport, including in the depiction by the media of Raheem Sterling. The Evra affair became another incident that symbolised that 'race' is not a word to play and that black voices in this debate remained marginalised.

Eight days after the Evra–Suárez affair, England and Chelsea captain John Terry and Anton Ferdinand, brother of Rio, got into an argument in a match between the southwest London club and Queens Park Rangers. The incident did not escalate. After the match, Terry responded to a video that allegedly showed him saying 'f**king black c**t' to Ferdinand.

'I thought Anton was accusing me of using a racist slur against him. I responded aggressively, saying that I never used that term,' said Terry.

A member of the public complained about Terry's use of language. QPR made a complaint too. Anton Ferdinand allegedly did not accuse Terry of making a racist remark but wanted the incident investigated.

Ferdinand issued a statement with the FA saying: 'I have very strong feelings on the matter, but in the interests of fairness and not wishing to prejudice what I am sure will be a very thorough inquiry by the FA, this will be my last comment on the subject until the inquiry is concluded.' The Metropolitan Police subsequently launched an inquiry into Terry's alleged racist abuse.

On 21 December 2011, Terry was charged with racially abusing Ferdinand by the Crown Prosecution Service. The following year, in February, soon after Terry pled not guilty to the charge, he was stripped of his England captaincy, a decision condemned by outgoing England manager Fabio Capello.

Terry was eventually cleared by Westminster Magistrates Court but charged by the FA for abusive language that referred to Ferdinand's skin colour. Terry received a £220,000 fine and was banned for four games.

Anton's career never recovered. Rio never played for England again. He would later reveal that: 'There were bullets in the post. My mum had her windows smashed and bullets put through her door and ended up in hospital because of the stress.'[5]

'Race' and football were not just confined to individual incidents. Something deep, something sinister lurked within the systems of the most powerful game in the world. You knew it. Suspected it. Couldn't quite put your finger on how it worked. But you knew it existed within the blood of the sport, behind closed doors, where decisions are made, where no one can see, where no one can complain, where there's no accountability. At the time, what lurked unseen would leak out. In 2004, when working for ITV sport, former manager Ron Atkinson said of French international Marcel Desailly that 'he's what is known in some schools as a lazy thick n****r', unaware that his microphone was on. When manager of West Bromwich Albion in the late seventies, Atkinson had been the man who brought together the Three Degrees – Laurie Cunningham, Brendon Batson and Cyrille Regis. He had been known as a pioneer, a progressive. Yet for him, a man who was very much a part of the establishment, to use the N-word and do so while using age-old stereotypes told me that the fight for real change would need to be systemic and that the individual incidents ended up being a distraction rather than change-making.

Manchester City defender Micah Richards had to close his Twitter account due to the racial abuse he had been receiving. Former England international turned pundit Stan Collymore, one of the most vocal and honest commentators on racism in football, had also been abused on social media platforms during the 2011–12 football season. Racism in football ran deep. On the pitch, in the terraces and in the boardrooms. Yet these incidents kept on being treated as isolated episodes and not systemic, institutional problems.

Talk of introducing the Rooney Rule had also started to emerge before the London 2012 Olympics. The difference between the number of black professional players in Britain (approximately 25 per cent) to black managers (3 per cent) had been stark. According to the website sportingintelligence.com, by the start of the 2012–13 football season, approximately 32 per cent of Premier League players could have been considered black. I take this to mean Black-British or black African, Caribbean or Other while potentially also encompassing mixed heritage (white and Caribbean or African). If you take the accumulated numbers of people within these ethnic categories then, according to the 2011 census, that would constitute about 4.5 per cent of the population of England. Yet Chris Hughton was the only black manager of a Premier League club (Norwich City) at the start of that season. There were 20 Premier League clubs in 2012–13 of which only one, Swansea City, was not based in England.

The Rooney Rule, named after Dan Rooney, the chair of the National Football League's diversity committee, had been introduced to the NFL in 2002 due to the lack of African-American or minority coaches (28 per cent assistant coaches, 6 per cent head coaches) in relation to African-American or minority players (70 per cent) in the game. The policy meant that NFL teams had to interview at least one African-American or minority candidate for head coaching or senior operational positions.

It was Johnnie Cochran, perhaps best known as O J Simpson's defence attorney, and labour law attorney Cyrus Mehri who had commissioned a report into the NFL's poor record on diversity in senior level positions in 2002. Pittsburgh Steelers' owner Dan

Rooney subsequently chaired the committee that introduced a policy that would see the number of African-American head coaches jump from 6 per cent to 22 per cent by 2006.

Peter Herbert, part-time judge and barrister and chairman of the Society of Black Lawyers, had been the one to take up the fight to introduce the Rooney Rule into English football. Herbert recognised the power of black footballers and their influence. If the likes of Regis and Cunningham had been symbolic of black people 'swamping' British society, by 2012 the economic case had been made for the value of the black player. The numbers were rising significantly and these players had wealth and influence.

But like many within the game, it had also been clear that opportunities to move from the pitch to the boardroom were limited. The football establishment appeared to adopt the same stereotypes and prejudices that once stopped black players from playing central roles, to now believing that black people could not be strategic enough to lead clubs.

The response from the football fraternity to the Rooney Rule was largely negative. The powers that be, from leaders of football's authorities through to club managers, were quick to shut down the conversation. American political sociologist Eduardo Bonilla-Silva's sentiment that, 'By regarding race-related matters as non-racial, "natural," or rooted in "people's choices," whites deem almost all proposals to remedy racial inequality necessarily as illogical, undemocratic, and "racist" (in reverse),' appeared to be true in the case of the mainstream response to the Rooney Rule.

*   *   *

I couldn't wait for the Olympics to arrive. The Olympics represented an escape. An escape from the injustice of the system. An escape from the depression of football and its non-racist racist acts. Like a holiday. Reality suspended for a moment. Suspended in sport with once-in-a-lifetime opportunities to see the greatest athletes on the planet compete in your home town. More than one person would tell me that the Games 'represented the best of London'. This was in part because so many people had left the country. The trains were empty. Morning rides to work pleasant. Work had not been so intense, bosses were happy for the television to be on during the day. And, of course, there were the lucky few of us who had been fortunate to attain tickets. My tension had been lifted. My rage dissolved. For a brief period, London had been smiling. And unlike Euro '96, the smile was not prompted by alcohol.

The Olympics was going to be a mask for what had really been going on in society. Earlier in the year, Doreen Lawrence finally gained some 'justice' when two of the suspected murderers of her son Stephen – Gary Dobson and David Norris – were convicted of stabbing the black teenager to death. Stephen died aged 18. It had taken Doreen and her family a further 18 years to secure partial justice.

The Olympics could do little to conceal such injustices. But at least the sports on display would feel a little less tribal, prettier, purer and, dare I say it, more romantic. That's what sport should be about, right? Romanticism. The romanticism of heroism. The romanticism of different communities coming together. The romanticism of sportsmanship. A place to dream; that's where sport had once taken me.

The Olympics meant more to me than watching Jess, Greg and Mo succeed. The Olympics was about Luol Deng, it was about Usain Bolt, it was about LeBron James. It would represent the multiple identities of me. The hyphenated me. The black me. The political me. That big complex pot of gumbo me.

I wrote an article for the literary website *The Weeklings* about my Olympic experience. I wrote about how I had, for the first time, supported a British team over opposition comprising black players. It had been a pre-Olympic basketball game in Manchester between Team GB and the United States. I had always felt a closer affinity to teams where shared experiences (blackness) or heritage (Jamaican roots) had been prominent. The African diaspora. But there I was, my body tingling as NBA legends Kobe Bryant and LeBron James were being announced. The star power of the United States had been such that the arena quivered as they appeared on court. They were superstars. Among the most famous sports people in the world. And they were on one team. It would be like an all-star football team comprising Lionel Messi, Cristiano Ronaldo and Andrés Iniesta competing against other countries.

That night, I watched Kobe bamboozle British defenders with his footwork, I watched the lengthy Kevin Durant shoot three-pointers as if they were lay-ups, I watched Chris Paul bullying the Brits with his defence and I watched LeBron James look about a foot taller, several inches wider, a lot stronger and wiser than anyone else on that court. The United States won 118–78. But when I talked to colleagues about the game the following day, I proudly said 'we' and 'us' when referring to Great Britain. That night, I felt that Team GB reflected the multiple me. There were black players. There were white players. There were Scottish players and naturalised Americans. Whether deliberate or not, the team played with the hurried intensity I had recognised from the Great Britain Olympic team in 1988. It had been a style that reflected the eclectic cultural mix of the team. American swag, inner-city toughness, British doggedness and a Caribbean work ethic although, in the 2012 version, there was also more of an African work ethic. No player exemplified the spirit of that team more than Luol Deng.

I had first interviewed Luol around 2000, when he was 14 or 15 years of age. I met him at the Brixton Rec during the Rough & Ready basketball tournament, an event created in 1996 by ex-Topcat Matthew Ryder, with sports apparel mogul Roger Hosannah and event organiser Junior Taylor.

Luol, who learned the game under the tutelage of Jimmy Rogers, had just gone to an American high school to pursue his NBA dreams. Watching him play, even to the untrained eye, Luol seemed to be everywhere on the court, a bit like Patrick Vieira when he played for Arsenal. Rough & Ready provided the ideal platform to showcase his skills and a new generation of hyphenated players.

At Rough & Ready, Jay-Z, DMX or UK garage was blaring from the speakers while hordes of young supporters came out sporting their finest wears. Fellas in tight turned-up jeans and matching denim jackets, with gleaming white Nike Air Flight Showbiz trainers or dark Nike tracksuit bottoms with crisp, baggy white T-shirts; women with oversized earrings, army fatigue croptops and pedal pushers, or matching tracksuit tops and bottoms with freshly styled hair, which could skilfully combine several different styles (Afro puffs, cornrows, beehives) in one.

The crowd swelled as word of mouth spread; it was hot and sweaty, like a house party on the verge of erupting. The players, each representing different parts of the country, would dive on the floor for loose balls, dunk with vain-popping energy; they were 'trash-talking' opponents and crowd members. It wasn't like anything I'd seen on a basketball court in England before. Rough & Ready provided an outlet for disaffected (by the basketball authorities) inner-city 'ballers to thrive.

Luol had only found his way onto a basketball court after being granted political asylum in England, having escaped the second Sudanese Civil War. He and his family ended up in Brixton via Egypt. With support from Rogers, Deng moved to New Jersey as a 14-year-old to attend Blair Academy high school. But Deng always returned. To play for England junior teams, to play in Rough & Ready tournaments, and to visit Rogers. I thought that Deng and tournaments like Rough & Ready and Hosannah's Pro-Am would be the future of British basketball, the legacy of Moore, the 'streetfighters', the Topcats and the Towers.

They put Britain's urban youth at their forefront, celebrated diversity as an asset, as the key to success, as the backbone of their business case. This had been different to mainstream basketball in Britain, which continued to lack stability, be disconnected from its urban audiences and still appeared to be utilising its resources poorly, bickering among themselves at the expense of its players.

When London won the right to host the Olympic Games in 2005, there wasn't even a Great Britain basketball team. It had long since been disbanded, with each British nation having its own national team. It had always been the case that the host nation of the Olympic Games would get a bye for the basketball tournament. A Great Britain team was hastily cobbled together, but FIBA, the governing body of international basketball, would not give this new team a bye given that it had no recent track record. From 2007 to 2011, the new Great Britain team would need to prove it was good enough to earn its place in the tournament.

Deng played in every tournament despite reservations and pressure from his NBA team Chicago Bulls. He was determined to help Great Britain be good enough to play at the Olympics, even at the expense of his NBA career.

On 3 August, Team GB played Spain in the qualifying round at the Olympics. Spain were the second-best team in the tournament behind the United States. They had been expected to defeat Great Britain with ease. It turned out to be arguably the greatest game of basketball played on these shores. I had never seen a British crowd so vocal, so alive, watching the national team play basketball. Great Britain lost by the slimmest of margins 79–78. Had Great Britain won, they would have almost certainly made it through to the knock-out stage but, more than anything, British basketball would have finally fulfilled its potential on the court and provided a positive vision of modern Britain off the court.

Deng led the team, but was ably assisted by Pops Mensah-Bonsu, one of the late Joe White's former charges. But British basketball had been like the Negro Leagues in baseball back in forties America. When Jackie Robinson broke the colour line in 1947, Major League Baseball teams ended up recruiting black players from the Negro League. But as Howard Bryant would point out in his book *The Heritage*, Major League Baseball recruited the black bodies but left the black brains (the Negro League coaches and managers) behind.

During the Olympics, I wrote, 'I guess the British basketball team said more to me about Britain than any other athlete or event at the Olympics. The reality. This team of London youths, immigrants, white boys as the minority, and naturalized Yanks; this minority sport (in both players and popularity) that lacks the resources to fully develop young working-class talent; the "gift of fury", the humility, the second-generation Caribbeans and Africans, the rejection of blacks from managerial positions, the renegades, the broken dreams, the dissolving presence of British African-Caribbean heritage, the untold story. The British basketball team travelled further than most during the Games and represented a reality of a Britain that struggles to be honest with itself around issues of race and multi-culturalism. More than anything, the team represented what it feels to be an outsider, it represented the fact that, many of these players – like many minority groups in the UK – succeeded not because of the system, but despite of it.'

While Luol Deng represented the 'othering' of hyphenated Britain, it had been his dedication to repaying Britain for granting him asylum that remained one of the most enduring legacies of the Games for me. As IT businesswoman and philanthropist Dame Stephanie 'Steve' Shirley once said, 'As an immigrant I love this country with a passion perhaps only someone who has lost their human rights can feel.'

*   *   *

If Luol Deng embodied the spirit of hyphen-nation, then the 2012 Olympics and sprinter Usain Bolt restored my faith and pride in Jamaican sport. By 2012, Jamaica's 50th anniversary of independence, Bolt had established himself as arguably the most famous athlete on the planet. During the 2008 Beijing Olympics, he won three gold medals with three world record times. The following year in Berlin, he broke his own world records in winning the 100 and 200 metres double at the World Championships. By the time of the London Games, Bolt's charisma, his signature 'Lightning Bolt' pose, his overwhelming dominance over opponents, his carefree attitude, his six-foot-five physical presence, his record-breaking feats (the first man to dip under 9.7 seconds and then 9.6 seconds for the 100 metres and the first and only man to go under 19.2 seconds in the 200 metres) had made him an icon and a saviour for athletics.

Athletics had taken over from cricket as Jamaica's primary sport. It had been many years since the West Indies had been a force in cricket. I'd dread calling my dad when the West Indies were playing a Test series. It wouldn't matter how serious our conversation would be, my father would always need a moment to comment on West Indies' poor play. 'They're rubbish. No pride,' he'd bark. 'Dearie, dearie me.' My father would always end up forgiving them for their poor play, but there had been one incident that he had struggled to come to terms with.

In 2009, Jamaican-born West Indian opening batsman Chris Gayle declared that 'I wouldn't be so sad' if Test cricket died out.

'He acts like Test cricket is of no importance,' my father said. 'It's just my personal opinion but I've grown up with Test cricket since the 1950s. It's rather sad that he would say something like that. I don't hold a high opinion of him. Belittling Test cricket.'

To my father, the West Indies had temporarily stubbed out colonialism, its legacy, its rule, its rules. The Test match was the ultimate platform where the West Indies (unbeaten in a Test series from 1980 to 1995) had proven its greatness, mastering its 'masters' as if they/we invented the game.

The Windies had also won Test matches (particularly against England) by doing what practically every West Indian parent had told their British-born children, that 'you have to be twice as good as your white counterpart if you want to succeed'. But this sentiment had seemingly been replaced by a distinctly American *Get Rich or Die Tryin'** mentality.

As Usain Bolt lined up for the greatest 100 metres race of all time at London's Olympic Stadium, I knew my father would be watching.

Prior to the final on 5 August, the day after 'Super Saturday', I had given my children a Jamaican flag to share. They had been fully aware of Usain Bolt and the importance of his races. My son, almost two, could do the 'Lightning Bolt' pose. He could also mimic the 'Mobot' and Jamaican sprinter Yohan Blake's 'Beast' roar. My son even had a pose for Jessica Ennis, a kind of frozen running posture, even though the heptathlete didn't have a signature move. Bolt's races had become family viewing in my household. A time for everything to pause.

---

* *Get Rich or Die Tryin'*, a 2003 album by 50 Cent (Shady/Aftermath/Interscope).

Bolt had not been in the best of form leading up to the Olympics and the final featured many runners capable of beating the Jamaican had he been subpar. The race featured double Olympic silver medallist Richard 'Torpedo' Thompson from Trinidad & Tobago; former world record holder and Bolt's Jamaican teammate Asafa Powell; American Tyson Gay, the only other man to go under 9.7 seconds; Yohan Blake, the fastest man in the world in 2012; Justin Gatlin, a former Olympic champion and twice a drug cheat; and Ryan Bailey, who looked more like a Hollywood actor than a sprinter.

It had been the first time that the five fastest runners in history (Bolt, Gay, Blake, Gatlin, Powell) had faced each other in a race. What made the race even more compelling had been the characters of the runners. Powell, a persistent record breaker who often performed badly when it mattered; Gay, nervous, twitchy, anxious even; Blake, Bolt's training partner who, at times, looked like he had been hallucinating before a race; Gatlin, with a slight stammer, arrogant and the villain of the race for failing two drugs tests.

When the race started, it took time for Bolt to uncoil out of the starting blocks. Gatlin led. He floated. Powell, Gay and Blake practically by his side. Coming to the midway point, Bolt was in fifth or sixth place. But he was upright. He was Ali, Sir Galahad, in a Yellow Jersey. Mounting. Mountain. Within three or so strides, he went from fifth or sixth to first. Within three or so strides, Bolt's legendary competitors diminished. Looked small. Bolt streaked away to victory in an Olympic record of 9.63 seconds. Blake crept into second place.

Bolt had reaffirmed his place as track and field's greatest athlete. For his competitors, diminishing had never been so dominant. In all, three men clocked under 9.8 seconds and five dipped under 9.9 seconds, both records for a single race. My house rejoiced. My mum and dad's house rejoiced. Bolt had won again. Jamaica had won again. For all his flash and riches, Bolt was old school, never shying away from his Jamaican roots.

What had also become clear at the Olympics was that the *Get Rich or Die Tryin'* mentality had not consumed all African-American athletes. A new generation of rap-influenced competitors emerged who were also not trying to Be Like Mike.

By 2012, NBA star LeBron James had become the greatest player and biggest name in basketball since Jordan. When he joined fellow superstar Dwyane Wade at the Miami Heat in 2011, the team had become so famous they were known as the 'Heatles'. Yet it would be his tribute to slain teenager Trayvon Martin in March 2012 that would indicate that LeBron would not be following Jordan or Tyson's pathway to success.

On 11 February 2012, 17-year-old Trayvon Martin was shot dead for being tall, black and wearing a hoodie. He had been carrying a drink and a packet of Skittles while walking to his father's house in Sanford, Florida when George Zimmerman, a neighbourhood watch volunteer, called the police. Zimmerman said Trayvon looked suspicious. What happened next, not quite sure. Zimmerman may have pursued Martin. A scuffle ensued and Martin, previously minding his own business, was dead.

His blackness had been a threat. His height had been a threat. His attire had been a threat. President Barack Obama would later comment that, 'If I had a son, he'd look like Trayvon.' As had been the case with Stephen Lawrence in England, there probably wasn't a black parent in America who didn't fear for their sons.

LeBron led his Miami Heat teammates in a tribute to Trayvon Martin by taking a photo of the team wearing hooded sweatshirts. It had been one of many significant statements made by African-American athletes in the wake of Martin's death.

LeBron's activism made watching the 2012 version of the 'Dream Team' that much more special. I sat courtside and watched the final between the USA and Spain and knew that there was something different about this version of the Dream Team.

This had not been like the first and original Dream Team comprising Michael Jordan, Magic Johnson and Larry Bird. That had been the greatest team ever assembled. But it had also been characterised as an all-American, superhero team.

London 2012 represented a return to a more political African-American athlete. LeBron would be joined by his friends and fellow Dream Team teammates Carmelo Anthony and Chris Paul in providing a voice for black athletes. LeBron was not the first contemporary black athlete to protest, but he had brought his contemporaries in basketball 'out from behind the tinted glass of their Escalades'.[6]

While the Olympics tried to mask tensions in British society, it had also been a celebration of black excellence. Romantic. It was not only the brilliance of Luol and LeBron, but British boxer Nicola Adams' charm, smile and dazzling footwork, American tennis player Serena Williams annihilating Maria Sharapova and Kenyan 800 metres runner David Rudisha's smooth brilliance.

The Olympics also seemed to signify that something had been changing in the approach of the black athlete. It felt as if the black athlete's political voice was becoming more prominent again. It felt as if black athletes were starting to change the narrative, creating a new blueprint, one in which whiteness would be questioned, scrutinised, spotlighted.

For those people who questioned my support of black athletes, I asked them who their favourite athletes were. For those who asked why I struggled to support the England football team, I asked who they felt more loyalty to, their club side or the national team. For those who asked whether black people were more athletically gifted, I asked why there were few black cyclists, show jumpers and skiers. For those who asked why black comedians always talked about their African or Caribbean upbringing, I responded by asking why white comedians always talked about their (white) upbringing. For those who questioned the victims, the Evras, the Ferdinands, I asked, who controlled the narrative, owned the narrative, made the choice about what to print. For those who said to me, why do you see 'race' all the time, I replied but *you* see 'race' all the time too, just not consciously.

The black athlete in 2012 had been demanding more, of themselves, of their sports and of the societies they had been living in. More than anything, these athletes had started to try and control their own narratives and to influence the narratives for black people in society. A change was about to come.

CHAPTER 9

DRIVEN TO THE POINT OF MADNESS

'I feel most colored when I am thrown against a sharp white background.'

Zora Neale Hurston

THERE'S A SCENE IN THE MOVIE *IF BEALE STREET COULD TALK*, adapted from James Baldwin's novel, where the main character Tish, a 19-year-old black woman living in Harlem, is harassed in a corner shop by a white man. It's late. Dark. Tish is trying to buy some tomatoes but this man, identified as an Italian man in the book, inches up behind her. On screen, the harassment clear, visible but subtle; he's so close that he's touching her inappropriately. In the book his hand touches Tish's behind and he says, 'I can sure dig a tomato who digs tomatoes.'

The harassment had not been obvious enough for Tish to alert anyone in the shop. Her boyfriend, Fonny, was not far away. He had gone to buy some cigarettes. Tish didn't want him to return to a situation where he might get into a fight. She was also aware that a cop had been lingering outside the shop, near this scene. The Italian man continues to say provocative things to Tish, objectifying her, ignoring her even as she makes it clear that his advances are not welcomed. He's in her way, close, too close, touching, undeterred, exercising his right, what he feels is rightfully his, her black body, a black body.

Fonny enters the store, sees what's happening, grabs the Italian, drags him out of the shop and tosses him onto some garbage laying on the road. The beat down is brief, incomplete, the harasser is on his back, distressed, but conscious, aware of his surroundings. The cop crosses the road to confront Fonny. Tish steps in front of Fonny, creating a slight wall between her man and the policeman. 'I was sure that the cop intended to kill Fonny; but he could not kill Fonny if I could keep my body between Fonny and this cop; and with all my strength, with all my love, my prayers and armed with the knowledge that Fonny was not, after all, going to knock me to the ground, I held the back of my head against Fonny's chest, held both his wrists between my hands, and looked up into the face of this cop.'

She tells the policeman that she had been attacked. But the copper is more concerned with Fonny, and starts questioning him in an accusing, provocative manner. Meanwhile, the Italian gets up and runs away. A guilty move. But the policeman is intent on continuing to exert his authority, his power over Fonny, wanting to take him to the police station. It is only when the corner-store owner, an older woman, comes out of the shop and tells the policeman what happened, and tells him that she knows the couple, and that he should leave them alone, that the situation diffuses. Not before the cop threatens Fonny, implies that he will get him at some point.

On the walk home, Fonny marches a couple of paces ahead of Tish, holding the tomatoes in a paper bag. He turns to Tish and says, 'Don't ever try to protect me again. Don't do that.' After a short exchange, he throws the bag of tomatoes on a wall. In that moment, as the juice from the tomatoes crept down the walls, like blood seeping from a wound, I realised that I had felt that way at some point practically every day of my life since I had been a child.

Baldwin captured the rage of powerlessness that is felt by any 'relatively conscious' black person. It had been the Spotlight, blackness amplified on a white canvas, it had been racism, it had been the unseen, the blatant, the unspoken, it had been the need for white validation in order to protect a devalued black body, it had been the lack of belief in our voice, our voiceless-ness, my emasculation, my need to be protected, my pain at not being able to protect myself, it had been the lessening of our experiences, our invisibility, my invisibility; it had been the system, a system we pay for protection that often treats us as a threat.

It happens every day. It's not always blatant. It's not always offensive. But always there, from the decisions that are made when you're not in the room to the denial of your experience; from the people who ask where you are from to those who notice when there's too many of you in a room but fail to notice when there's none of you in a room. It's the way complaints from black people have little credibility unless uttered from the mouths of whites; it's the way black culture and intersectionality are misappropriated by mainstream institutions; it's black and brown people's diverse networks, experience/s of Britishness and knowledge of its history against a power structure with limited diversity in its networks, a fundamental belief in the virtues of Empire, with limited of experience of our history, our collective history, our hyphenated history, our side of the story; it's our social exclusion in the workplace, being accused of positive discrimination when promoted, being de-prioritised, de-racialised, being in spaces where 'race' is never mentioned and when it is mentioned someone saying 'what about other equality issues?' or 'can we stop using the term "race"?' It's the way in which people will not mention 'race', but when you speak of diversity, they immediately think of 'race'. It's the discomfort you see in white people's eyes when you mention 'race', when you mention 'race', when you mention 'race', when you mention 'race', when you mention 'race', that tells you that an honest conversation will not occur, that the fix is in, that humanity does not quite extend itself so easily to you; it's being the canary in the mine, it's your guilt, your Empire, your fear, your lack of understanding, your lifelong frame. My silence. Your frame that silences me.

Black and brown people are invisible in the places that matter, where decisions are made, and our visibility is amplified in areas of concern to this nation. And no one wants to talk about it because those with the power to be most vocal, they are either ideologically opposed or they just don't know. I ain't mad at ya. My rage comes from the unwillingness to listen. That inability to listen denies my experience and it invalidates my experience. I rage at the diversionary tactics. I rage at the notion that no one feels they can win with 'race', win this 'race'. I rage because, as business psychologist Binna Kandola and others have said, racism mutates. But racism is treated in British society as something static, a thing of the past, black people's problem, a thing perpetrated by a few, an issue resolved and only relevant because we black folks won't shut up about it.

Before we knew it, the nation had sleep-walked into Brexit and Donald Trump had become the voice of white America. Brexit had been in part sold to the public as a warped return to the Empire, an empire that enslaved black folks while Trump's rallying call to make 'America Great Again' had an undertone of making America white again. In both cases, like any old-school sci-fi movie, there was no vision of blackness in the future.

Trump may have been sacked from most jobs in the UK due to his racist and sexist statements. Yet he became the President of the United States. This was a man who had been taken to court for discriminatory practices against minorities, a man who once funded anti-Native American ads, called Mexicans 'rapists' and 'criminals', claimed that African-American young people 'have no spirit', planned to ban people from Muslim-majority countries, criticised Puerto Ricans after its hurricane, said that Haitian immigrants 'all have AIDS' and allegedly called African and Central American nations 'shithole countries'.

The rise in 'race'-related hate crimes after the EU Referendum suggested that Britain now had carte blanche to say what it really felt about immigrants. There were many places that voted to Leave that had low immigration numbers, yet immigration had been among the main issues of concern to people. It felt as if for years the English had tolerated black, brown and now Eastern European folks while harbouring resentment at people they felt were taking their jobs, putting too much of a strain on the NHS, diluting Britishness while not saying anything through fear of being accused of racism.

Soon after Brexit, I was coming out of the front door of my house in southeast London with my kids when a group of white youths in a car shouted racist abuse at me and my family. Fortunately, my kids did not hear but wondered why I'd shouted something back at them as their car sped off. My parents faced a similar situation in Essex, a place where they had lived for almost 30 years, without incident. My kids support England. My parents have spent more time in England than in their place of birth, Jamaica. Yet in both instances, all the assailants saw was the colour of our skins.

As mad as Brexit made me, at least I knew I wasn't going mad. For years I had felt silenced by the overwhelming denial of 'race' as a factor in the disparities faced by the black community. Brexit told me that everything I felt had been real, and there had been a sense of relief. But it was not a lasting satisfaction, only a somewhat depressing illustration of how little we had progressed and how bold we would need to be to change things significantly.

When footballer Eniola Aluko lodged a complaint in 2016 to the FA regarding racist language she reportedly had experienced from the England women's football coach Mark Sampson, the case encapsulated some of my rage at how racism was increasingly being silenced.

Aluko, born in Lagos, Nigeria and raised in Birmingham, had established herself as one of England's best female footballers. She had won 102 caps for England, scoring 33 goals. She had competed in three World Cups, represented Great Britain at the London 2012 Olympics, became the first woman to be a pundit on *Match of the Day*, and achieved all of this while gaining first-class honours in law and qualifying as a solicitor. Aluko represented her England teammates in negotiating improved terms for women from the FA's central contracts system. Women's salaries have since increased from £16,000 per year in 2013 to £25,000 per year in 2017. It's fair to say that Aluko's record on and off the pitch had been impressive.

Sampson had allegedly made inappropriate remarks with 'derogatory, racial and prejudicial connotations' to Aluko and a player of mixed heritage, Drew Spence. These allegations emerged after Aluko had been asked to take part in a confidential 'Culture Review'. She was asked to share her experiences playing for England, including what it had been like playing for Sampson. Soon after making her revelation, Aluko was dropped by Sampson from the England team due to her attitude and behaviour. Aluko then received notice that she would be under investigation for her work as a sports lawyer. The FA said that none of these incidents were related to what Aluko had said in the review.

The FA launched an independent inquiry after Aluko's revelations, but her grievance was dismissed. Aluko was awarded £80,000 compensation related to, as would later be revealed, 'loss of earnings and future earnings'. The FA said they had agreed to pay her the money to avoid any distractions ahead of the women's European Championships in the Netherlands in 2017. The case was dismissed, so was Aluko. She was not picked to play for England in the Euros.

That appeared to be the end of it, until the Culture Review and subsequent case leaked to the press. It reveals what Aluko had reported in the review about Sampson's racially insensitive remarks. Aluko told Sampson that her family would be attending the England versus Germany game at Wembley to which he replied, 'Make sure they don't come over with Ebola.' Sampson had also at one time said to Spence: 'How many times have you been arrested? Four times, isn't it?' Spence, who has never been arrested, had been the only person of colour in that meeting. Aluko felt that this was a 'negative prejudicial comment'.

After the press revelations, the FA continued to defend their initial inquiry decision and Sampson. Sampson would say that his conscience was clear. He would also say that he could not recall the Ebola comment, which had been at odds with a statement he had given to the inquiry earlier. Meanwhile, the FA had re-opened a safeguarding case against Sampson from 2014, made while he had been working at Bristol Academy. The FA sacked Sampson based on the safeguarding allegations. Soon after, the FA changed its mind about the Aluko case. The FA said that Sampson twice made 'ill-judged attempts at humour, which, as a matter of law, were discriminatory on grounds of race'.

Aluko had won. Well, sort of. A bit like coming third in a race only to find out later that the runners ahead of you were busted for drugs. Despite the evidence, the FA or its initial investigation did not conclude that Sampson had been ill judged in his humour. It appeared to come out at the point it became major news, at a point when the government's Department for Culture, Media and Sport (DCMS) was involved, at a point when Aluko's name had been 'trending'. Aluko had been vindicated. She had exposed, and she had done so, somehow, by keeping her sanity, maintaining a high level of poise and not breaking at a point when most people would have thrown the towel in. Third had become first, but something was lost in 'victory'. But a 'victory' nonetheless and one that would highlight some systemic problems deep in the heart of English football.

I was glad that she won because too often in the past, when black sports men and women had gone up against the establishment, they had lost, even if they had won. When I say establishment, I'm not only referring to the authorities like the FA. I'm also talking about battles against the media, and battles against individuals who in some way represent elements of the establishment. Such encounters against the establishment always felt like a no-win race.

It was how I felt when middle-distance runner Sebastian Coe criticised sprinter Linford Christie in 2001. Christie had been banned for two years for the use of the banned substance nandrolone in 1999. He had been cleared of any guilt by UK Athletics but the International Association of Athletics Federations (IAAF) overturned the decision. On the week that the ban had been lifted, Coe penned an article for *The Times* questioning the former Olympic champion's character. In the article, Coe called him 'boorish'. He said that when Christie had been Great Britain captain, he isolated British officials with his 'jive' talking. It had been like a nail in Christie's reputation.

Christie had always had a patchy relationship with the media and the public. Yet he had been Olympic, World, European and Commonwealth champion in the 100 metres, arguably the most competitive and certainly most revered event in track and field. He was also one of the most outspoken athletes. Despite what the press may have thought of him as a person, he had been highly respected as an athlete. In the December 1995–January 1996 issue of *Total Sport*, Christie ranked third in a poll of the 100 greatest

British sports people of all time. *Total Sport* polled 1,000 sports journalists, broadcasters and personalities, and he finished behind George Best and Ian Botham.

In February 2002, Coe and Christie battled on Simon Mayo's show on BBC Radio 5 Live. The two went back and forth without a resolution.

Coe, a former Conservative MP, would end up becoming chairman of London's bid to host the 2012 Games in 2004. Christie was not involved in the bid. Even though his drugs ban had been cleared by UK Athletics, even though it had come at the tail end of his career when semi-retired, Christie had no recourse for redemption. Against the prototypical English gentleman that was Coe, Christie had no chance. It had not been a matter of 'race' to me whatsoever. It just did not feel like it could be, would ever be, a fair argument. I also thought it some-what unfair that Christie, as a figurehead, has been missing from mainstream athletics ever since. I'm not sure Christie would still poll in the top-ten greatest British athletes now, and I'm not sure he would be so absent from our screens had it not been for his conflict with Coe. But who knows. When you sit on the outside of these things, you never quite know the full story. It just felt like a shame that two decades on from polling third in the *Total Sport* list, we just don't see enough of Christie anymore.

I also felt that the biggest loser in the Anton Ferdinand–John Terry case had been the Ferdinands. Terry had been fined and banned for using discriminatory language. Many people condemned him, although not strictly, I believe, because of what he said to Anton. There had been many incidents in the past where Terry's character had been called into question. When in 2010 it was reported that he slept with England teammate and good friend Wayne Bridge's former girlfriend, paid for her abortion, paid her money to keep quiet and tried to impose a super-injunction to stop the press from revealing details of the incident, Terry's popularity plummeted. He was stripped of the England captaincy as a result, replaced by Anton's brother Rio Ferdinand. Terry would later regain the captaincy.

John Terry is the antithesis of Coe. But he too represented an aspect of Englishness widely adored; he was the bulldog, the fighter, the warrior, the captain of the army, the heart and soul who would take a bullet for the team. In contrast, his teammate in the England football team, Rio Ferdinand, had a reputation for playing like a continental footballer, the type you'd see from Italy; stylish, technical, composed, comfortable on the ball. Terry appeared to be the working-class hero, a grafter who made something from nothing, conquered against the odds, everything an English player should be, a bleed-for-your-country type.

Through much of their careers, Terry and Ferdinand had been rivals. Terry's Chelsea and Ferdinand's Manchester United dominated the game through much of the noughties and early 2010s, interchanging league titles and scooping the Champions League. Terry always appeared to present a conception of Englishness that everyone was more comfortable with. To me, Ferdinand represented the future; a patriot with a bit of bulldog himself (though Terry, for all his bulldog qualities, had hardly been a crude, Captain Caveman player, for he too had been technically gifted) but with a hyphenated style and a modern approach to defending.

Despite the charges, after the Anton Ferdinand incidents, then England manager Fabio Cappello sought to excuse his captain's behaviour and felt the FA had been wrong to again strip him of the captaincy. While Anton's career faded, and while the Ferdinands dealt with threats, it would be Rio Ferdinand's England career that would also pay the price. While never proven, it felt as if the England management team had to pick between the two. Ferdinand would later express his disappointment to the *Guardian* (24 September 2014) at being overlooked by England manager Roy Hodgson over what Ferdinand perceived as worries about the 'working relationship' between him and Terry. I don't think that either player had been approached about the possibility of playing together again. What we do know is that they were the two best centre-backs in the country, but the preference had been for Terry. Ferdinand was not selected for England's Euro 2012 squad, even after Gary Cahill picked up an injury and had been ruled out of the squad. Roy Hodgson, who had taken over from Cappello, picked a novice in Martin Kelly over Ferdinand as Cahill's replacement. Rio had paid the price and no one it seemed had a sensible reason why this had been the case.

Despite Eniola Aluko's 'victory', it was not without consequence. Her international career seemed to be over, even though she had been the victim, even though the FA had apparently fluffed the original inquiry, even though Mark Sampson had reportedly made racially insensitive remarks. Worse still, it appeared that no one within the system, not the FA, not anyone within England's senior management set-up nor anyone involved in the inquiry, could quite grasp how flawed and insensitive Sampson's comments had been and the implications of what he had said coming from someone in a position of power. Sampson's sacking, the FA's back-tracking, stunk of a cover-up, an attempt to sweep the incident under the carpet.

Aluko appeared in front of a select committee convened by the DCMS. Allegedly only an hour before the committee, it was revealed by barrister Katharine Newton, who originally carried out the independent report, that they now found Sampson's remarks to be discriminatory. But Aluko's appearance and the written evidence she submitted revealed more about the England women's setup.

I have known a lot of black people over the years who have not complained about or reported racist incidents through fear of being marginalised, through fear of not having their complaint taken seriously, through fear of being stereotyped as 'chippy', through fear of the incident being covered up, through fear of being ruled out of gaining top positions, through fear of jeopardising their careers. I'd make a bet that for every major racist incident in sport or otherwise that makes the press, there are hundreds more that never see the light of day. We whisper. We whisper because the price you pay is too steep. You're in the minority. Even if you win, you're unlikely to win because you've rocked the boat, because not many people truly believe or understand the severity of your complaint, because you will be perceived as some sort of radical. Aluko could have stayed silent. At one point, FA Chief Executive Martin Glenn allegedly asked her to issue a statement saying that the FA was not institutionally racist, at which point they would release the balance of her compensation money (a claim Glenn denied). But she didn't stay silent and risked marginalisation as a result.

Aluko's written statement revealed that, from 2014 to 2016, the time in which she played under Sampson, she scored 15 goals in 16 starts for England. In her written evidence submitted to the DCMS, Aluko suggested that she had been targeted negatively by Sampson's staff, bullied and, worst perhaps, she had been systematically marginalised during Sampson's tenure.

'28. In February 2014, one month into Mark Sampson's management, I was at home watching my individual performance clips on a Replay Analysis system that hosts a full video of England games. At the time, staff members wore microphones to communicate amongst themselves.

'29. Whilst watching the game I clearly heard staff members Lee Kendall (Goalkeeper coach) and Naomi Datson (Former Sport scientist) discussing me on the microphones. Whilst I was on the ball, Naomi Datson could be heard saying, "Her fitness results are good," and Lee Kendall replied, "Yes, but she is lazy as f**k." Lee Kendall can also be heard later in the game shouting, "Oh f**k off, Eni" after I gave possession of the ball away ("Replay Analysis incident").

'30. I scored a goal and assisted in that particular match that finished 3–1 against Finland. No positive comments can be heard from either staff member at the time of either goal or assist.

'31. Furthermore, Lee Kendall did not use such language about any other member of the team throughout the 90-minute match.'

Aluko would later state:

'55. My evidence regarding the Ebola Comment was referenced in a legal letter to the FA in November 2016 (see Appendix 5), but was not requested by the FA legal team. Given the particularly serious nature of my complaints, the November 2016 letter was copied to FA Chairman Greg Clarke and Chief Executive Martin Glenn in an email. We felt that it was entirely appropriate to include the Chairman and Chief Executive of the FA in the email. However, Greg Clarke replied in an email about my complaint: "I've no idea why you are sending me this. Perhaps you could enlighten me?" I found the dismissive and disrespectful tone of Greg Clarke's response to my complaints extraordinary. I submit to the committee that Greg Clarke's response, as the ultimate leader of the organisation, is reflective of the unprofessional, disrespectful and dismissive attitude of senior members of the FA in relation to my grievances.'

Aluko's stance had been brave. She had a lot to lose. You're not talking about a footballer earning millions of pounds with millions of Twitter followers playing in front of thousands every week for a Premier League club. She had been fighting deeply patriarchal structures as well as a racially discriminatory culture. Aluko's stand appeared to go unnoticed by her England teammates. Allegedly none of them contacted her through the case. The reasons why, only they will know. When England defeated Russia 6–0 during a World Cup qualifier, every member of England women's team publicly ran off the pitch and embraced Sampson. 'United as a team,' said Nikita Parris who, after scoring, joined the rest of the team on the pitch to go over to Sampson. It appeared that football trumped ethics. Patriarchy trumped feminism. Feminism trumped racism. There shouldn't have been a hierarchy. Whether intentional or not, the gesture by the women's team suggested that they had sided with Sampson over Aluko.

In response, Aluko tweeted: 'For the most together team in the world, tonight's "message" only shows a level of disrespect that represents division and selfish action.'

In the press, most writers praised Aluko. There had been negative press too, focused on whether Aluko had been a good teammate or not, whether she was good enough to play for England and whether the comments by Sampson really deserved such attention. Sport's unwritten code of 'unethics' tended to underpin such commentary. *This is sport, you wouldn't understand. Things are different in sport, you cannot apply the same rules to sport as you would in other industries. PC gone mad. It's only banter.*

Through much of the debate, I cannot recall many footballers expressing much of an opinion on the case. It had only been former England goalkeeper David James who'd broken the silence when he tweeted: 'Mark Sampson sacked as @England women's manager?! Seems some wasted talent can't deal with the fact they aren't good enough! #enialuko.'

James also said: 'Basically, Mark Sampson is being told, "even though you may have changed, you are being F**KED because of your past". #bollocks.'

It was left to grime artist Stormzy to use his voice to defend Aluko. He criticised David James when he tweeted: 'Where's David James the absolute chief?'

He added: 'YOU ABSOLUTE DICKHEAD.'[1]

As with the Evra–Suárez and Ferdinand–Terry cases, the victim's lens had been lost. The Aluko case had become less about what she had experienced and more about what she must have done wrong. It had become more about the FA trying to avoid being called racist and less about the facts surrounding the case. Through it all, I can't recall hearing much support for Aluko come from within the sport's world and the voices that tended to be heard the most happened to be white, male and privileged.

I had heard and read all the negative comments about Aluko. For me, it was simple. A person of colour had been treated differently to others within the team. Her protest and I think her education made those within football's fraternity deeply uncomfortable. If she had, as some in the press suggested, been a bad teammate then provide concrete evidence and drop her or give her an opportunity to improve. But to suggest that she brought the case forward because she had not been picked for England was hardly a move that would get her back in the team. She would have been better off staying silent. She wouldn't have been any happier, but she wouldn't have been marginalised.

'Race', people's fear of it, people's lack of understanding of it, people's unwillingness to confront it, people not knowing how to talk about it, had blurred the situation and the victim, in this case Eniola Aluko, had paid the price. Mark Sampson had ultimately been sacked over a safeguarding issue, not the Aluko case. Aluko had ultimately 'justified' the compensation she had been paid, although this covered loss of earnings. As said, victory had come in the fact that Aluko had been vindicated. But the case needn't have transpired the way it did. Aluko's case also illustrated that there had been a clear lack of understanding of the experiences of black women in sport.

I thought Aluko's case was an important moment for British sport. As a black person, there are normally three ways in which you deal with racism. You confront it, tolerate it or joke about it. I've tried all three. When I've confronted it people have been either too scared to deal with me or accused me of having a chip on my shoulder. When I've tolerated it, nothing changes in that situation except for my mental wellbeing. When I've joked about it, I've maintained relationships, appeared like a good sport, but I've never felt good about myself.

Historically, the Black-British sports person has rarely confronted racism head on, not in the manner that Aluko took on the FA. We had seen Devon Malcolm, footballer Stan Collymore and Rio and Anton Ferdinand confront racism, report incidents, but in each case it had generally been an individual incident. I certainly had not seen anyone in sport in England take a stance as radical as the Newham 7 or the Race Today Collective in the eighties. Most sports stars had generally tolerated racism, often with great dignity, for which they had won great acclaim, or laughed it off, been a good sport, provided a comfortable example of how blacks should treat racism. Aluko gave me hope that more British athletes would confront it; but do so in a more systematic way.

After many years of apathy and fear of losing what is ultimately a time-limited career, African-American athletes had started to take up the fight against racism too. They had been inspired by the Black Lives Matter movement. The movement evolved after George Zimmerman had been acquitted for the murder of Trayvon Martin on 13 July 2013. When the activist Alicia Garza wrote a response to the acquittal on Facebook, Patrisse Khan-Cullors re-posted using the hashtag #BlackLivesMatter and Opal Tometi would further spread the word across social media. The female trio's call to action would result in the development of over 40 Black Lives Matters chapters, including movements in England and Canada, birthing, for some, the civil rights movement for the twenty-first century. The deaths of Eric Garner, who had been filmed being put in a chokehold by police while repeatedly saying to the officers, 'I can't breathe', and 18-year-old Michael Brown at the hands of white police officer Darren Wilson, which sparked the protests in Ferguson, Missouri in 2014, and many more, furthered a movement that refused to be silenced, refused to be hierarchal, refused to let people forget the names of the victims, refused to dilute their message and refused to let patriarchal approaches to black activism in the past dictate the future of this movement.

African-American athletes followed. Most famously in 2016, American footballer Colin Kaepernick refused to stand during the national anthem before NFL games. He said, 'I am not going to stand up to show pride in a flag for a country that oppresses black people and people of color.' Kaepernick kneeling while the national anthem played became the most distinct political gesture since Tommie Smith and John Carlos's Black Power salute at the 1968 Mexico Olympics. The movement spread with more NFL players kneeling in protest against police brutality, and divided opinion in America. Kaepernick's stance squarely put politics back on the sporting agenda, although at a cost to his career.

'The seminal issue, from about 1975 to 2010, some thirty-five years, was the absence of a defining ideology and movement that would frame and inform activist positions,' said Harry Edwards, the sociologist and activist who had been at the forefront of the Black Power protests at the 1968 Olympics.

During a year, 2016, when Muhammad Ali, perhaps the greatest symbol of athlete activism, had died, his spirit lived on in a whole new generation of athletes who had started to recognise that while progress had been made, black people remained severely disadvantaged in American society. Like the Black Lives Matter movement, many of these athletes, like Ali, Smith and Carlos in the sixties, had been widely condemned, often being branded as racists and unpatriotic for protesting against systemic racism.

Few elite athletes carried the fight as much as Serena Williams. I stopped watching Serena Williams play tennis after 2012. More than any athlete, she was the one who had been the most excruciating to watch. The athlete whose every success filled me with joy, whose every failure made me upset. After a time, I couldn't watch.

Perhaps it was because Serena was doing Serena. Little or no façade. Didn't hide, mask, veil, lessen herself in the way I had to progress through my career. She did not try to present blackness in a way that would be palatable to us, to them. Didn't try to impress, to woo. Watching Serena had been like watching some sort of reality no longer confined to the 'hood, but in the whitest of white environments. Tennis. This had been, like, blackness on prime-time television, in the House of Lords, in your office.

So, I couldn't watch Serena. I couldn't watch what I had been, aspired to be: unfiltered, undiluted, bigger, higher, wider. I could have been more forceful in my convictions like Serena. When I watched Serena, I realised that I had been searching for myself through the eyes of my oppressors. I found this deeply uncomfortable. I found watching her deeply uncomfortable.

She grew up in Compton, started playing tennis at three, was coached by her father Richard, became a child prodigy, suffered racist snubs and boos frequently, sported those braids. She had been booed so unmercifully in Indian Wells that she would not return for over a decade, she became the world's number one female tennis player, survived the murder of half-sister Yetunde Price, completed the 'Serena Slam' (holding all four Grand Slams in a calendar year), endured vile and racist comments about her body, continued to win Grand Slams, continued to show dignity, continued to face snubs and micro-aggressions on tour from her peers and from commentators, continued to win Slams, continued to show dignity, was treated as if she had some kind of unfair advantage over the other 'girls', continued to be unfavoured by crowds, watched less successful tennis players like Maria Sharapova scoop big sponsorship deals, occasionally cursed in matches, suffered a pulmonary embolism (blood clot in her lung) then developed a hematoma in her stomach, was called a gorilla, shamed even more because of her body, became an Olympic champion, won more Grand Slam singles titles than any women in the Open era, won the Australian Open while pregnant, had severe complications during the birth of her daughter, and exposed the double standards in umpiring at the US Open.

American sportswriter Dave Zirin penned an article called 'Serena Williams is Today's Muhammad Ali'. Serena Williams was not today's Muhammad Ali. She is Serena Williams. An original. The GOAT. The blueprint for other athletes to follow. Serena would become a supporter of black rights, of women's rights, and would do so through a torrent of racist commentary from the media, biased judging from umpires, unequal treatment when juxtaposed with her male counterparts. Through it all, Serena kept on being Serena. Didn't play by anyone's rules, kept on winning, remained outspoken, held her poise as lesser talents garnered bigger endorsement deals.

I understood how difficult it could be to blend, to fit in, to dim the Spotlight, to overcome over-scrutiny, to have no room for error, to be profiled, to see those sneers and stares, to never quite belong, to having a sense of injustice long before you're old enough to go to the corner shop alone. But I never had to face those issues on television, in front of thousands of people, while being booed while dressed in white, while being black, female and from the 'hood. Serena had, along with a number of black female athletes, become a figurehead in the resurrection of activism in sport.

To my knowledge, no sport or indeed league carried the fight against systemic racism and sexism more than the WNBA, the Women's National Basketball Association. I am not sure there is a league in a major sport across the globe that could match the WNBA in terms of diversity and activism. And, as is often the case, the WNBA's athletes had more to lose than their male counterparts.

The top female basketball players in the WNBA will pull in around $110,000 per season in comparison to the top NBA players who will earn upwards of $28 million a season. Yet in 2016, many WNBA athletes, including its best player at the time, Maya Moore, wore black T-shirts while warming up for games in support of Black Lives Matter. The WNBA initially fined the women $500 for violating the league's uniform policy. The players would not relent. They continued to talk politics at press conferences and openly protested on social media until WNBA Commissioner Lisa Borders retreated, then backed her players. Howard Megdal, Editor-in-Chief of *High Post Hoops,* said: 'When you have a league with so many women of color, so many of them educated and attuned to social justice issues, the league realized there was no neutral ground.'

In addition, there had been a great deal of solidarity between African-American and white players around the Black Lives Matter protests. The WNBA now openly celebrates the activism of its athletes. The WNBA's leading players have protested against Trump's travel ban, largely aimed at Muslim-majority countries, supported charitable causes dealing with sexual assault or LGBT+ communities (many of the WNBA's leading players are publicly out). These athletes in the WNBA, black and white, had shown that you could protest without fear, that diversity in sport did not need to mask realities in society, that sport could provide a vision of what a more cohesive society could look like and that none of this was easy. It has been, can be, messy. The WNBA had also shown, like the Black Lives Matter movement, that black activism in the future would be intersectional in approach.

Two years before the Eniola Aluko case broke, I hosted a roundtable at the House of Lords chaired by Baroness Grey-Thompson titled 'Non-white, poor, disabled … So what?' It was a deliberately provocative title. So many of the conversations I'd been having in sport had been about power (who held it), narrative (who owned it) and practice (who homogenised it). These conversations tended to take place in silence. Whispered. Thompson had been among the most vocal advocates for more inclusive practices in sport.

At the time, I had been involved heavily in sport, but in the development side, supporting and funding programmes that used sport to help young people facing disadvantage. I had worked for many elite athletes who wanted to use their name to help young people. But I also realised that while the sport for development world, the world I had been in, was a million miles away from the elite level, there remained many barriers to inclusion that ran right through the bloodstream of the sport's industry. I wanted to have an open conversation. I wanted to challenge, to be challenged.

There were many leaders in the field present that day. Some had been athletes, others had watched and campaigned from the margins. They understood about sexism in sport. Racism in sport. Ableism in sport. Homophobia in sport. They also understood that when gender intersected with 'race', ability, sexual preference and/or class, it created multiple barriers to inclusion, something rarely discussed in sport. But many of the people around the table that day had been openly challenging the status quo in sport. This included Rimla Akhtar from the Muslim Women's Sports Foundation, Maria Bobenrieth, Executive Director of Women Win, which uses sport to achieve gender equity, Joyce Cook, Founding and Managing Director of the Centre for Access to Football in Europe (CAFE) with a vision of 'Total Football – Total Access' for disabled people; former Paralympic gold medallist Tara Flood, the Chief Executive of Alliance for Inclusive Education (ALLFIE) and Kevin Hylton.

The roundtable had been facilitated by Thompson and Michelle Moore who opened the session by stating that people in sport needed to recognise that 'when intersecting forms of oppression overlap in terms of multiple levels of discrimination this is not often discussed, especially in relation to the engagement of ethnic minority, disabled girls participating in sport … when there are competing forms of oppression i.e. sexism, racial, homophobia, disableism, cultural and religious bias – what is it that can be learnt from each form of oppression – to fully understand the barriers which exist for women and girls and their access and engagement with sport? Furthermore, if we understand the barriers but not the experiences and intersections of discrimination, how can we ensure practice is inclusive?'[2]

It had been a stimulating session and incredibly open. We knew we were speaking to the converted, even if many of us were coming from different perspectives. We knew that the people who needed to be around the table next time were the suits, those with the power to change, many who would probably not even recognise the terms we had been using or the experiences we had been talking about through the day. They probably would not realise that these barriers to grassroots and elite sport existed. They probably would not recognise how complicit they were. I'm not sure they would even realise that, if not for ethical reasons, a more nuanced approach to inclusion at all levels would get more people active, widen their talent pool, help retain talent, get the best out of their talent pool and help the country excel in sport.

Moore would later write about intersectionality, a term coined in 1989 by American professor Kimberlé Crenshaw, and how this can play out in sport. 'By the age of 14, girls drop out of sport at twice the rate of boys. Research from Women in Sport emphasises factors that include social stigma, lack of access, safety and lack of positive role models. Barriers to participation for young women are heightened when gender intersects with race, low economic status and/or disability, with dress-code, poor or culturally inappropriate coaching, non-segregated activities, lack of specialist equipment, prejudice, lack of user group consultation and non-inclusive practices.'[3]

Aluko would later say that, 'Some of this is lack of appreciation of what racism is. A lot of this is, "it hasn't happened to me, I can't relate to that, so I'm not going to comment". That, to me, can't be a team. That can't be sport either.'

For those who say that we need to keep politics out of sport, that would mean that sport is somehow exempt from the institutional biases that pervade our society. An island on its own. Escapism. Little else. A place where you dare to dream. But that is not a reality for many people in or on the periphery of sport. I have never met an athlete who entered sport to get into politics.

It is clear, however, that once a Black-British athlete enters the politics of sport, the likelihood of that athlete remaining in sport is limited. Former basketball player John Amaechi is probably the most vocal athlete of colour I have personally known. I have interviewed him several times over the last 20 years. He was the first English player to start in an NBA game and the first NBA athlete to come out. He is also a psychologist who invested £2.1 million in the Amaechi Basketball Centre (ABC) to support a new generation of players from Manchester to fulfil their potential in the sport.

Amaechi has been vocal about British basketball, hyper-masculinity in sport, racism, homophobia and sport's capacity to tackle social issues among many topics. He is, alongside Steve Bucknall and Luol Deng, one of the three most important English basketball players. Amaechi has remained vocal because he knows he can earn a living outside of sport. Had this not been the case, he would have been severely compromised.

'You really have to decide that you don't ever want to have anything to do with sport,' he said. 'I really am not interested in having a career in sport, but there is no possibility of me having a career in sport ever because I am persona non grata in sport in every significant way.'

For most black athletes, activism is understandably difficult. They are managing what is ultimately a short career while trying to fulfil their dreams, often with limited exposure to the real world. Being vocal is often a price that is too heavy to pay.

'I will not criticise athletes, people of colour,' said Chris Grant. 'Anyone who copes and retains their sanity and some shred of dignity with pressures, I take my hat off to them.'

It has yet to be seen whether Black-British athletes will follow in the footsteps of their African-American counterparts, who had been inspired by Black Lives Matter and other campaigns. Black and brown people's activism in the UK has also been reignited in the 2010s. Although nowhere near as famous as Black Lives Matters, there were many groups that once more started protesting against structural racism. These groups were happy to exist on the margins. They were not seeking approval from the mainstream. This felt like a return to the seventies and eighties, when you had groups like the Newham 7, Race Today Collective and the Organisation of Women of African and Asian Descent (OWAAD) who were direct in their politics and their methods to achieving social change. The big difference this time round had been the prominence of participants with multiple identities, that more of these movements were led by women of colour and that the primary frame had been distinctly intersectional.

While the level of hostility directed at black athletes has subsided since the early eighties, I am not sure conditions to be more vocal about 'race' issues have improved.

But this is Britain. Am I proud to be British? I am, but on my own terms. For me to be a proud Brit, I would need to be a native son, and I am not. It would mean having to compromise a part of me, a part of my history that is integral to my identity because that conflicts with British society, the institution. I can loosen when the situation requires me to do so. Compromise a little. But I refuse to lose my heritage and the value of shared experience. Blackness. I am what I am. I am not what you want me to be.

I can only hope that the things I teach my kids, about post-war immigration patterns and the true legacy of colonialism, will be common on the school curriculum one day, so we have a better understanding of each other. I only hope that black folks recognise how moveable our culture has become and will not be so reactive to the Spotlight or the Shadow. I hope that we as a black community focus less on 'selling out' and 'what's cool' and focus more on the commonalities of our struggles, which will include people from backgrounds other than our own. I hope that people will read this as openly and honestly as I've written it and are willing to listen and debate without being defensive. I hope that people accept that difference is fine, appreciate the true value of difference, that difference does not necessarily dilute but can enhance. I hope that we all accept that we often judge each other by our own flawed moral standards but that conflict is not necessarily always a bad thing. I hope that when I take my children to museums or to historic buildings that our side of the story is being told. I hope that Britishness shifts because of values not economics. I hope that more people realise that the current conception of Empire is flawed and a return to it would be about as realistic as nineteenth-century pugilist Tom Cribb defeating Anthony Joshua. I hope that there is a move towards an intersectional lens in how we tackle social and sporting issues. I hope that one day black boys will not be the canaries in the mine. I hope that mass disaffection and anger does not spiral out of control and that we stop attacking each other. I hope that more people realise how governments stack poor folks on top of each other like Russian nesting dolls and how this causes so much conflict. I hope that apathy dies. I hope that Black-British athletes find their voice, whatever that may be, enough so they can feel some ease.

I accept Britishness on my terms. I rarely use the words 'we', 'us' and 'our'. I find it hard when I'm made to feel like I do not belong. I cannot talk about 'we' when it comes to football, although my son openly can. I do not stop him from doing so. I do not see myself, my culture, my conception of self within the England football team. My son does. My family has changed through the generations. I guess I had been hopeful that British or English society and its attitude towards black people would evolve as swiftly too.

I feel British when I watch the Great Britain basketball team. While I accept that 'black brains' have been systemically marginalised from the centre of decision making in basketball, at least when I go to see Great Britain play – and before you ask, it is always a mixed team, a blend – I see me, the hyphenated me.

But sport rarely shifts things fundamentally in society. Back in 1998, we all celebrated the French national side winning the World Cup because the team included players from Algerian, Senegalese and Ghanaian backgrounds. It had been a celebration of multiculturalism. How so many colours could unite under one flag and win, be national heroes. Yet this has not necessarily improved 'race' relations in France. Black folks are still being arrested for congregating together, still being disadvantaged systemically, still being perceived as a threat.

I can see why sport is symbolic and always political. It masks the realities. It will not change anything politically. But it can provide a vision. It can create visions of national identity, give people an idea of what things could be like, bring people round the table who wouldn't normally do so. We have seen it in the power of the West Indies, the pathways opened by Michael Jordan, the vision created by the French national team, the way in which the charity Fight for Peace bonds previously troubled communities. We have seen how Cyrille, Justin and Garth 'swamped' English football and changed the racial make-up of the game in ways no one could have perceived in the early eighties. We have seen Serena Williams, a black woman on top who has not tried to be 'perfect' to succeed, opening up pathways to gender equity for women of all shades. Aluko has no doubt opened the door for Black-British athletes to be more vocal about their experiences, to confront more, tolerate less. John Amaechi and ex-footballer Jason Roberts have shown that athlete activism in the UK is alive.

Maybe in the future there will be more leagues like the WNBA, which treats its female athletes' voices as an asset and not something to suppress. I question whether sport can change the world. I know, as a tool, it can be incredibly powerful in achieving social change, engaging the hard to engage and in bonding communities. I also know that, for all the positive images, it is easily manipulated, used for propaganda, and reinforces many of the power structures that exist in society. It is not a meritocracy as some would believe. The image of black athletes on the field is not some indication of progress off the field. We have wealthy black footballers, but their capital and power in no way compares to the owners of the football clubs. The absence of black faces in the boardroom also tells a story that we remain more comfortable with blacks in positions that reinforce stereotypes than in positions of power.

As John Amaechi said: 'The presumption [is] that negroes are magic in only one way, in that their muscle fibres are somehow magical. That's a really comfortable place for the vast majority of people, and there is a racial dimension to this, no doubt, of the white governance of the sport. They're really comfortable with athletes being notable for their athleticism. Once it transcends into a point where what they're doing with their brain starts to match what they might have done with their body, the balance is all wrong because where are we in this world if white people don't have the brains to be in charge of stuff. In sport that is particularly challenging.'

What sport does provide is an example of what society could be. It disarms enough that people cannot see restrictions. The images of Viv, Cyrille and Justin had not been fruitless. They sensitised the public to a more multicultural Britain, to a Britain where blacks were less of a threat. It had been the way with Jackie Robinson and with Muhammad Ali. But it will not fundamentally change things. As said, racism mutates, the system, the Spotlight finds ways to respond, to adapt. Sport can, however, show a way, and this is powerful and valuable.

It is probably the reason why Donald Trump has frequently clashed with black athletes, trying consistently to put them in their place. At times, it feels as if this is one of his key policies. Trump, in reference to the kneel-down protests in the NFL, said, 'Wouldn't you love to see one of these NFL owners, when somebody disrespects our flag, to say: "Get that son of a bitch off the field right now. Out. He's fired. He's fired!"' Trump rescinded on the customary White House visit for NBA champions after Golden State's Stephen Curry said he wouldn't go. Trump also had a war of words on social media with LeBron James, the greatest basketball player on the planet.

But that's the point. While the public face of sport suggests that progress has been made, the continued marginalisation of black folks from positions of power remains a constant, which is why Aluko's case had been so important. If sport can show us the way, then Aluko's challenge to the system is just as powerful as a Mo Farah or Anthony Joshua victory. I agree with what John Amaechi said, society is comfortable with progression in sport because of the stereotypes that exist around black and brown people's supposed physical superiority. This isn't true belonging. Its adoration, admiration, an acceptance that great athletes can disarm to the point where they go beyond 'race'. But this isn't a reality. It says little about how people feel in their everyday lives. But sport is hugely symbolic. It can, even in shreds, show a way forward.

If the Aluko case, the WNBA, the activism of John Amaechi, the practices that can be found in sport for development and other movements tell us anything, it would say that this battle needs to be tackled systemically, and that the institutions in which these archaic values are preserved need to be dismantled. It would tell us that, in all likelihood, Britain and England would be more successful, more inclusive and more powerful because its soul will encompass a future generation of black and brown people who will be reclaiming Britishness on their own terms and will be crying for Britain on their own terms. Why? Because generations of black and brown people have evolved far swifter than the institutions that govern us. But there's little in waiting for a generation of Empire preservers to die out if a new generation of Brits think that the impact of 'race' – racism and white supremacy – no longer exists. It will mean nothing if future generations of British people, those with little knowledge of black activism historically, think that better is good enough. In sport, we are continuing to win races. In society, we are not winning with 'race'. True acceptance will only come by winning, by destroying the latter.

CHAPTER 10

MORE THAN MAGICAL

'If you think about the history of the development of sport in this country and its connection to empire and class, you can see what we're describing as a failing or you could see it as it's absolutely doing what it was designed to do, which was to reinforce power structures, to reinforce the class system, to let the natives play but keep them in their place.'

Chris Grant, former Chief Executive of Sported!

In January 2017 my six-year-old son declared that he wanted a boys' night out. With Anthony Joshua scheduled to fight Wladimir Klitschko for the IBF and WBA world heavyweight titles in April, we decided to have a boys' night in. It was customary for my brothers-in-law and I to pile round to my mum and dad's house to watch the big fights. Over the years we had stayed up until late morning to see the likes of Manny Pacquiao, Ricky Hatton and Floyd Mayweather. Joshua–Klitschko would be my son's first major boxing fight with the boys. I couldn't think of a better way for us all to bond.

That night, my mum cooked curry goat, chicken, coco, rice & peas, and potatoes with coleslaw. I made the rum punch. After devouring the food, we reconvened in my parents' living room, with the heaters turned up, carpet and cushions seemingly covering the entire floor space, pictures and ornaments adorning every wall and plants surrounding us. It was a living room so homely, it embraced you like a hug from a loved one during a moment only they would understand. A living room you never wanted to leave.

That night we talked about our favourite sporting events, politics, Jay-Z, racism, work woes, *The Wire*, grime, enterprise, Alesha Dixon, food, motorbikes, Jamaica, local government. We joked, we laughed hysterically, we lamented, we reminisced, we wound each other up.

My son joined in as best he could, continually asking questions, playing with his Lego when bored, drifting off to sleep on occasion, and enjoying the rare opportunity in which he could drink some juice. Through the night, there was an ease. Always was. Ease to talk about anything, without judgement. Ease in each other's company. An ease that enabled us to escape temporarily from our everyday realities. Ease. I didn't want to be anywhere else.

We watched Klitschko outbox and outfox Joshua early, before the Brit of Nigerian heritage knocked the Ukrainian down. Klitschko returned the favour and looked on the way to victory before a searing uppercut by Joshua in round 11 almost took his opponent's head off. It was over soon after, Joshua, the 2012 Olympic champion, battering Klitschko against the ropes before the referee stopped the fight. The two fighters embraced at the end, they shared kind words. We agreed that this had been the greatest night of boxing we had witnessed together.

It had been sport at its best. Exhilarating, unpredictable, emotional, raw, revealing, real life. And in Anthony Joshua, we had found a boxer who appeared to epitomise the soul of modern Black-Britain, a personality who had been embraced by the British public on his own terms, a boxer who was more than just hype, an athlete we could all root for.

When Joshua fought bitter rival Dillian Whyte in 2015, Stormzy performed 'Shut Up' as AJ was making his way to the ring. For me it had been close to the Black-British equivalent of Marvin Gaye's performance at the 1983 NBA All-Star Game. Gaye famously turned the 'Star-Spangled Banner' into a sultry, seductive number that put the blackness into the American national anthem. It was audacious. Crazy. Sexy. Cool. A moment. A moment that took the most American of things, its national anthem, and reclaimed it for the souls of black folks.

Watching Joshua and Stormzy in the ring that night, I saw the sound and the fury of Black-Britain's hyphenated identity, embraced by the type of patrons whose fathers, uncles and relatives may have been at the Hagler-Minter fight some 37 years earlier. If only symbolically, if only temporarily, it felt like a dimming of the Spotlight, our emergence from the Shadow; it felt as if we had more choices than just the Codes and the Tiers.

My son's experience of the fight – well, the moments when he had been awake – were joy, not despair. Unlike my Minter–Hagler experience, Joshua–Klitschko had not made him question himself or his identity. No fright. No fight.

Just over a year after the Joshua–Klitschko fight, England played Croatia in the semi-final of the World Cup. I had never seen my son so immersed in a sport. The World Cup had been his true discovery of the highs and lows of sport. Croatia came from behind to seal a 2–1 victory in extra time. My son cried.

The tears uncontrollable. He, inconsolable. Without question, without questioning, he was England through and through and defeat had been agonising for him. No disgust. No distrust.

In truth, Gareth Southgate's England team had been an easy one for us all to get behind. Southgate keenly acknowledged the multiple identities of his players, highlighting this as an asset and not as some perverse dilution of 'true' Englishness. This approach had been the antithesis of the old 'two World Wars and one World Cup' mentality that had traditionally followed the England team. Southgate recognised that he had 'a team that represents modern England' and that his players could 'affect other things that are even bigger'.[1]

Soon after the World Cup, however, my son started to see black and white more vividly. He started asking questions about black and white, and the difference after hearing about the number of homicides in London on the radio. The radio show host had been linking the 'epidemic' of serious youth violence to black youths.

At home, he sees positive images of black people, from the pictures on our wall and the literature on our shelves to the music we listen to and the documentaries we watch. But blackness and brownness is not a minority. Ease. Yet outside of home, his first real encounter with 'race' had been overwhelmingly negative. It was heartbreaking.

I had always classified myself as black. I was brought up at a time when the term had been a force, a force against racism, a unifying force, a force that bonded the African diaspora (at the time, primarily from the Caribbean and West Africa), a force that connected the African diaspora with South Asian communities (primarily those of Indian, Bangladeshi and Pakistani descent). It was empowering, even if it had been reactive, patriarchal and, at times, failed to fully acknowledge difference.

Yet for the British majority, blackness continued to be a threat, something they feared, and white fragility around all things to do with 'race' had been a burden I had endured since primary school. I didn't want my son to carry this weight.

Despite a rise in black and brown people from many other nations outside of the Caribbean and West Africa in recent years – some who would not have classified themselves as black, some who were born into a completely different context to me and my generation, some whose experiences would have been completely different to mine, even if the tone of our skins looked similar – as far as the mainstream media had been concerned, we were all black, all the same, all a threat. During my father's generation, black men were perceived as pimps. In my generation, we were classified as muggers. Now my son's generation were being written off as gang criminals.

The analysis in the media of gang and knife crime tended to be all too simplistic. Solutions tended to locate the problems solely on the individual not the system. There had not been, to quote Kalpana Krishnamurthy, policy director at Forward Together,* solutions addressing the 'structural barriers using an intersectional analysis'.

* Forward Together, an organisation whose mission statement is 'rights, recognition and resources for all families'.

The creation of a moral panic around black culture remained a pervasive frame. This is not to excuse the actions of the perpetrators and causes that lie within our communities. But blackness as the underlying blame frame provided a highly racialised and distorted narrative.

But that is what the Empire state of mind had done historically. If fragility is the common state of those in power to control what we see, what we consume, what we hear, how we understand the world, how we understand other people, then fear will be the lens through which this nation, particularly those with little or no contact with black or brown people, will view our presence.

By the beginning of 2019, it was difficult to refute the burden black folks have had to bear as a result of white fragility and the power of Empire. Perpetual hostile environment. We knew this after the sickening treatment of the Windrush generation, many of whom faced detainment, deportation, loss of rights and citizenship due to circumstances created by the government. We knew this after the Grenfell tragedy, which highlighted the disparities between rich and poor and the systemic failures resulting in negative outcomes for those of low socio-economic status, of which many people of colour reside. We knew this because anti-Muslim racism had become practically acceptable in mainstream media and political discourse. We knew this because of Brexit, where immigration had been a key reason why people voted leave, the majority of whom were not fans of multiculturalism.

We knew this because of statistical data highlighted in the Race Disparity Audit of 2017, set up under Theresa May's government, which found major disparities in school exclusions, employment, in the criminal justice system and other areas. We knew this from the excessive policing of black youths. We knew this from the continued absence of black people in top positions in universities, in and on television, and in the press. We knew this because further research revealed that Black-Britons and people of South Asian origin faced similar levels of discrimination in the job market today as they did 40 years ago in 1969.

We knew this after a wave of excellent books in recent years, including Binna Kandola's *Racism at Work*, Akala's *Natives* and Afua Hirsch's *Brit(ish)*, highlighted these historic disparities from evidence-based and personal perspectives.

We knew this after Raheem Sterling had been racially abused at Stamford Bridge and when a banana was thrown on the pitch by a Tottenham fan at the Emirates stadium. The media and general public were outraged. Sterling made a stand by highlighting the role the media play in inciting problems through their negative portrayals of black players.

We knew this. We had always known it. Been made to feel crazy for acknowledging it and talking about it.

But this has been our everyday reality.

On 3 December 2018, the *Guardian* revealed findings from a survey of 1000 people from minority ethnic backgrounds and their experiences of racism in Britain. From stop and search policing to treatment in clubs and restaurants, from opportunities for promotion at work to being wrongly accused of shoplifting, it had been clear that the Spotlight was still shining bright.

Yet a YouGov poll in 2018 revealed that up to 40 per cent of British people did not think that ethnic minorities faced more discrimination than white people. They couldn't see it, not in television or film, not in the workplace, employment or in education. Denial? Defensiveness? *A few rotten apples. Things are better.* When it came to the legacy of the Empire, Britain had a long memory. When it came to the oppressive nature of the Empire, that memory became clouded, deluded. And somewhere along the line, the majority of white Britain stopped listening.

The silence came from all sides, all classes, all generations, both sides of the political divide.

It appeared that British society had reverted to implicit or PC ways of saying black and brown people were reverse racists, had been indulging in identity politics. The most powerful and controlling identity in this country is the Empire state of mind, which marginalises black and brown people, working-class people and anyone who does not look like those who fundamentally control and own power in this country.

It had become exhausting, maddening even, to constantly fight against British history, the overwhelming power of the media's narrative, to constantly reinforce that our reality is not some character fault or an illusion.

My father, son and I still bond by watching sport. Still love it. Still find magic amid the politics. My father still hates basketball. Whenever it is on, he will still groan, 'money for old rope', and then gasp when a player dunks the ball. The West Indies still brings him joy and pain, in equal measures. He has become more forgiving of the West Indies due to their success in T20 competition, winning the World Cup in 2012 and 2016. It offered a glimmer of past glories.

He had been ecstatic when the West Indies beat England in the 2016 final. When Carlos Brathwaite hit four consecutive sixes in the final over to win the game, causing commentator Ian Bishop to roar, 'Carlos Brathwaite, Carlos Brathwaite, remember the name!', it had been one of my father's favourite sporting moments. He even begrudgingly chuckled when Chris Gayle performed the 'Gangnam Style' dance after the 2012 victory.

But he found real pleasure when the West Indies crushed England in the first two Tests early in 2019. The Windies won the first Test by 381 runs and the second by 10 wickets. The West Indies, for many years the underdogs when playing against England, had won the Test series, with ease. This perhaps surpassed the happiness of the T20 victories because the Windies had beaten England in the true test.

My son watches football incessantly. Australian, German, Premier League, he doesn't care. He currently supports Manchester City and Paris St Germain. At the time of writing, Sergio Agüero, Raheem Sterling and Kevin De Bruyne are his favourite players. Kylian Mbappé, Lionel Messi and Paul Pogba had been demoted. He likes who he likes. A little less tribal than in my day. A positive thing. He is a British citizen of Jamaican and Nigerian heritage. In our house, he is surrounded by James Baldwin, Angela Davis, Nijinsky, Fanon, Luciano, Nina Simone, Chris Ofili, Toni Morrison, Fela. He is also surrounded by aunties, uncles, grandparents, cousins and godparents of Chinese, Serbian, Irish, Egyptian, Ghanaian, English and Australian descent. This is not another country. This is his country. His reality. I cannot help but think how powerful this is. How powerful this conception of Britishness could be.

Me, I'm still a sucker for British basketball. I take my kids to watch Great Britain and the London City Royals and London

Lions play. It has been an almost 40-year affair for me. While at times it feels like unrequited love, I will forever remain fond of this marginalised sport because of its cultural power and immense potential to transcend sporting boundaries.

I also continue to find the magic of sport away from the elite level. I could see it when I was in China, assisting sport for development trainer Rubel Ahmed. He effortlessly blended children and young people of mixed ability in his sessions, providing opportunities for peer support, emphasising teamwork, providing constant and instant feedback and ensuring that every participant had a role to play, irrespective of ability, while making the reluctant participants feel safe in physical activity.

I could see it when I attended PeacePlayers' International Exchange Summer Camp at the Rodon Mount Hotel and Resort in Agros, Cyprus. I watched Israeli and Palestinian teenagers, Greek-Cypriot and Turkish-Cypriot young people, children from Northern Ireland and South Africa, girls and boys, all from historically divided communities, come together under the common language of basketball to compete, discuss, laugh, mix, share stories, feel at ease. It had been more meaningful for me than watching Roger Federer, Mo Farah, Magic Johnson or Brian Lara.

Few people intentionally watch sport for politics. It certainly had not been my intention to watch sport because it reflected what I had been facing growing up. I have never met an athlete who entered sport because they wanted to be a political voice either. You chose us, we didn't choose you. But that had been so true of many black and brown people's experience of Britain.

As much as sport tries to hide problems in society, it cannot help but reflect it, too. It is still managed by governing bodies that fail to acknowledge black brains and is more comfortable with black bodies. It still treats the symptoms of racism, not the root causes. It still has a fundamental mistrust of black people in power.

Branding has at least broken the narrow and reductive choices of the Codes and the Tiers for the black athlete. Black athletes are more activist. Some happily play to stereotypes. Not quite what I had expected or indeed desired. But if America has shown us anything in recent years, it has told us that adhering to the Codes need not be a career killer, while conforming to the Tiers would not guarantee you eternal favour.

But for real progression, we should not be just talking about increasing numbers on the field of play or tackling isolated incidents of racism. It's about breaking those archaic structures, it's about creating new narratives of national sporting success, but through the lens of the marginalised. It's about converting symbolism on the field of play into systemic reform off it. Sport matters.

'If you wanted to change this country, if you wanted to make this country feel more at ease with itself, find its place in the world and bring to the front policies and behaviours that are more about justice and fairness and access, sport is still the best way to do it,' said Chris Grant. 'Sport is a lever for social change. There isn't a bigger one in this country. In its various forms, it attracts more of the country to it than anything else. It's built for symbolism … Sport has endless capacity to create those moments … If you want to change the country in the next 10–20 years, there'd be no better place than sport.'

The Black-British athlete has amplified our presence in this country, our contribution to this country. And they have done so playing games that had not been created for them to win. For many years, I hadn't quite recognised how deep their struggles had been. I had been harsh in my assessment of some of these athletes, which was wrong and at times unfair. But then sport tends to heighten emotions, it heightens feelings, it moves you beyond your conscious self, often revealing parts of your true self. There's a lot of truth in sport. Our own truths. How we truly feel.

Change will not come without a challenge. If there's no long term vision and no change in leadership, there will be no movement, no promise, no hope. It will take those on the inside at an elite level in management positions to nudge doors open. It will take those on the periphery to provoke, to innovate, to chip away. It will take communities mobilising behind athletes, behind causes, behind progressive initiatives. It will take a long-term, concerted effort and a demand. The same is true of society.

When I see what sport for development can do to transform young people's relationship with others, with their bodies, with their communities, when I see Eniola Aluko not hiding, when I think of the West Indian cricket team and the Topcats, I see hope, I see magic. But this is not just confined to the field of play.

We are not just magical. We are more than magical.

CHAPTER 11

IS IT IN THE BLOOD?

*'Issues of race and gender are not extra credit points in
being a good Democrat, they're a core part of the
competencies that a president needs. You have to
understand that our country is one of the biggest
experiments in a multi-racial democracy in the history of
humanity and if you don't understand the multi-racial
or the multi-identity part of a multi-racial democracy,
it can severely hamper your capacity to govern.'*

Alexandria Ocasio-Cortez, US Representative for
New York's 14th congressional district[1]

An addict, I believe, smelling like burnt rubber, face obscured by a black, brown and cream hoodie, grinds his teeth as he walks up and down the carriage of a moving train. He stops near the doors and, in a high-pitched tone shouts, 'CRAIG DAVID. CRAIG DAVID. CRAIG DAVID.' Piercing. Unusually melodic. As the early-evening train stops, he strolls towards the seating area, close to where I'm sitting. His hands are shrivelled. Grey. Ashy. No nails.

The smell, the closer he gets, is less rubber-like and more like an unflushed toilet. I see a glimpse of his face, a face, not so much his features. He's bearded. He was originally black, brown, now more a Blu Tack colour. Cracked face. Frankenstein. But with the soft lips of a better past. 'CRAIG DAVID,' he shouts again.

A white guy sitting next to me in a buttoned shirt and fitted jeans barks, 'Be quiet, you're annoying.'

The man in the hoodie turns to him and says, 'Do you like Craig David?'

Those within listening distance start giggling. Muted, though. No one wants to draw too much attention to themselves.

A young dark-skinned black woman, hair slicked back, with gentle features, dressed in business attire, is sitting opposite me. She puts her headphones in her ears, then shuts her eyes. The man in the hoodie somehow spots this as he immediately turns and moves towards her. He stops in front of where she is seated and stares at her. Not so close as to be threatening, though.

'CRAIG DAVID,' he shouts. 'Do you like Craig David?'

She jumps. Eyeballs seemingly leave her face, as if in a cartoon. Mouth opens. Nothing comes out. He moves on.

How do people end up this way? I thought as I watched him drift away. Well, that was my initial thought, only because that is what I thought the other people in the carriage wanted me to think. In such moments, paranoia seizes me. I hold on to some crazy belief that every black man, in this case, the man in the hoodie, is me and I am the man in the hoodie. We are, to many. We're not; not in the way you try to define us.

I hold on to this crazy belief that we reflect each other, and the only way I can indicate that I'm different is to conform with what the others – the white majority and the 'suits and ties' in this carriage – want me to think. To condemn, with compassion. Bad black. Good black. Creating a separation between the two. A survival tactic. A code-switch. A progression tactic. Self-loathing.

As if to leave no doubt about where I stand, I furnish the people on the train with a facial expression to accompany my initial thought. But it wasn't what I wanted to think at all. When I saw the man in the hoodie, I did see myself. Not in the same way the folks in the carriage might have viewed us. I saw what little margins we – as black people – have in this society. I saw not what this man had become. Didn't think about how he'd ended up in this state, in such a state, or where he may end up. I thought about how narrow his margins for error probably were. How, in different circumstances perhaps, in a different environment, with greater access to support, services, opportunities, he may not have been in this state.

I thought about the poetic way in which he had said 'Craig David', his timing and humour; how aware he had been of everything around him, even the woman with the headphones, and yet what little awareness he had had of how everyone felt around him, and what wonderful qualities people would have thought these were if he had been wearing a suit, if he had been white, Oxbridge educated; if he had been in a position of power.

I suppressed any further thoughts about the power of privilege, the privilege of power, the ugliness of it, the outright unfairness of it all, and why those with greater margins for error are more likely to dictate and more likely to escape, to recover, to avoid being a 'threat'; to become a poet, a banker, a comedian, a politician.

We are programmed in such a way that this story, his story, a story that may not end well, will not change us because of what and who we value in society. And I could tell, by the look on the faces of those on this train, that we were each reinforcing this value-judgement during the minimal time we shared with this man. It is reinforced through the images we consume, our education and by the choices the media makes on our behalf, the stories they decide to tell and how they tell it; it is reinforced by the ineptitude of those who have the power to decide, by those who have greater freedom to free their speech, by those with inherited wealth, those with infinitely wider margins. And they reinforce narrowness and reinforce these value-judgements, rupturing Britain's ability to be as great as it desperately wants to be, and its ability to reverse inequity created by the wealthy, by colonialism, by whiteness; it is created by those who prefer to preserve, which is as much a game of masking and retaining mediocrity in positions of power as it is habitually racist. This is British society. British history. Britain's conscience. Britain's everything. But Britain will claim it is nothing.

No Win Race started with my father and I watching a boxing contest. A contest that was infected by racism. For many I spoke to, who read the book, it started and ended with racism. In sport. My father and I, and, to some degree, society's racism, were obscured. Racism obscures. That is part of how Britain is programmed.

Acclaimed geneticist Bruce Lahn is quoted in Angela Saini's excellent book *Superior* as saying, 'Before there is data, these are just possibilities.'[2] I disagree. Before there is data, before most things that are human-made, there are ideologies. And 'race', one of the biggest lies in history, and racism can obscure to a point where this belief in human superiority and inferiority contaminates possibilities, humanity, science, sport, everything. And what is lost is us. All of us. Black and brown folks, foremost. We end up being lost because, for any person of colour in Britain, we are treated as if we are occasional. And disposable. Most white folks cannot see past 'race', they cannot see past racism or their own privilege, or their own response to 'race', because they are not occasional, and they will not permit their elite to be disposable. Despite the many ways in which the elite oppress them, they think they will be, must be, benefactors, and if not benefactors, at least not the canaries in the mine, because they are the norm, because they think they are permanent.

Blackness is trending. Diversity is trending. But trending is not permanent. It is not the norm. It is occasional. The 'post-racial' bliss of the Obama years surrendered swiftly to Ferguson, Trump, Brexit, Grenfell, Euro-nationalism, Boris, Dominic and the harsh reality that racism has barely suffered a minor abrasion. The absurd voyage from Obama to Trump in the US, and from London 2012 to Brexit in the UK, opened the way for more mainstream commentary from people of colour. But while the doors have opened and more black and brown people have become visible, we have not gained much in the way of power to disturb the status quo. We are commodified by the same 'extractivist' culture of Empire, one that also glorifies our pain; one that blames our pain on us and creates a narrative to save us. And yet the choices about what black and brownness are consumed by the masses is, overall, not in people of colours' hands. As such, we are still susceptible. We are still delivered through Britain's narrow lens, culturally through our bodies and in society through our pain.

So, even with greater visibility, mainstreaming, sales, sponsorship and some influence, we are still occasional, because trending does not lead to the type of sustained change required to disrupt the Empire state of mind. It is a building block, but also vulnerable to and endangered by the co-option, exploitation and misappropriation of those in power before it can fully form and gain control. And this is a pattern we have seen all too often in the past.

In 2019, it felt as if athlete-activism was trending, with no clear route to establishing permanence. Sport is news-led, intentionally sensationalist; the only thing that matters is the last result, the last incident, and whether you can milk three or four days' worth of content from it. Solutions are little more than headlines. Occasional. Not change-making.

Raheem Sterling continued to speak out about the problems in football, particularly the media's veiled bigotry in the way it portrays young black players and how this fuels negative behaviour on terraces. He advocated for more stringent penalties for racially motivated incidents, including points deductions or teams being thrown out of tournaments. It was the first time that such a high-profile Black-British sporting figure had spoken out so vehemently about racism at the height of his or her career.

Sterling's stance occurred at a point when he had been enjoying his best season. He won the Football Writers' Association (FWA)

Player of the Year award, bagging 17 goals and 12 assists during Manchester City's 2018–19 Premier League-winning campaign. He established himself as arguably the best player in the Premier League (certainly the best British player), and perhaps one of the top five footballers in the world.

Supported by his sponsors Nike, it would be difficult to find any Black-British footballer historically who has had as much of an impact on and off the pitch as Sterling. The likes of Viv Anderson, Emma Clarke, Arthur Wharton, Paul Ince and Eniola Aluko spring to mind, but Sterling, in a short time, had established himself as a true icon of British sport.

It's a shame, then, that the football authorities could not be as brave as the players. When Bulgarian football fans mocked England players with Nazi salutes and monkey chants during a European Championships qualifier in Sofia in October 2019, UEFA responded by ordering Bulgaria to play one game behind closed doors and fining them €75,000. During the game, the England football team had followed protocol, responding to racist chants by notifying officials, which led to the game being halted twice. For all the noise made by players, including threats to walk off the pitch, UEFA's sanctions had been meek, administering – seemingly – the minimum viable penalty. Aluko said it best when she tweeted: '"(Insert name) do not care about black people" – Kanye West. Yes I said it. @uefa know this fine is pitiful. It's an insult to every player that followed their protocols that day.'

Once more, the biggest opposition to progression was the institution that governs the sport. The protests and campaigns by black footballers led to great headlines and front-page news.

They likely made some journalists mildly more thoughtful, but they fundamentally did little to change *who* would be responsible for dispensing sanctions, or who would be making those editorial decisions. This is not to dismiss the players' efforts. It's not actually on them. More to recognise the limitations of blackness trending. The same is true of wider society, which addresses racism by trying to 'fix' individuals, with short-term solutions but no thirst for challenging the structural or systemic issues required for lasting change.

It is difficult to know what will force the sport's authorities to change the way they address racism. In the case of the Bulgaria incident, it became all too easy for folks in Britain to point the finger and ignore (and obscure) its own problems with racism. Another part of the Brits' game. Athlete-activism will only go so far, unless the players collectively elect to walk off the pitch, which would hit the authorities where it hurts, in their pockets. Unless they pool their wealth to create the type of infrastructural body that could truly and independently hold the governing bodies to account.

We need to decolonise sport. Just like we need to decolonise every other institution in this country; a deep process of 'undoing' racism and these racist structures and their historical harms. The response to racism from football's major bodies has and continues to be abysmal. Yet there is little that really challenges the lack of concern and accountability in leadership and their power to manage the short-term news cycle.

I get it. It gets me. For some, it's easy to forget the problems that lie in sport. Sport is alluring, absorbing, mind-altering. It continues to occupy an unhealthy amount of space in my thoughts. Few things can beat the thrill of watching the burrowing illusionism of Barry Sanders' 47-yard touchdown run against the Dallas Cowboys in 1992; or Paul Ereng striding past competitors in the 800 metres as if they were standing still while breaking Seb Coe's indoor record in Budapest; or seeing the original Ronaldo in 1996 driving through the Compostela team from the halfway line, leaving his manager, the late Bobby Robson, looking on in disbelief; or Jamaican Bert Cameron literally stopping with what looked like a hamstring injury during the semi-final of the 400 metres at the 1984 Olympics, only to continue on and qualify for the final; or the pain of love watching my son elegantly marauding in central midfield, like former French international Jean Tigana, for his football team every Sunday. It's easy to be distracted by epic sporting feats, booing on the terraces, world records, riots and rivalries, and the escapism or tension that comes with that. It's easy to forget those administrators who sit in the background and do little to enhance workers' rights and more harm by refusing to hold anyone in power to account for racism.

The hyphenated identity of the England football team continued to offer some hope of change. England's 1966 World Cup win remains the country's greatest sporting moment, more so than 'Super Saturday' at London 2012 or the Ashes victories in 1981 and 2005 or Andy Murray's Wimbledon victory in 2013 or England's victory at the 2003 Rugby World Cup. What had become abundantly clear was that for England to win the 2022

World Cup in Qatar, a significant number of black or mixed heritage players would need to be in key positions. This would include Raheem Sterling (voted as the world's best winger in the 2019 ESPN 100 poll), Jadon Sancho (voted the fourth-best winger), Trent Alexander-Arnold (voted the number-one right back), Marcus Rashford and Dele Alli.

If a team with a significant number of black and mixed heritage players were to win the World Cup, would they be as revered as the '66 team? Would this, symbolically, destroy the myth of Empire if a hyphenated England were to win a major championship? Would it erase such questions as, 'Is it in the blood?' Would we rid ourselves of the notion of hyphenation altogether and start progressing towards a more wholesome and progressive national identity? Would it encourage the English football authorities and sports funding bodies to revise their policies and provide better access to opportunities for black and brown people?

I don't think an England victory – with Sterling, Alexander-Arnold and Sancho at the helm – would legitimately address these questions. But it may do more to address racism, representation, identity or any other issue that systematically disadvantages black and brown folks more than anything else, which is kind of sad. After all, it's football, it's a game, and as with most games, there is a clear beginning, middle and end, and, unfortunately, 'race' and racism doesn't work that way.

What we do know is that the number of black footballers in Britain will continue to increase. And with that increase, these players will develop more confidence and assume greater power. There will come a day when the Premier League will start to look like the Majority World* or the NBA. Although history also tells us that, at some point, a coded rule will be introduced that will reduce the influence and numbers of black players in British football. Not even the commodification of our black bodies in the sport will escape the hostile environment.

What this generation of black sports stars will no doubt do is open the pathways for future generations, enabling them to be more confident while establishing a clear identity for the Black-British athlete. It matters. There are not many African-American athletes of note who've been fully able to ignore its legacy of activism in sport. In the future, we will see more Black-British sports stars hiring agents and advisers from within closer friendship circles. We have seen this in the United States where NBA stars like LeBron James have worked closely with their friends to build their brands and multiple empires, following Jay-Z's ethos, *I'm not a businessman, I'm a business, man*.† James has gone on to use his platform to address politics in a way that Michael Jordan didn't when at the peak of his playing career. We've already seen Black-Brits in the entertainment industry, like Stormzy and Jamal Edwards, use their wealth and influence for social good. Whether these wealthy sports stars can build significant enough empires, do good and move into ownership is another matter.

---

* Majority World is a more positive and accurate way to describe countries in Africa, Asia, the Caribbean and South and Central America. It is used as an alternative to more negative terms such as Developing World or Third World.
† 'Diamonds from Sierra Leone (Remix)' by Kanye West featuring Jay-Z, released in 2005 (Roc-A-Fella Records).

But the platform in 2019 for our athletes had never been greater. Beyond Sterling's brilliance, Anthony Joshua and Lewis Hamilton were reaching almost unprecedented heights of popularity for the Black-British athlete globally. Joshua lost and then regained his world titles against Andy Ruiz. The Brit had allegedly banked some $55 million in his career after the first fight with the Mexican slugger. It is estimated that Joshua took home $60 million for the rematch with Ruiz. Lewis Hamilton, meanwhile, cemented his position as Britain's greatest ever sports star and arguably the greatest racing driver of all time, having won 84 Formula 1 races (second to Michael Schumacher's 91), gained 88 pole positions (a Formula 1 record) and won six championships (second to Schumacher's seven) with a win percentage that surpasses recent greats such as Ayrton Senna, Alain Prost and Schumacher.

Sterling and Hamilton were joined on the Sports Personality of the Year (SPOTY) shortlist by track and field athletes Dina Asher-Smith and Katarina Johnson-Thompson. In 2019, Asher-Smith became the first British female athlete to win an individual sprint gold at a World Championship, winning the 200 metres while also scooping silver medals in the 100 metres and 4 x 100 metres relay. After years of disappointment, KJT won her first major senior world title, winning the heptathlon gold. Like Asher-Smith in the 100 metres and 200 metres, KJT broke the British record and threatened to become only the fifth woman to top 7,000 points in the heptathlon. Four of the six shortlisted athletes for the 2019 SPOTY award were black or of mixed heritage.

The margins for error for black people, however, remain thin. The fact that a few of us have better lifestyles does not remove the fact that most of us remain at the sharp end of 'life and death' issues.

Until the death of the Empire state of mind and complete acknowledgement of the damage it has caused and continues to cause, power, privilege and preservation will inhibit progression. The Empire state of mind devalues black and brownness, and that has not changed. That is why, typically, we are still perceived as a threat by the police, a beneficiary by the charity worker, a natural by the sports coach, a folk devil by the politician, a low prospect by the teacher and another author by the BBC reporter.

Alexandria Ocasio-Cortez's quote and sentiments at the beginning of this chapter have far broader implications than just the Democratic leadership race. It's a point for every institution in Britain.

Leadership needs to change, with more people who understand what it means to be in a multi-racial and multi-identity society at the helm. To combat racism – individually, structurally, systemically and institutionally – you need to take an anti-racist approach. You need an equity lens or to adopt strategies like targeted universalism, created by American academic john a powell. In short, if you create a universal goal, for example, ensuring that a local meeting reflects the demographics of your community, then you develop targeted approaches to reach people according to where and how they are situated in relation to that goal. Your recruitment strategy, for example, will vary depending on whether you want to reach someone with a disability or someone without the economic means to attend the meeting. If you fail to reflect the community in this meeting because you have taken a one-size-fits-all approach, then you're not doing your job properly and therefore you should not be doing your job. *It's simple ain't it, but quite clever.**

In sport, if you're scouting for talent, but your reach is limited to the privileged few or your practice is discriminatory, it really does not matter how successful your team is; it could be better if your recruitment strategy was better.

And it doesn't stop there. Once you've recruited, you then need to know how to retain and develop talent, which goes beyond just skills development. If you want, for example, a world-class team, do you have the personnel to develop the talent on your roster? Without any accountability or any measures or targets related to this, it means that all our services operate at a deficit for marginalised folks, particularly people of colour, particularly those at the intersections. And none of this will change if those in charge think that we are situated further from these opportunities because there must be something in our blood.

The absence of a major race equity institution – independent of government – that can represent the needs of black and brown people from a legal and policy perspective is another problem. When you go back to the eighties and indeed the nineties, and you look at the black newspapers, the supplementary school movement, the record labels, etc., that vibrancy of independence has been severely reduced in recent years, largely the result of marginalisation or mainstreaming. But, apart from the Commis-

---

* 'Move the Crowd', a song by Eric B. & Rakim, released in 1987 from the album 'Paid in Full' (4th & Broadway/Island).

sion for Race Equality (1976–2007) – which was an arms-length government body – there has never really been an independent institution with significant resources to truly hold the authorities to account.

How good would it be to have an independent, central body or indeed a dedicated, endowed foundation that could have responded to the Naga Munchetty–BBC fallout, or Elsie Owusu's case against RIBA, or the Windrush scandal, or racism in football, or to challenge the ethics, efficacy and existence of Prevent? How good would it be to have an independent body or a foundation that could provide a vision for a better future?

What we cannot measure is just how much damage has been done by the absence of these groups, this independence, a body. And the absence of our brains in positions where decisions are made. Multi-culturalism was deemed problematic, and this has been the dominant narrative now for over twenty years. For many years, race relations have not improved, while countless governments have tried to legislate multi-culturalism out of being. It has unquestionably been racist social policies that have been the cause of further social divisions, tensions and segregation in Britain. Inertia, prejudice, poor leadership and low accountability in all British institutions, including sports institutions, have meant that racism has largely gone unchallenged, except for three or four days' worth of news content. Let's face it, no one in high places loses their job because of racial injustice. Not in government, housing, the police, education or sport. Think: the hostile environment, Grenfell, the Eni Aluko case. Pseudo-scientific racism still drives many policies. Millions are invested in reinforcing racist ideologies, yet anti-racist organisations struggle to raise £10,000 from funders. Britain still feels pride in the Empire and has little or no knowledge about the impact of its colonial past. Fans on terraces still use old racist tropes when taunting black players. You can be a racist, a eugenic thinker, and still climb to the top of any institution in this country. This is not the profile of a progressive society. Nor is it ambiguous. It's racist. And it lies at the core of British society. Is it in the blood? No. But this is Britain's game. The elite's gain. British history. Britain's conscience. Ultimately, Britain's loss. Britain's lost.

ENDNOTES

INTRODUCTION

1. Taken from a speech by former Deputy Prime Minister Geoffrey Howe, when he resigned from Thatcher's government.

CHAPTER 1: HYMN OF HATE

1. Reynolds, A (2016), *The Battle of the Southpaws: Race, Rioting, and Beer on the Canvas.* Fightland. Fightland.vice.com.
2. Newham Monitoring Project/Campaign Against Racism and Fascism (1991), *Newham: The Forging of a Black Community.* Newham Monitoring Project/Campaign Against Racism and Fascism. 24.
3. Reynolds, *The Battle of the Southpaws.*
4. Campbell, C (2015), *Minter v Hagler: The Night That Shamed British Boxing.* Sabotage Times. Sabotagetimes.com.
5. *Guardian,* 3 October 2013.
6. Institute of Race Relations (1987), *Policing Against Black People.* Institute of Race Relations. 4.
7. Newham Monitoring Project/Campaign Against Racism and Fascism, *Newham.* 51.
8. Ibid. 58.

CHAPTER 2: BLACKWASHED

1. Vaidyanathan, S (2006), *Never Another Like Collie.* Cricinfo. ESPN-Cricinfo.com.

2. Marqusee, M (1994), *Anyone But England: Cricket and the National Malaise*. Verso. 145.
3. Lister, S (2016), *Fire in Babylon*. Yellow Jersey. 270–1.
4. www.dawn.com/news/617920.
5. Beckles, H and Stoddart, B (1995), *Liberation Cricket: West Indies and Cricket Culture*. Manchester University Press. 157.
6. August 2006 issue of *Cricinfo* magazine. Siddhartha Vaidyanathan is assistant editor of Cricinfo.
7. www.cricketcountry.com/articles/herbert-chang-the-jamaican-of-chinese-origin-who-wasted-his-life-in-south-africa-188792
8. Lister, *Fire in Babylon*. 305.
9. Marqusee, *Anyone But England*. 146.
10. Lister, *Fire in Babylon*. 302–3.
11. Marqusee, *Anyone But England*. 146.
12. Lister, *Fire in Babylon*. 248–9.
13. Marqusee, *Anyone But England*. 146.
14. Lister, *Fire in Babylon*. 249.
15. Marqusee, *Anyone But England*. 146.
16. Lister, *Fire in Babylon*. 302.
17. Marqusee, *Anyone But England*. 137.
18. Ibid. 18.
19. Lister, *Fire in Babylon*. 3.

CHAPTER 3: THE SHOT

1. Gilroy, P (1993), *The Black Atlantic: Modernity and Double Consciousness*. Verso. 16
2. *Basketball* (1982), Cheerleader Productions. Channel 4.
3. Bryant, H (2018), *The Heritage*. Beacon Press.
4. Wetzel, D and Yaeger, D (2000), *Sole Influence*. Warner Books. 2.
5. LaFeber, A (2002), *Michael Jordan and the New Global Capitalism*. W.W. Norton & Company. 27.
6. Sported. https://sported.org.uk/about-us/what-is-sport-for-development/.

7. Baker, A (2000), 'Hoop Dreams in Black and White: Race and Basketball Movies.' In T Boyd and K L Shropshire (eds), *Basketball Jones*. New York University Press. 223.
8. Rhoden, W C (2006), *Forty Million Dollar Slaves*. Three Rivers Press. 204.
9. Ibid. 200.

CHAPTER 4: SO MANY TIERS

1. *Sunday Times*, 23 December 1986.
2. Bardowell, D A, 'Can't, Don't, Never … The Melancholy of Manhood'. *The Weeklings* (3 September, 2012). https://theweeklings.com/dbardowell/2012/09/03/cant-dont-never-the-melancholy-of-manhood/
3. *Guardian*, 7 February 2018.
4. Fryer, P (1984), *Staying Power: The History of Black People in Britain*. Pluto Press. 135–6.
5. Ibid. 446–7.
6. Ibid. 447.
7. Smith, K (date unknown), 'Black Dynamite/American Bare Knuckle Champion.' *Cyber Boxing Zone Journal*. Retrieved November 2009 from www.cyberboxingzone.com/boxing/tom-mol.html.
8. Edwards, P and Walvin, J (1983), *Black Personalities in the Era of the Slave Trade*. Macmillan. 203
9. Fryer, *Staying Power*, 447–8.
10. Some of the text first appeared in Bardowell, D A, 'Lennox Lewis: A Question of Nobility over Notoriety'. *Cyber Boxing Zone Journal* (April, 2000). http://www.cyberboxingzone.com/boxing/box4-00.htm

CHAPTER 5: NEW NATION

1. Onuora, E (2015), *Pitch Black: The Story of Black British Footballers*. Biteback Publishing. 10.
2. Ibid.
3. Barnes, J (1999), *The Autobiography*. Headline. 83.

4. Ibid.
5. Ibid. 84.
6. Ibid. 116.
7. Ibid.
8. Carrington, B (2002), 'Postmodern Blackness and the Celebrity Sports Star.' *Sports Stars*. Routledge. 105–6.

CHAPTER 6: BEYOND SPORT

1. Marqusee, *Anyone But England*. 295–6.
2. Carrington, B (2010), *Race, Sport and Politics: The Sporting Black Diaspora*. Sage. 139–40.
3. Ibid.
4. www.theguardian.com/world/2009/feb/24/racism-police-lawrence-met

CHAPTER 7: THE GREATEST WEEK EVER IN BLACK HISTORY?

1. Cole, C L and Andrews D A (2001), 'America's New Son'. *Sports Stars*. Routledge. 70.
2. Ibid.
3. Carrington, *Race, Sport and Politics*. 158.
4. Ibid.
5. *Guardian,* 24 November 2014.
6. Warmington, P (2015), 'The Status of Race and Racism in Policy: An Analysis of Project Interviews.' Working Paper. 31. Gargi Bhattacharyya was interviewed for and quoted in this working paper.
7. Ibid. 13. Quote from Maxie Hayles, a community activist in Birmingham.

CHAPTER 8: POOR PEOPLE'S OLYMPICS

1. *Beautifully Human: Words and Sounds Vol. 2* by Jill Scott (Hidden Beach Recordings, 2004).
2. Lammy, D (2012), *Out of the Ashes: Britain after the Riots*. Guardian Books. 207.

ENDNOTES

3. Lammy, *Out of the Ashes*. 130
4. *Daily Telegraph*, 22 December 2011.
5. *Guardian*, 14 September 2014.
6. Bryant, *The Heritage*. 99.

CHAPTER 9: DRIVEN TO THE POINT OF MADNESS

1. *Independent*, 19 October 2017.
2. http://michellemoore.me/blog/.
3. Ibid.

CHAPTER 10: MORE THAN MAGIC

1. *Guardian*, 7 July 2018.

CHAPTER 11: IS IT IN THE BLOOD?

1. *The New Yorker: Politics and More* (2019). *Alexandria Ocasio-Cortez on the 2020 Presidential Race and Why We Should Break up Homeland Security* [Podcast]. 15 July. Available at https://podcasts.apple.com/us/podcast/alexandria-ocasio-cortez-on-2020-presidential-race/id268213039?i=1000444536256 (Accessed: 9 October 2019).
2. Saini, A (2019), *Superior*. 4th Estate. 277.

ACKNOWLEDGEMENTS

THIS BOOK STARTED OUT AS a dedication to British basketball. My first love. A huge thanks goes out to the many people I interviewed over the years, many who are in this book, including Joel Moore, Junior Taylor, Roger Hosannah and Paul Philp. Thank you to Laureus Sport for Good and the Stephen Lawrence Trust for some amazing opportunities and experiences, City University for seeing me through the first draft, Roger Fairman at the Basketball Heritage Archive, and to Michelle Moore, Chris Grant, Rimla Akhtar, John Amaechi, Binna Kandola, Ruth Ibegbuna, Immy Kaur and Frances Jessop for your wisdom, words and honesty. There are way too many writers and academics to list here; many are acknowledged in the endnotes. But an extra special thanks goes to Ben Carrington and Kevin Hylton, academics who have very much created the foundation of thinking around 'race', sport and British society, and how the three intersect. This book would not have been possible without the wonderful Jennifer Kabat and the freedom she gave me to be me at The Weeklings. Got to pay respect to the Powermoves crew for being the first people to show faith in my work and give me a break in journalism. While there are way too many friends for me to list here, people whose thoughts, comments and wise words are sprinkled throughout this book, I have to say a special thanks to Shivanti, Darren Crosdale and Anisha for always having my back, and to Sunny, Fedj and Al for the fight nights, and to Farzana and the Melanin fam, the 5% fam (you know who you are) and the UK Portfolio. And, of course, thanks to my agent Oli Munson for your enthusiasm and advice and to Ed Faulkner, Zoe Berville and the whole HarperNonFiction team for listening, believing and never trying to 'edit' my voice.

Most of all, a massive thanks to my family. To Meadow, Marlowe and Mya for your patience and support, your hugs and your humour. To Elle and Keithus, for everything, literally, the endless love, the stories and the many nights of sport and great food. To my big sisters, Paula B Stanic for reading my work and the fab advice and to Ka for always making me feel like I can conquer this world. You are both inspirations. And to Diana Evans, for the overwhelming support and patience and for being the wonder that you are.